Major Spiri[...] and Delivera[...] Principles

Separating bible-based principles from harmful non-biblical spiritual warfare and deliverance teachings

* Second Edition *
An ultimate spiritual warfare and deliverance manual for all

Eric Isaiah Gondwe

JesusW.com and SpiritualWarfareDeliverance.com (Jesus Work Ministry),
Cambridge, MA, USA

Major Spiritual Warfare and Deliverance Ministry Principles
Second Edition, 52nd Revision/Update (December 28, 2006)

Published by JesusW.com and SpiritualWarfareDeliverance.com
(Jesus Work Ministry)
Cambridge, MA, USA

Registered with the United States Copyright Office, Library of Congress:
TXu1-250-489 2005

International Standard Book Number (ISBN):
978-0-6151-3755-1
Paperback, Second Edition

Acknowledgments

I'm grateful to numerous individuals who've been part of this work directly and indirectly. Your prayers, suggestions, time, and other sacrifices have made this assignment possible.

To Dr. Michael Gondwe, David Kofsky, Jeanneth Angel, and my entire extended family. Only God can thank these amazing people enough for their undying faith, love, sacrifices, and inspiration throughout my life.

And above all, to our Lord Jesus Christ, our Shepherd in life, who is the way, the truth and the life. May he use this book that he inspired, among many others throughout history, in equipping his church and prevailing against the gates of hell. "I will build my church, and the gates of Hades will not overcome it," Matthew 16:18.

Table of Contents

Introduction

INTRODUCTION - SUB-TOPICS:

    -Origins of the Erroneous Warfare and Deliverance Teachings
    -Nature of False Doctrine and False Teachings
    -Indirect confrontation Vs direct confrontation
    -The Sovereignty of God and His Set-up of Spiritual Laws

This book could save you avoidable heartache in your life, in the lives of your loved ones, or in your ministry. It covers on what some of us in evangelical circles have assumed to be Christian spiritual warfare and deliverance ministry teachings. It cautions on the potential dangers, consequences, and points to what bible based spiritual warfare and deliverance ministry principles are.

The biblical interpretation of spiritual warfare and deliverance ministry principles endorsed by this book are supported by the entire 2000 year church history -from Christ's time up to now.

On the other hand, the new end-time spiritual warfare teachings that advocate for direct confrontation with Satan emerged in the 1980s. They are mainly prescribed by two or three denominations among our various evangelical branches.

Evangelicals include Charismatics, Baptists, Pentecostals, Methodists, AME, Presbyterians, Assemblies of God, Lutherans, and so on, including most non-denominations. Our uniting beliefs include emphasis on spiritual rebirth through accepting and following Jesus Christ as Lord and Savior, and in upholding the inerrancy of the bible. Together we constitute the body of Christ, the church of our Lord that transcends denominational and geographical boundaries.

This book is empowering on major biblical principles on spiritual warfare and deliverance. It is also valuable in avoiding the spiritual attacks that are caused by applying erroneous teachings on spiritual warfare and deliverance. It's better learning through the easier way of understanding than through an avoidable shipwreck or crisis that enforces a change of perspective - like some of us once faced.

You will be amazed at the findings as we test the spirit and truth behind each version of spiritual warfare and deliverance ministry principles. Needless to say that the fruits or consequences from each version of teachings speak for themselves.

Origins of the Erroneous Warfare and Deliverance Teachings

Beginning in the 1980s we, in some evangelical circles, have followed matters we have called spiritual warfare teachings with little or no biblical scrutiny. C. Peter Wagner is considered among the chief architects of the spiritual warfare doctrine of direct confrontation with evil spirits.

The doctrine of direct confrontation advocates for making verbal proclamations against Satan and his fellow fallen angels (demons) in thin air, binding them up in the spirit realm, in geographical territories, and so on. Chapter 4: True Biblical Spiritual Warfare = Indirect Confrontation explains why this is nowhere in the bible. It shows the formula the bible gives: God's role = direct confrontation, and our role = indirect confrontation

Wagner went on to establish the Wagner Leadership Institute where Strategic Level Spiritual Warfare (SLSW) was taught as a major warfare strategy of winning territorial spiritual warfare against spiritual principalities. Scriptures have been taken out of context, given new meaning and the new spiritual warfare teachings became what we have today - among some of our fellow believers.

The zeal and sincerity for God's kingdom is not being disputed among advocates of teachings that misinterpret scripture. Our main concern is the fact that the body of Christ cannot afford erroneous and harmful teachings. As watchmen and women we have a mandate to reveal erroneous and harmful teachings circulating in the body of Christ.

The new movement in the eyes of its advocates began to be known as the "Third Wave," or "Signs and Wonders" movement. They called it a new move of the Holy Spirit in the body of Christ. Says Dr. Wagner, "The first wave was known as the Pentecostal movement, (p.16) the second, the Charismatics (p.17), and now "I see the Third Wave distinct from, but at the same time similar to the first and second waves."(p.18) C. Peter Wagner, *The Third Wave of the Holy Spirit: Encountering the Power of Signs and Wonders Today.* (Note that due partly to heavy criticism from fellow evangelicals this book is out of print. For any reference purposes used copies are available at online stores like Amazon.com and Half.ebay.com).

The Third Wave movement not only introduced the new spiritual warfare teachings, it also emphasized that baptism in the Holy Spirit is verified through speaking in tongues. No tongues no baptism, no heaven, even if you were Billy Graham. Although speaking in tongues re-emerged in the early 1900s it received a new association by the Third Wavers in the late 1900s.

Says Dr. Wagner, "The Third Wave is a new moving of the Holy Spirit among evangelicals who for one reason or another have chosen not to identify with either the Pentecostals or the Charismatics. Its roots go back a little further but I see it as mainly a movement beginning in the 1980's and gathering momentum through the closing years of the 20th century.

"I see," says Wagner, "the Third Wave as distinct from, but at the same time, very similar to the first and second waves. They have to be similar because it is the same Spirit of God who is doing the work. ***The major variation comes in the understanding of the meaning of "Baptism in the Holy Spirit" and the role of tongues in authenticating this. I myself, for example, would rather not have people call me a Charismatic,*** I do not consider myself a Charismatic, I am simply an Evangelical Congregationalist who is open to the Holy Spirit working through me and my church in any way He chooses," C. Peter Wagner, cited by John F. MacArthur Jr in his book *Charismatic Chaos.*

Wagner disassociates himself from being a Charismatic or Pentecostal not primarily because of any doctrinal distinction, but primarily because of the stigma attached to such names (during the 1980s).

But not only did Wagner's teachings gain prominence among our Charismatic and Pentecostal evangelical churches we also became the major crusaders of his teachings. Without the support of Charismatics and Pentecostals Wagner and other pioneers of the non-biblical spiritual warfare teachings would have largely gone unnoticed.

Sincere believers of high prominence endorsed the non-biblical spiritual warfare and what followed is what we have today. The deception flood of the erroneous spiritual warfare and deliverance teachings got so high that many of us easily found scripture to back up our resolve to directly fight evil spirits.

Believers were zealous in their resolve to directly confront demonic spirits that scripture was easily taken out of context without even realizing it. Some are still zealous in the non-biblical spiritual warfare and deliverance teachings. The consequences among believers of following these teachings have been disturbing and unfortunate.

The mistaken understanding has been that spiritual warfare implies directly confronting Satan and his demonic spirits (fallen angels), making verbal proclamations in thin air against them, binding them up in the spirit world, in geographical territories, and so on. This, it has been assumed, was our responsibility according to the bible. Unfortunately the consequences speak for themselves on whether or not the bible supports this belief. This book covers on the potential dangers, consequences and points to the true biblical spiritual warfare we have always followed throughout church history.

True biblical spiritual warfare is what we have held all along before the misinterpretation came in. It maintains that God fights our battles us we seek his intervention rather than confronting Satan ourselves. Our role in dealing with evil spirits in the spirit realm is indirect in nature, while God's role is direct. The only exception is when casting out evil spirits out of people. The book outlines all these areas.

Some changes towards biblical spiritual warfare and deliverance have been occurring as we have been learning from these unfortunate experiences. However we still have some way to go as fundamentalist evangelicals. This book, among others, facilitates our return to biblical principles of spiritual warfare and deliverance. Without a true understanding we will continue facing avoidable consequences that our mistaken spiritual warfare and deliverance teachings invite.

Nature of False Doctrine and False Teachings

False doctrine in the body of Christ refers to teachings with biblical half-truths containing errors that misinterpret the scripture. Presence of false doctrine does not imply a particular church or denomination is a cult. Far from it. A cult in its broadest meaning represents groups that worship or give reverence to a deity other than God, Father of Jesus Christ and deny the basic doctrines of the Christian faith.

False doctrine and cults can therefore refer to two separate matters, even though cults by their nature follow false doctrine. As Chapter 1 shows, church history has shown that every church body has had some level of error uncovered at some point or another. That error constituted false doctrine but did not imply that believers who fell for it were part of a cult.

This book is therefore, not about exposing cults but about false doctrines in the body of Christ. It is primarily about revealing and correcting one area of false doctrines: on spiritual warfare and deliverance principles.

The book is also not about attacking or condemning any individual, church or denomination in body of Christ. It is about pointing out erroneous and harmful teachings that pose major hindrances to believers and ultimately the entire body of Christ.

The book uncovers the errors on spiritual warfare and deliverance principles that have entered the body of Christ trapping many sincere believers who practice them. The biblical truths contained in this book proclaim their freedom from all consequences of the false doctrines on spiritual warfare and deliverance teachings.

False doctrines or false teachings at their lowest level are a hindrance to true Christian living. At their worst level they are severely destructive to a believer spiritually, emotionally, socially, materially, or even physically. For example, the false doctrines on slavery and gender biases brought psycho-social humiliation of inferiority complexes and economic deprivation on discriminated groups. Although other religions and cultures still embrace primitive gender biases our focus here is where scripture is misinterpreted in order to justify false beliefs.

One of our most recent false beliefs in the body of Christ are on spiritual warfare and deliverance teachings. Parts of this book explain why the spiritual warfare and deliverance errors have the worst consequences among false doctrines currently circulating in the body of Christ. Thankfully there is a way out.

Indirect confrontation Vs direct confrontation

The vicious cycle of strange problem after another befalls many sincere, heaven destined believers who assume scripture authorizes us to fight Satan ourselves. Thankfully there is a solution to whatever befalls anyone trapped in this false doctrine. It is in ceasing the practice of the assumed spiritual warfare and fighting the enemy the way scripture authorizes us to. This is through indirect confrontation.

Indirect confrontation is what scripture prescribes for us. Chapter 4, "True Spiritual Warfare = Indirect Confrontation," shows how God has made indirect confrontation as our only spiritual warfare. Indirect confrontation implies that we do not fight with Satan and his evil forces by approaching them directly. We confront them by applying indirect means and ways that God has established for us.

Applying and fulfilling our required indirect roles secures our standing before God and allows him to directly act on our behalf. Attacks from Satan against us become God's battles as we obey and fulfill the roles required of us. In this spiritual battle God's role is direct in nature as he is able to directly deal with the spiritual forces unseen to our human eyes.

God through his heavenly government that has the authority and access to the kingdom of hell is able to directly deal with the enemy and his works. Indirect confrontation is how we can petition God in the name of Jesus to fight on our behalf over our lives or the lives of others.

Indirect confrontation seems simple yet it has the most powerful deliverance ministry tools given to us. Our weapons of warfare, which from a correct scriptural interpretation are indirect in nature, are the most powerful weapons God has entrusted us with. Scripture says they are more powerful than human weapons, able to devastate the activities of Satan on earth. May we effectively use them in setting captives free and practicing true deliverance ministry.

The Sovereignty of God and His Set-up of Spiritual Laws

Our God is almighty, all sovereign. This makes him in charge of everything, including over Satan. He thus has not left his throne to Satan to do whatever he pleases. Satan operates *within* the boundaries that God allows and has set-up as spiritual laws. Outside these boundaries he has NO means, authority, nor power to enforce his wishes.

That is why he uses traps to bring people into his boundaries -so that he can attack them. *Within* his boundaries he gains legal access to attack in whatever way he has access to –spiritually, socially, materially, physically, etc. The methods he uses to gain legal access to people include deception, sin and ignorance. The false teachings on spiritual warfare and deliverance are therefore among his doorways. Other traps he uses among believers include love of money, pursuit of worldly pleasures, power, fame, knowledge, etc.

Deliverance comes when people understand that direct confrontation with Satan takes us into his forbidden territory. Being outside the boundary brought by the assumed spiritual warfare ends his legal access to an individual or ministry. It closes the door he used to hinder a person's life.

God can still permit Satan to operate outside his boundary, e.g. in the case of Job. However, Satan had to first obtain permission from God because all avenues of legal access were closed. The same applies to all believers who walk in truth and are under the righteousness of Christ. Satan can only gain entry into our lives only after getting permission from God.

God giving Satan permission is an exception rather than a rule. God does not delight in our affliction, especially in areas that Satan has no legal entry. The ultimate outcome when God gives Satan permission always brings victory rather than defeat for the believer and for God's kingdom. We know how Job ended up with more than he lost. Similarly, our Lord Jesus got the greatest victory for all humanity after being innocently oppressed and killed by Satan. God ultimately upholds his faithfulness and righteousness.

1. The Fallibility of the Church

The Church (body of Christ) is Liable to Err

To begin with, every *sincere* and *practicing* born again believer in evangelical circles is heaven-bound. Not even hell can contest that. We are sealed as God's children in the body of Christ and the Spirit in us bears witness to that.

However, it would be wrong to assume that all the doctrinal beliefs held in our various evangelical denominations are infallible or free from error. The church, the bride of Christ, is fallible and liable to err.

By the end of this book you'll understand how fallible we are and that in our fallibility we are still 100 percent God's children and his elect. You'll also learn that being in err has its consequences in this life. It may not affect our place in eternity if we are innocently deceived yet it does affect our outcomes in this life. That is why it's not worth entertaining erroneous teachings when they are revealed.

No single denomination can claim to be free from error on all its doctrines and beliefs. Such a claim would be at best naïve and at worst an expression of pride. It is a false assumption even when we may not know what the major error(s) may be.

The Lord has exposed some level of error in every church and denomination throughout history. Thus even today no single denomination can be the exception, not in this fallible life. *The International Standard Bible Encyclopedia* says "The history of the church shows that it has been as liable to error, and as readily influenced by natural conditions, as any other human institutions," (ISB Encyclopedia, "Authority in Religion: V. Classification of Theories").

Exposing the errors has been our Lord's way of building, growing and maturing his church. Those that made changes have steered the church to higher levels of obedience, truth, and usefulness.

The Bible says we do not yet have perfect knowledge of everything, until this present world passes away. "For we know in part and we prophesy in part, but when perfection comes, the imperfect disappears." 1 Corinthians 13:9-10. The imperfect knowledge we have will be replaced by the perfect.

We therefore only know in part, according to the level the Lord chooses to reveal. More revelation brings more freedom and more power in the body of Christ against Satan's works on earth. "If you hold to my teaching, you are really my disciples. Then you will know the truth, and the truth will set you free," John 8:31-32.

A truth revealed to correct an error is therefore a sign that the Lord is taking us to a new level of freedom. It's a sign that he is closing the door Satan legally used to attack us through our ignorance. We understand that hell will stop at nothing in attempting to rob or even destroy God's elect. Deception has been his major weapon of attack. Deception feeds on ignorance. Our level of deception therefore depends on our level of ignorance.

The Lord also allows that we remain ignorant on particular truths we may not be able to handle. "I have much more to say to you, more than you can now bear," John 16:12. At each point in church history and even in our individual lives the Lord has been revealing more to us in relation to what we can effectively bear.

There is therefore more to be revealed to us in the measure that we can handle. He reveals to us the amount we can handle per time. This often happens when dealing with revelations that will drastically change our understanding. By the time we get the whole truth we're able to accept it without it seeming controversial. It's able to replace old beliefs we had always assumed were true.

Consequences of Church Errors on Believers

Unfortunately every error has had its level of negative consequences. Being outside God's will it opens legal access for Satan to attack. In the body of Christ, errors limit our effectiveness, fruitfulness and triumph over evil on both an individual and corporate level.

For example, the Pope of the Catholic Church was in 1870, declared to be infallible. He was said to be immune from liability to error or failure. He exalted himself above humanity and equated himself with heavenly beings. At some point something had to bring the papacy (church government of the Roman Catholic Church) to the truth before their claim to infallibility brought more chaos.

Combined with other errors this infallibility false doctrine/teaching added to the decline of the reign of the Catholic Church. It continued to lose its immense political authority God entrusted it with over the most powerful nations at the time.

By 1929, the Catholic Church's political influence was reduced to what is now the Vatican nation, a tiny piece of land. This is a church that once controlled the power and wealth of numerous nations throughout the world.

Since its downfall the Lord has never entrusted any other church body with so much political, economic, social, and spiritual authority. The gospel would have been evangelized throughout the world by now had such immense authority remained to the body of Christ, particularly with the evangelical denominations.

With few of the major errors on scripture corrected the Catholic Church has been labeled by many Protestants as a modern day Pharisee. Obedience to maintaining established tradition became more important than the willingness to change when errors were revealed. It has been accused of resisting to move with the Spirit of God.

We, in the evangelical circles, will not be spared from consequences of embracing errors if we fall in the same trap. This includes embracing errors on spiritual warfare and deliverance teachings.

The erroneous spiritual warfare and deliverance teachings advocating for direct confrontation against the kingdom of hell started primarily in the 1980s. The enemy showed up, disguised as an "angel of light" to add in his poison as the Body of Christ has been advancing and preparing the soon return of Christ.

Many of the deceptive kinds of spiritual warfare strategies that infiltrated the church have been revealed in the body of Christ. These include scolding Satan, repeated chants of binding and rebuking him, stomping on the ground in a symbolic expression of crushing him, chaining him or his demons and casting him into some imaginary place like fire, hell, a pot, etc. It's amazing what we, in the body of Christ, have been doing in the name of spiritual warfare and deliverance for the past few decades.

Such erroneous spiritual warfare and deliverance has only led us to stray into spiritual territory that's not in our realm of authority (domain) and led to unfortunate counterattacks. The counterattacks could have been avoided if we had not trespassed into forbidden territory. This has been much to the enemy's pleasure to see God's people being destroyed for lack of proper knowledge.

Consequences of the Erroneous Spiritual Warfare Teachings

The negative consequences may sound like science fiction to observers who do not practice this spiritual warfare. However these are real matters that people involved in the false doctrine on spiritual warfare and deliverance ministry experience. The experiences may be spiritual, social, material, physical or any combination.

John Jackson in his book, *Needless Casualties of War*, gives a list of problems among believers that testified about their involvement in the erroneous spiritual warfare and deliverance teachings. They include troubled careers, businesses and ministries, unexplainable church conflicts, tormented families, divorces, marital unfaithfulness, runaway children, strange illnesses, miscarriages, untimely deaths and unstoppable sinful habits. Speak of terror. These are not trials of faith, nor persecution for righteousness' sake.

Thankfully, for some of us, God remained faithful in preserving us from falling out of faith. Many have given up though, in their spiritual lives, marriages, vocations, ministries and so on. Fortunately most of the believers that testified in Jackson's book experienced healing and restoration after making amends in their approach over erroneous spiritual warfare and deliverance teachings.

The experiences are the devil's direct acts of coming to "steal and kill and destroy," (John 10:10) using the spiritual warfare and deliverance deception of direct confrontation. The unfortunate experiences tell us that there is something wrong with the spiritual warfare and deliverance teachings we are applying.

Even when a "breakthrough" happens through the erroneous spiritual warfare and deliverance teachings twice the trouble comes out elsewhere. If we cannot learn from the scriptures we're at least enabled to learn from the experiences the erroneous spiritual warfare and deliverance teachings bring.

Perry Stone, a prominent evangelist that went through much trouble in his early days of ministry says, "Focus on the devil and he shows up, focus on Christ and he shows up," (3:00 in the Morning: Tapping into the Spirit World). He was warned about his preoccupation with the evil spirit realm in his early years of ministry but never listened. He experienced much trouble from following unscriptural practices concerning the spirit realm.

Some of us may identify with Perry Stone from various troubles we may have gone through as a result of being caught up with the erroneous spiritual warfare and deliverance teachings that advocate for direct confrontation. It is quite simple to spot these experiences.

Firstly they really can never be classified as genuine marks of Christ. They're more marks of the enemy than anything else. Secondly, they leave this uneasiness in us that somehow the Lord ought to have stopped these matters from turning out the way they did. This is regardless of whether or not they eventually worked to our good. The Lord works even our past sins and negative backgrounds to our good yet he never ordained or orchestrated them for us to go through.

The marks of Christ come from enduring persecution and living a sacrificial life. They do not come from crippling illnesses, tormenting setbacks and losses, divorces, church setbacks and so on. Unless one believes that God delights in giving good gifts to his children then only to allow the enemy to steal or destroy them. Such theology is not biblical. Even the book of Job has its own contextual meaning. It is not intended to be easily used to justify such terror.

John Jackson, author of *Needless Casualties of War,* says these strange experiences are more prominent among believers who're burdened for the lives of others and engage in the assumed erroneous spiritual warfare and deliverance teachings. The problem is that we have been swayed by the lie that the attacks are mere acts of the enemy trying to put a counterattack that he'll eventually loose.

The enemy loves to play the deception card which works on ignorance to trap God's people. Ignorance is no excuse in the realm of the spirit. That's why God says his own blood bought and heaven-bound people are destroyed for lack of proper knowledge (Hosea 4.6). It may be destruction spiritually (God forbid), socially, physically or materially.

It is our burden and prayer that this book will put an end to consequences resulting from practicing the erroneous spiritual warfare and deliverance teachings that advocate for direct confrontation against Satan. It is also our burden and prayer that fellow believers will be armed with true biblical spiritual warfare and deliverance principles that advocate for INdirect confrontation against Satan.

Many believers may already be familiar with controversial experiences in their Christian lives that contradict scripture a bit too far. Have you experienced or are experiencing strange problems in your life that seem to have no scriptural basis?

The experiences could be in any area or combination of spiritual, emotional, social, material, or physical areas. They usually follow after some time of practicing the assumed spiritual warfare. The strange experiences are neither trials of faith nor persecution for righteousness' sake. No other scriptural basis seems to fit in. Not even sin, with the righteousness of Christ covering your blemishes.

Or you have no peace, with your self or even with God. No smooth road promised in the bible, yet much inner peace usually accompanies us in the midst of our various trials. It may also include a spiritual heaviness where you are seeing or hearing spirit beings. And the "spiritual warfare" or "deliverance seminars" from a "deliverance ministry" only keep making things worse. Strange dreams and nightmares maybe a norm for some believers. Any explanation of your experiences to someone unfamiliar with what's going on makes him/her think you have some mental problems.

Some strange problems may be in the lives of your loved ones or ministry. Years of prayer have had little or no fruit. It's like receiving a snake after having asked for a fish. Many snakes in some experiences.

Have you ever considered your involvement in what many of us in some fundamentalist evangelical circles have called "spiritual warfare?" How about the "deliverance seminars" that some ministries practice on believers?

There is nothing wrong with us being radical for Jesus yet many things go wrong if misinformed. "*My people* are destroyed from lack of knowledge," Hosea 4.6.

This book uncovers the effects of the practice of the unscriptural spiritual warfare and deliverance teachings, its background, and points to the true spiritual warfare and deliverance principles from the correct biblical interpretation. It will be a lifesaver for many sincere believers innocently caught up in false teachings on spiritual warfare and deliverance ministry.

2. Our Territory and Nature of Our Christian Authority

CHAPTER 2 SUB-TOPICS:

-Sphere of Influence
-Exercising our Christian Authority on Earth
1. Our Christian Authority through Binding and Loosing
 a) True Binding and Loosing
 b) Limitations of Binding and Loosing
2. Our Christian Authority through our Roles in Body of Christ
 a) Implies Divine Choice
 b) Implies Representation
 c) Implies Offering Living Sacrifice (ourselves)

This is quite a boring chapter with its detailed coverage on church doctrine and 2,000 years of interpretation of particular scriptures. It is nonetheless essential to understanding our boundaries of authority according to the bible in relation to matters we deal with in life, both physical (seen) and spiritual (unseen). It's also a short chapter compared to the book's principle chapters.

God has his unlimited sphere of authority, we have our limited one, and Satan too has his limited authority. We cannot afford to go beyond our limited sphere of influence because we end up straying into unauthorized territory that does not have heaven's backing.

Without heaven's backing we end up merely operating in our own strength, a sure strategy for defeat. This chapter explains where our limited sphere of influence lies.

Sphere of Influence

Knowing our sphere or territory of influence is important to avoid going into unauthorized territory and matters. Much error has arisen here in the body of Christ. On the extreme right some have assumed we could exercise authority over everything on earth and in the spirit realm except God.

One example is that the church as an institution assumed it had the authority to forgive (loose) or withhold (bind) the sins of its members. Another concerns spiritual warfare and deliverance teachings where believers assume they have authority to directly confront evil spirits that live outside people and in the heavenly realms. Both have used scripture to justify their understanding.

On the extreme left some have assumed we are mere passengers in God's master plan that only he dictates while we follow. He is the Porter while we're the clay so we have no say in how our lives unfold. Whatever experience or matter in our lives, good or bad, big or small, he predestined it to come our way. All we can do, like Job, is to trust him that he knows what he is doing even though we may not understand. By faith we keep going. This assumption also uses scripture. Both extremes, plus the other extreme given above, are harmful to believers in the Body of Christ.

The authority or influence assigned to the Body of Christ belonged to all mankind from the beginning of creation. God told Adam and Eve, "fill the earth and subdue it. Rule over the fish of the sea and the birds of the air and over every living creature that moves on the ground," Genesis 1:28.

The earth was ours to rule over while God retained authority in the heavens. "The highest heavens belong to the Lord, but the earth he has given to man," Psalm 115:16.

However, through sin that came by Satan's deception on Adam and Eve we lost this authority on earth. What Jesus did on the cross was to restore it to us. He was restoring the authority mankind lost by giving it to his church. Unbelievers however, are still under the influence and authority of Satan who stole our birthright of ruling the earth. The church on the other hand, is immune to Satan's authority. He can try to influence us but cannot rule over us. Through the Holy Spirit living in us we have the final say in determining our decisions and ultimately the course of our lives.

Although the sphere of authority changed very little when Christ restored it to us, the assignment for using the authority changed. The sphere or realm of authority remains on the earthly realm. However, the purpose for using the authority changed. We now have a higher purpose than just populating the earth and releasing our creative potential to better manage our lives.

Our new purpose is to populate God's kingdom. It is a priestly purpose. It involves fulfilling all our priestly duties assigned to each one of us in the body of Christ. Through our various priestly duties people are set free from their bondage to Satan, spiritually, socially, physically and materially. It is deliverance ministry in its totality from Satan's kingdom into God's kingdom. Each one of us in the body of Christ has a form of deliverance ministry we've been commissioned to fulfill.

The only addition to our authority on earth concerned confronting evil spirits living in people. This is not the same thing as confronting evil spirits living in the spiritual realm, in geographical areas, or in thin air where they do not occupy any human vessel. The chapter on "Exception for Direct Confrontation" explains the authority on confronting evil spirits living in people. Going outside its boundaries has recently been getting us into trouble.

Exercising our Christian Authority on Earth

1. a) True Binding and Loosing

A scripture that helps us understand how we exercise our assigned authority is in Matthew 16. Our Lord said, "I will give you the keys of the kingdom of heaven; whatever you bind on earth will be bound in heaven, and whatever you loose on earth will be loosed in heaven," Matthew 16:19.

Matthew Henry's Concise Commentary says, "This binding and loosing, in the common language of the Jews, signified to forbid and to allow, or to teach what is lawful or unlawful."

John Wesley's Bible Notes say, "Under the term of binding and loosing are contained all those acts of discipline which Peter and his brethren performed as apostles: and undoubtedly what they thus performed on earth, God confirmed in heaven."

The Matthew Henry Complete Commentary says the authority to bind and loose among the Jews, "signified to prohibit and permit; to teach or declare a thing to be unlawful was to bind; to be lawful, was to loose.

"Now the apostles had an extraordinary power of this kind; some things forbidden by the law of Moses were now to be allowed, as the eating of such and such meats; some things allowed there were now to be forbidden, as divorce; and the apostles were empowered to declare this to the world, and men might take it upon their words. When Peter was first taught himself, and then taught others, to call nothing common or unclean, this power was exercised."

It says the authority to bind and loose, "is a power which Christ has promised to own the due administration of; he will ratify the sentences of his stewards with his own approbation; It shall be bound in heaven, and loosed in heaven: not that Christ hath hereby obliged himself to confirm all church-censures, right or wrong; but such as are duly passed according to the word, clave non errante—the key turning the right way, such are sealed in heaven; that is, the word of the gospel, in the mouth of faithful ministers, is to be looked upon, not as the word of man, but as the word of God, and to be received accordingly, 1 Th. 2:13; Jn. 12:20." (sorry for the difficult old English version)

Binding and loosing therefore implies making decisions on allowing or forbidding matters on earth which once agreed upon would be supported in heaven. These matters could be in *whatever* area of life –spiritual, social, political, physical and material. They have largely been spiritual or religious matters throughout history. Unfortunately we recently (in the past few decades) took the binding and loosing to imply the authority to go after evil spirits.

Before this assumption, there was another error of using the authority given to the church. The church, under the Roman Catholic Church, as an institution used it to forgive (loose) or withhold (bind) the sins of its members. After the Lord revealed this error many Christians, led by Martin Luther, protested. They called such acts as blasphemy, since religious leaders were acting as God, able to forgive or retain sins.

What would we then call the act of going to bind and loose evil spirits? We were never assigned to do it. The book of Jude calls it "slander" against "celestial beings," because "men speak abusively against whatever they do not understand," Jude 1:8-10. It is spiritual slander. We cannot afford taking scripture out of its context and assigning it a different meaning just to justify a point that we have authority over evil spirits.

Authority over evil spirits is given in another passage of scripture and not in Matthew 16. This authority is however, limited in its nature –like any other form of authority. The chapter on "Exception for Direct Confrontation" explains this area of authority.

Notice also that the binding and loosing power given to Christians involved the church. The church in its literal meaning is a council or a congregation of the "called out ones." *The Matthew Henry Complete Commentary* defines it as "the children of men called out of the world, and set apart from it, and dedicated to Christ."

The church is a representative congregation of people who decide on matters that affect their lives and the lives of people they represent before heaven, not hell. They render the matters as binding or loosed in the sense of annulling whatever was considered bound. As the council or church presents its decisions before heaven once agreed upon on earth God in his heavenly government also considers them binding in the heavenly realms.

How these matters are enforced as bound or loosed in the heavenly realm may not be a big issue to know. All we know is that God's angels are involved in fulfilling what he has considered binding. The angels do the work of fighting any spiritual beings that oppose his will. We do not have any business to directly deal with these heavenly beings.

The authority of binding and loosing was therefore not intended for going after evil spirits. It was Christ giving the power of agreement on matters between us in the church (body of Christ) and heaven. The minimum number to operate in this authority is two. "I tell you the truth, whatever you bind on earth will be bound in heaven, and whatever you loose on earth will be loosed in heaven. Again, I tell you that *if two of you* on earth agree about anything you ask for, it will be done for you by my Father in heaven. For where two or three come together in my name, there am I with them," Matthew 18:18-20.

Two or more people thus constitute a church with enough power on earth to receive the full backing of heaven on whatever matters they're entrusted with. Whatever they agree upon is then left to heaven to fulfill the rest. This includes heaven's role in directly overcoming the evil spiritual forces that try to oppose what has been considered a binding matter between heaven and earth. We're not to interfere how God's government deals with these matters in the heavenly (celestial) realm. Our jurisdiction is down here - authority over whatever (spiritual, social, political, physical) matters that exist on earth. "*Whatever* you bind *on earth*..."

"*Whatever* you bind *on earth*..." It is "on earth," not in the spirit realm, nor in the heavenly and nor in the unseen world. It is also "whatever" matters or issues, not "whatever" spirits nor demonic beings. Taking the original meaning out of context invalidates what Christ actually meant. Changing what he meant creates a totally different scripture that's not in the bible and one that does not have the backing of heaven.

1. b) Limitations of Binding and Loosing

The authority of binding and loosing on whatever matters that exist on earth is limited by our level of obedience to God. Even in the secular world, anyone given authority is answerable to the one who gave him/her the authority. Presidents are answerable to the people, managers to shareholders and so on. Once they start making decisions that are contrary to those who have given them the authority their legitimacy or claim to be in office is compromised. The bigger the violation of authority the higher the risk of being dismissed even with severe punishment.

The same is true for us. God who gave us authority over affairs on earth is only committed to fulfilling his will on earth and in each of our lives. He has a will for us on who, where, when, how, why and what needs to be done. When we submit to his agenda for our lives and for others we receive his full support in the matters we have been assigned to represent him.

Binding and loosing whatever matters that exist on earth in whatever way we desire would be a permit to representing our on wishes on earth. Not only would that be a license to anarchy, it would reduce God to a mere observer as we use our given authority to advance our agendas. Our Lord remains in charge and thus remains the one giving the orders on where, when, how, why and what matters need to be bound or loosed on earth.

Many of us who have proceeded to fulfill whatever our minds considered have gone through unnecessary stress. Heaven's support was not with us and it became our own struggle to fulfill them. The key to binding and loosing whatever matters that exist on earth is therefore obedience to the will of God on earth. We're able to receive his plans as we submit to him in prayer, by allowing his Spirit to work through us and through his word.

As believers we can always bring all our thoughts, plans and convictions before the Lord. He will be faithful to give us the right understanding. We have access to his throne of grace for wisdom and every provision for fulfilling our purposed callings. "Let us then approach the throne of grace with confidence, so that we may receive mercy and find grace to help us in our time of need," Hebrews 4:16.

Just us we're able to know more of each other as we spend more time together, we're also able to know and understand the language of the Holy Spirit the more time we spend with God - in prayer, his Word, evangelism and so on.

The Holy Spirit who lives inside every one of us born again is able to speak more clearly to us the more we submit to God. "Do you not know that your body is a temple of the Holy Spirit, who is in you, whom you have received from God?" (1 Corinthians 6:19). He is able to more effectively fulfill the purposes of heaven through us on earth. "God is at work in you, both to will and to work for his good pleasure," (Philippians 2:13).

The Scriptures have many examples of people who had a close relationship with God. It illustrates how God leads us on an individual level and on a corporate level. The people spoke to him and heard him speak to them in words and ways they understood it was him speaking. The presence of God was what characterized people that submitted their lives to him.

Tom Marshall in his book, *Free Indeed*, says, "We may not be able to explain or describe how we know but we "just know" in a certain and unshakable way that God has spoken to us, or that God has heard our prayer, or that we are in presence of God. Many times, because we do not understand this, we are not aware that it is God who has been speaking to us."

The inner witness of God registers in the conscience which is the unseen spiritual part of us. The bible says, "The Holy Spirit himself testifies with our spirit that we are God's children," (Romans 8:16).

When this reliance on God's Spirit to testify (bear witness) with our spirits over issues becomes habitual our minds become tuned to the voice of the Holy Spirit. We are able to be led by the Spirit because we give him first priority over our thoughts and desires.

Scripture says that, "Those who live according to the sinful nature (the flesh) have their minds set on what nature desires; but those who live in accordance with the Spirit have their minds set on what the Spirit desires," (Ro 8:5-6)

2. Our Christian Authority Through our Roles in Body of Christ

Another area that enables us to understand our given authority on earth is by examining our roles in the body of Christ. Our duties show us where our authority lies. This authority enables us to effectively fulfill our responsibilities in our assigned areas. Our major obligations can all be summed up into one role –priesthood. The nature of the priestly office is as follows:

2. a) Implies Divine Choice

"You are a *chosen* people, a royal priesthood, a holy nation, a people belonging to God, that you may declare the praises of him who called you out of darkness into his wonderful light," 1 Peter 2:9.

Whatever role we may have in the body of Christ will not be by our own choosing or an appointment from others. It will be from God. Any matter that we involve ourselves outside his appointment will at best not have lasting results. At worst it may have negative consequences on us, like the sons of Sceva experienced (Acts 19: 15-16). Since there will be no support from heaven it will be a labor or battle under our own strength.

God will use people, various experiences and imparting necessary gifts to confirm to us the areas of work he has for us per time. Ultimately it is him who orchestrates everything to ensure we end up knowing our assigned duties. Our burden for particular matters or people, level of commitment and other marks will show that the areas are not our choosing but a divine choice. We are enabled to effectively fulfill our priestly role in those areas and to put up with any opposition Satan tries to use against us.

Even our Lord Jesus was sent by God. He received his commission and his authority from God. He was able to declare, "The Spirit of the Lord is on me, because he has anointed me to preach good news to the poor. *He has sent me* to proclaim freedom for the prisoners and recovery of sight for the blind, to release the oppressed," Luke 4:18.

Jeremiah was ordained before his birth, "Before I formed you in the womb I knew you, before you were born I set you apart; I appointed you as a prophet to the nations," Jeremiah 1:5. Paul was chosen in spite of the initial controversy it brought among the early disciples. "This man is my chosen instrument to carry my name before the Gentiles and their kings and before the people of Israel," Acts 9:15.

2. b) Implies Representation

The International Standard Bible Encyclopedia says, "A priest is one who is duly authorized to minister in sacred things, particularly to offer sacrifices at the altar, and who acts as mediator between men and God," (ISB Encyclopedia, "Priest").

Our primary representation is the work of Jesus on earth. He was sent to sacrifice his life for the sin of humanity. He offered the last and most perfect sacrifice for the sins for all people: himself. That is why sin offerings are no longer necessary. He was the ultimate sacrifice for all the sins of people who receive him and accept him as Lord and Savior.

"Christ did not enter a man-made sanctuary that was only a copy of the true one; he entered heaven itself, now to appear for us in God's presence. Nor did he enter heaven to offer himself again and again, the way the high priest enters the Most Holy Place every year with blood that is not his own... Just as man is destined to die once, and after that to face judgment, so Christ was sacrificed once to take away the sins of many people; and he will appear a second time, not to bear sin, but to bring salvation to those who are waiting for him," Hebrews 9:24-28.

Jesus served the role of High Priest by offering up a sacrifice to God – his life. "He became the source of eternal salvation for all who obey him and was designated by God to be high priest in the order of Melchizedek," Hebrews 5:9-10. The role of high priest now belongs to Christ while our priestly work is to serve under him. He is our head in the priestly office. "Christ is the head of the church, his body, of which he is the Savior," Ephesians 5:23.

The High Priest who offered his sin offering has assigned us to fulfill the other priestly duties that facilitate his mediation for all mankind. "There is one God and one mediator between God and men, the man Christ Jesus, who gave himself as a ransom for all men," 1 Timothy 2:5-6.

Through us, his body, he is able to reach the lost and disadvantaged spiritually, socially, materially, physically and so on. He is also able to reveal to them his ultimate sacrifice for our sins. Whatever role we have been assigned in his body, big or small, is useful in his outreach to all humanity. We are Christ's representatives or ambassadors to all humanity here on earth.

2. c) Implies Offering Living Sacrifice (ourselves)

Offering of sacrifices was the most important priestly duty. Blood sacrifices served to reconcile men to God by making atonement for their sins. Jesus became our high priest by completing the major purpose of sacrifices through his death on the cross (Hebrews 5:1,4-5)

The requirement of offering of sacrifices for our sins is now irrelevant. However his work on the cross did not abolish offering of all sacrifices to God. In the Old Testament God commanded the children of Israel to make five types of offerings and sacrifices to him:

i. Trespass or guilt offering (Ended with Christ)

A trespass or guilt offering was made to seek forgiveness both from God, and the person wronged when people sinned against their neighbors. The trespassers who violated the rights of others were also required to return any stolen property or service, plus 20%, to their neighbors on the day that they offered up their guilt offering. The priest then proceeded to make restitution between the sinner and God by making a blood offering before God.

ii. Sin Offering (Ended with Christ)

This included both sins of ignorance and sins committed unintentionally. The offerings gave the people and the priest a way to confess their sin before God and to be cleansed from their inequity.

iii. Burnt Offerings

The burnt offering mainly served as an act of worship to God. The offering was burnt entirely as a surrender to God of the individual or congregation, while the one presenting the offering received nothing. It served as a thankful prayer to God, an acknowledgment of his mercy, wisdom and love. Unlike the other offerings Gentiles could participate in the burnt offering sacrifice. However their presence was prohibited during the burnt offering ceremony.

We are still required to make sacrifices to God of worship. Unlike in the Old Testament our sacrifice to him is in form of giving ourselves to his service spiritually, physically, materially and socially. "Therefore, I urge you, brothers, in view of God's mercy, to offer your bodies as *living sacrifices*, holy and pleasing to God - this is your spiritual act of worship," Romans 12:1-2.

Our service in the body of Christ serves as a spiritual offering. "You also, like living stones, are being built into a spiritual house to be a holy priesthood, offering *spiritual sacrifices* acceptable to God through Jesus Christ," 1 Peter 2:5.

Our highest level of worship is when we endeavor to live at the obedient and submissive level Christ walked with God in his earthly ministry. "A time is coming and has now come when the true worshipers will worship the Father in spirit and truth, for they are the kind of worshipers the Father seeks. God is spirit, and his worshipers must worship in spirit and in truth," John 4:23-24.

iv. Grain Offerings

Offerings brought were meant to satisfy God by honoring him with the provisions he made for his people. The offering is known by various titles such as the cereal, grain, meat, meal, and drink offering. It was the only bloodless offering of the Israelites. They included fine flour, unleavened cakes, with oil.

Although the format may have changed we are still required to honor God with all that he provides for us spiritually, materially, socially and physically. We honor him by sharing our gifts with those less privileged. "And do not forget to do good and to share with others, for with such sacrifices God is pleased," Hebrews 13:16.

Through our sacrificial service to those in need we indirectly offer sacrifices to God. Whatever acceptable form of service to them whether spiritually, materially, socially or physically is a form of service to God. "I was hungry and you gave me something to eat, I was thirsty and you gave me something to drink, I was a stranger and you invited me in, I needed clothes and you clothed me, I was sick and you looked after me, I was in prison and you came to visit me," Matthew 25:35-36.

It is actually our righteous living and Christian service to others that the Lord, our High Priest, will judge on Judgment Day, put in the fire as an offering for us. Sacrifices founded on Christ as a genuine cross that we carried for the sake of others will be revealed.

Sacrifices made merely for selfish gain will also be revealed. "If any man builds on this foundation using gold, silver, costly stones, wood, hay or straw, his work will be shown for what it is, because the Day will bring it to light. It will be revealed with fire, and the fire will test the quality of each man's work. If what he has built survives, he will receive his reward. If it is burned up, he will suffer loss; he himself will be saved, but only as one escaping through the flames," 1 Corinthians 3:12-15.

iv. Peace Offerings (Ended with Christ)

The peace offerings indicated right relations with God. They were of three types that consisted of thanksgiving, votive ("vow"), and freewill offerings. Jesus became our ultimate peace-maker. Through him we find peace with God. Our priestly role is to lead people to the Peace-Maker. "For God was pleased to have all his fullness dwell in him, and through him to reconcile to himself all things, whether things on earth or things in heaven, by making peace through his blood, shed on the cross," Colossians 1:19-20.

Summary on Our Christian Authority through Roles in Body of Christ

Elaborating on our priesthood can be a lengthy topic. The point we see is that the priestly office had no time being preoccupied with Satan or directly confronting him. The same pattern of priesthood can be seen in the New Testament, though in a different format. The change is mainly in terms of animal and food sacrifices, and rituals that characterized the old covenant. Christ was our ultimate sacrifice.

Part of the similar pattern is that consecration, obedience, and fellowship with God, for our own sake and for the sake of others remains the major role of the priestly office. This office equips us with weapons of righteousness.

For example the passage in Ephesians 6:11-18 shows a spiritual amour that is composed of Truth, Righteousness, Gospel of Peace, Faith, Salvation, and the Word of God. All these are matters of consecration, obedience and fellowship with God. The Lord uses our consecration and obedience to overturn Satan's legal hold over matters in our lives and the lives of those we've been assigned to minister to –spiritually, socially, materially and physically. The chapter on "True Spiritual Warfare = Indirect Confrontation" elaborates on this.

There is no role where the priest is assigned to have any form of dialogue with Satan or to make proclamations to Satan. Fulfilling our priestly roles to God and to people represented is what enables God to bring the blessings and enables him to overcome Satanic opposition.

3. Heavenly Access: Prohibited and Permitted Areas

CHAPTER 3 SUB-TOPICS:
- **Prohibited Areas**
- **Exception for Heavenly Access: Permitted Areas**

Prohibited Areas

"The *highest heavens belong to the Lord*, but the *earth he has given to man*," Psalm 115:16.

The heavens or the spirit world, or the unseen world, are a restricted territory to us human beings. Our primary business is here on earth as the scripture above says. If the heavens were not so restricted to us we'd be able to see, hear and talk with the spiritual beings that exist in this spiritual world. These are God's angels on one side and the fallen angels, including Satan, on the other side.

It is therefore for a reason that the Lord closed our eyes, ears and other senses from having any contact with the spirit world. The main reason is that it's his business to handle matters in the spirit world while it's our business to focus on matters on earth.

John Jackson in his book, *Needless Casualties of War*, distinguishes between terrestrial (earthly) and celestial (heavenly) realms, showing were our jurisdiction lies and where it does not. He shows where our given authority is – the earthly (terrestrial) realm. Jackson says, "Sending us into the world to preach the Gospel, Jesus commissioned us to cast out demons, heal the sick, cleanse the lepers and raise the dead –all warfare activities in the terrestrial (earthly) sphere."

It may be easy for some to understand this distinction between the two realms. The Lord is keeping you from danger in a good way. For some of us, understanding may have come through associating the avoidable experiences encountered in the years of active duty in the erroneous spiritual warfare and deliverance teachings. We're able to see that certain types of "spiritual warfare prayers," and "deliverance seminars," are unscriptural and dangerous.

Most of the erroneous spiritual warfare and deliverance teachings trespass into celestial (heavenly) realms that are outside our domain. Jackson says, "Only God has power to command his heavenly realms. Therefore, we who at present remain a little lower than the angels ought not to presume to command those spiritual beings who are higher ranking in the created order. This includes all of God's heavenly hosts – Michael, Gabriel, or even any lesser angel. Remember, Gabrielle struck mute Zacharias, the high priest, because he spoke presumptively and simply questioned the angel (Luke 1:11-20).

"If we can't even question angels, why do we think we can speak pre-sumptively to command celestial beings?.... Since scripture is clear that angels only follow commands from God, neither will their counterparts in the second Heaven (i.e. principalities, etc.) respond to our commands. The consequences of such behavior maybe grave." (*Needless Casualties of War*, p. 92-93)

The bible says that destruction will come upon people who "speak abu-sively against whatever they do not understand." It says, "These dreamers pollute their own bodies, reject authority and slander celestial beings. But even the archangel Michael, when he was disputing with the devil about the body of Moses, did not dare to bring a slanderous accusation against him, but said, "The Lord rebuke you!" Yet these men speak abusively against whatever they do not understand; and what things they do understand by instinct, like unreasoning animals--*these are the very things that destroy them*," Jude 1:8-10.

The scripture above may be difficult to think it also refers to sincere be-lievers since the people mainly mentioned are "dreamers" who pollute their own bodies (with sin) and reject authority (including in the heavenly realm). But those who "slander celestial beings," end up falling in the same category because they "speak abusively against whatever they do not understand."

This sin may not take us to hell like the other "dreamers" being referred who also pollute themselves by pursuing evil desires. However it still brings destruction in our lives because we operate outside the will of God by trying to confront these celestial beings ourselves. God's setup in his heavenly govern-ment is that he is the one to deal directly with the spiritual forces while we mind our business here on earth, living the Christian life.

Scripture says these beings are higher ranking in the created order than we are. Yes they are fallen angels yet we are not, in this life, entitled to rule over them in their various ranks. Even the archangel Michael, in disputing with Satan about the body of Moses, had to follow protocols that God has set up. And we being "a little lower than the angels," (Hebrews 2:7) deceive ourselves when we assume we can do otherwise –with serious consequences.

Another similar scripture to the one given earlier from the book of Jude is in 2 Peter. It says, "Bold and arrogant, these men are not afraid to slander celestial beings; yet even angels, although they are stronger and more powerful, do not bring slanderous accusations against such beings in the presence of the Lord. But these men blaspheme in matters they do not understand. They are like brute beasts, creatures of instinct, born *only to be caught and destroyed*, and like beasts they too will perish," 2 Peter 2:10-12.

Satan's territory is therefore outside our given realm of authority. Ours is on earth and only God has power and authority over the celestial beings in heavenly realms or the spirit world. Anything done outside our given realm of authority is, as the book of Jude says, considered rejection of authority. It is rejection of God's authority on the limited spheres of influence he gave us.

The consequences of this behavior can be catastrophic as many of us have experienced. It still came even if we did not willfully or knowingly go outside our given realm of authority. Virtually all of us were merely enticed by the enemy, through false teachings, to directly confront him as a way of exercising our assumed authority in spiritual warfare and deliverance matters.

Jackson says, "We need not vent our anger, shake our fist, stomp our feet, and revile Satan. The Bible encourages us to humble ourselves, repent and ask God to remove principalities that curse our land. (p.57)

"Jesus focused on intimacy with God, thus establishing prayer as a form of worship and communion. And he said (in the Lord's prayer (Matthew 6:9-13)) to petition God for the establishment of his kingdom on earth…When Jesus encouraged his disciples to petition God the Father, he was recognizing God's authority and protection in our lives –to deliver us from the evil one. When we pray, we are entreating God to act on our behalf." (p.108-109)

Thus to avoid unnecessary negative consequences we remain in our own realm of authority (terrestrial (earthly)) and commit the Lord to deal with the heavenly (celestial) structures the enemy has set up to influence certain people, matters, places and times. As we do our assigned obligations in the warfare against the enemy the Lord will commit his forces to pull down and demolish these spiritual strongholds.

We therefore seek God to "deliver us from the evil one," Matthew 6:13 in all matters Satan is working against us. We cannot deliver ourselves from the evil one. Only God has the power over the evil one, Satan and his hosts. As we do our part of fulfilling what God requires of us in walking uprightly he is able to do his part of overcoming forces that we humanly are unable to fight nor have access to.

Exception for Heavenly Access: Permitted Areas

The kingdom of God is the only celestial (heavenly) realm we have access to. Our Lord Jesus even gave us the keys to God's heavenly kingdom: "I will give you the keys of the kingdom of heaven; whatever you bind on earth will be bound in heaven, and whatever you loose on earth will be loosed in heaven," Matthew 16:19.

(On what binding and loosing means according to the bible, please read the previous chapter, Our Territory and Nature of Our Christian Authority. Some in the body of Christ recently began to assume it implied binding and loosing evil spirits in geographical territories, in the heavenly realms or the spirit world).

"I will give you the keys of the kingdom of heaven," Matthew 16:19. This means that there're certain places and matters that unbelievers and Satan's hosts cannot have access to in heaven. It's our Father's house that only his children have access to.

What a priestly privilege we have to stand for unbelievers by going to heaven (through prayer) and to petition their case of salvation for them. The entire kingdom of God is on our side. As we pursue their case the way the Lord requires we'll be able to see Satan's works destroyed in their lives.

We also have access to God's throne of grace for wisdom and every provision for fulfilling our purposed callings. "Let us then approach the throne of grace with confidence, so that we may receive mercy and find grace to help us in our time of need," Hebrews 4:16.

Though we have the keys to God's kingdom we were not given the keys to hell or Hades, the residence of Satan and his hosts. We therefore have no access to the territory where these celestial beings live and exercise their influence of evil. Only our Lord does. "I hold the keys of death and Hades," Rev. 1:18. The enemy doesn't have any keys even to his own house!!

However he has been cunning enough to have us think we can enter his celestial (heavenly) territory and fight him there. The consequences have brought much terror. Only our Lord has access there after he disarmed the principalities and took all their authority away. Our obligation is to present to God matters that only his heavenly government has the power and access to deal with.

Jesus who has access to hell can go there at will and overcome forces behind certain people and matters. Since he took their authority away he is able to overcome even their legal claim over the people and matters. He has a mighty army with his angels from God's heavenly government.

Scriptures say Jesus can open and close any door he pleases. "These are the words of him who is holy and true, who holds the key of David. What he opens no one can shut, and what he shuts no one can open. I know your deeds. See, I have placed before you an open door that no one can shut," Rev 3:7-8. He is able to open doors for us to fulfill his work regardless of the enemy's legal claim over the people and matters we're assigned to.

4. True Biblical Spiritual Warfare = Indirect Confrontation

CHAPTER 4 SUB-TOPICS:

-God's role = direct confrontation, verses our role = indirect confrontation
-Examples of Indirect Confrontation in the Bible
-More Scriptural Objection for Direct Confrontation
-Weapons of Spiritual Warfare –Part 1
       1) The belt of truth
       2) The breastplate of righteousness
       3) The shoes of the gospel of peace
       4) The shield of faith
       5) The helmet of salvation
       6) The sword of the Spirit
       7) All kinds of prayers
-Weapons of Spiritual Warfare –Part 2
- Spiritual warfare Vs spiritual slander; Deliverance ministry Vs demonic ministry

By this time, based on the previous chapters, you likely have a solid foundation on understanding the biblical nature of spiritual warfare and deliverance. With the foundation now in place you'll be able to build a solid biblical interpretation of spiritual warfare principles that are not diluted with erroneous and harmful teachings.

God's role = direct confrontation, verses our role = indirect confrontation

This chapter is an answer to: what is spiritual warfare according to the bible? Or what is Christian spiritual warfare?

True biblical spiritual warfare is simply indirect confrontation with Satan our principle enemy. Indirect confrontation implies that we do not fight with Satan and his evil forces by approaching them directly. We confront them by applying indirect means and ways that God has established for us. These will be covered shortly.

Applying and fulfilling our required indirect roles secures our standing before God and allows him to directly act on our behalf. Attacks from Satan against us become God's battles as we obey and fulfill the roles required of us.

In this spiritual battle God's role is direct in nature as he is able to directly confront the spiritual forces unseen to our human eyes.

God himself does not necessarily fight Satan. He is too big to go out and fight a creature he himself created and allowed to exist after his rebellion. The Lord uses his angels, Satan's equals since Satan is also an angel, only a fallen one.

God through his heavenly government of angels has the power, authority and direct access to the kingdom of Satan and his fallen angels. We do not and we only deceive ourselves to assume we do. However, we have a very special role to play in setting the stage for God to send out his angels to minister (carry out) his will.

This special role comprises of fulfilling our expected part in our walk with God. The combination of our walk with God and committing life's battles into his hands constitutes our indirect role. God becomes our defender and acts on our behalf in dealing with matters confronting us and the people we commit to him.

True Christian spiritual warfare is living a life of consecration, obedience and fellowship with God in such a way that we enable God to effectively deal with the evil working against us and against other people. It is a form of abiding in Christ that overcomes Satan's legal and illegal grounds against us and others. This is seen in the outline of our spiritual armor given in Ephesians 6:11-18 (outlined below).

Biblical spiritual warfare is therefore indirect confrontation against Satan. We approach God to intervene for us against Satan on matters in our lives and the lives of others.

It's true that Satan and his demonic spirits (fallen angels) are our primary enemies we wrestle against. It's also true that God has given us certain ways in the Bible of confronting these evil beings whose full time ministry is scheming to ruin our lives. Working outside these biblical ways only increases their effect in our lives. One of these non-biblical ways is the assumption that direct confrontation against Satan is our role.

Examples of Indirect Confrontation in the Bible

a) Examples of indirect Confrontation During Jesus' Time on Earth
Nowhere in the scripture do we see Jesus or the apostles bombarding demons in thin air and calling it spiritual warfare prayers or deliverance prayers. When Satan sought to sift Peter and finish him off Jesus prayed to God. Jesus prayed that Peter's faith would not fail and when he'd turned back from the attack he'd strengthen his fellow disciples.

"Simon, Simon, Satan has asked to sift you as wheat. But I have prayed for you, Simon that your faith may not fail. And when you have turned back, strengthen your brothers," Luke 22:31-32.

Jesus Christ, God made flesh, prayed to God, the Father, for Peter's deliverance. His spiritual warfare prayer or deliverance prayer was addressed to God not to Satan. How much more should we follow his example of indirect confrontation.

The events that followed showed the results of Jesus' prayers of deliverance addressed to God, not Satan. Peter rose to be the foundation of the early church. His faith in his teacher and master, Jesus Christ, was preserved. God did his spiritual warfare part in fulfilling Jesus' deliverance prayer by directly confronting Satan in the spirit realm.

In a major prayer by Jesus for himself, his disciples and for all Christians there is not a hint of him being preoccupied with demons and their activities (John 17). The entire prayer of Jesus in John 17 is given below. Yet this is a classic spiritual warfare prayer and deliverance prayer. His focus was on God as the deliverer. He desired that his disciples and all believers would walk in unity and be protected from evil spiritual influence. "My prayer is not that you take them out of the world but that you protect them from the evil one," John 17:15.

We don't see Jesus binding and loosing demonic spirits, familiar spirits, generational spirits, Jezebel spirits, territorial spirits, spirits of division, spirits of unforgiveness, spirits of this and that. Yet his version of spiritual warfare prayer and deliverance prayer has kept the church united to this day, for over 2000 years.

Some may say the church is totally divided. However we agree on more issues than we disagree. We agree particularly on the major matters –who God is, Jesus is, the Holy Spirit, who Satan is, demons, angels, hell, heaven, the Bible and so on. There are wolves around us but the sheep outnumber the wolves. Together as God's sheep we comprise the Body of Christ, the global church that transcends geographical and denominational boundaries.

John 17 in full from New International Version (NIV) bible (headings are as marked in NIV):

Jesus Prays for Himself
JN 17:1 After Jesus said this, he looked toward heaven and prayed:

"Father, the time has come. Glorify your Son, that your Son may glorify you. 2 For you granted him authority over all people that he might give eternal life to all those you have given him. 3 Now this is eternal life: that they may know you, the only true God, and Jesus Christ, whom you have sent. 4 I have brought you glory on earth by completing the work you gave me to do. 5 And now, Father, glorify me in your presence with the glory I had with you before the world began.

Jesus Prays for His Disciples

JN 17:6 "I have revealed you to those whom you gave me out of the world. They were yours; you gave them to me and they have obeyed your word. 7 Now they know that everything you have given me comes from you. 8 For I gave them the words you gave me and they accepted them. They knew with certainty that I came from you, and they believed that you sent me. 9 I pray for them. I am not praying for the world, but for those you have given me, for they are yours. 10 All I have is yours, and all you have is mine. And glory has come to me through them. 11 I will remain in the world no longer, but they are still in the world, and I am coming to you. Holy Father, protect them by the power of your name--the name you gave me--so that they may be one as we are one. 12 While I was with them, I protected them and kept them safe by that name you gave me. None has been lost except the one doomed to destruction so that Scripture would be fulfilled.

JN 17:13 "I am coming to you now, but I say these things while I am still in the world, so that they may have the full measure of my joy within them. 14 I have given them your word and the world has hated them, for they are not of the world any more than I am of the world. 15 My prayer is not that you take them out of the world but that you protect them from the evil one. 16 They are not of the world, even as I am not of it. 17 Sanctify them by the truth; your word is truth. 18 As you sent me into the world, I have sent them into the world. 19 For them I sanctify myself, that they too may be truly sanctified.

Jesus Prays For All Believers

JN 17:20 "My prayer is not for them alone. I pray also for those who will believe in me through their message, 21 that all of them may be one, Father, just as you are in me and I am in you. May they also be in us so that the world may believe that you have sent me. 22 I have given them the glory that you gave me, that they may be one as we are one: 23 I in them and you in me. May they be brought to complete unity to let the world know that you sent me and have loved them even as you have loved me.

JN 17:24 "Father, I want those you have given me to be with me where I am, and to see my glory, the glory you have given me because you loved me before the creation of the world.

JN 17:25 "Righteous Father, though the world does not know you, I know you, and they know that you have sent me. 26 I have made you known to them, and will continue to make you known in order that the love you have for me may be in them and that I myself may be in them."

b) Examples of Indirect Confrontation after Jesus' Ascension and During the Early Church

Some may say direct confrontation with demonic spirits, binding and loosing them became necessary after Jesus ascended to heaven. How come the apostles did not practice it? When confronted with threats that could have closed the emerging church they turned to God.

At one point they prayed so much that, "After they prayed, the place where they were meeting was shaken," Acts 4:31. In our time fellow believers assume earth shaking breakthroughs will come after binding and loosing demonic spirits, familiar spirits, generational spirits, Jezebel spirits, territorial spirits, spirits of division, spirits of unforgiveness, and so on. This only ends up taking us outside our biblical limits.

It also ends up summoning demons to interfere with our lives because we confront them in their spiritual territory where only God and his hosts have access to. We have direct access to God when confronted with evil. However we do not have direct access to the spirits of darkness. The previous chapter covers this in depth from God's word.

Paul, the apostle whose inspired words on spiritual warfare have confused some, never directly confronted demonic powers. He received a thorn in the flesh from Satan that brought much pain and discomfort in his life. "There was given me a thorn in my flesh, a messenger of Satan, to torment me," 2 Corinthians 12:7.

None of us would like to have a demonic attack that is illegally operating against us. More so for a person of his spiritual stature with one of the greatest anointing on him. He is probably the greatest spiritual warfare prayer warrior in Christian history. His spiritual warfare prayers where addressed to God. He indirectly confronted the enemy.

In dealing with the demonic thorn in the flesh Paul turned to God instead of confronting Satan and the ranks of principalities he identifies in Ephesians. He turned to God, not once but, "Three times I pleaded with the Lord to take it away from me," Corinthians 12:8.

If direct confrontation was scriptural we would have seen at least one direct encounter between Paul and demonic spirits. But he kept turning to God, his only source of salvation, who had the authority to directly confront these evil beings in the spirit realm.

Ultimately God, not demonic spirits, had the final say over Paul's torment. "He said to me, 'My grace is sufficient for you, for my power is made perfect in weakness.' Therefore I will boast all the more gladly about my weaknesses, so that Christ's power may rest on me," (verse 9). God delivered him in a non-traditional way, by giving him the grace to endure his affliction.

On another major occasion requiring deliverance Paul and his team were so badly hindered in their ministry that they preferred to die (2 Cor. 1:8). They knew the spiritual forces that were working against them in the spirit realm. Yet they did not address these forces. If there was any suitable place to address so called territorial spirits and demonic forces it was at this time. They were in parts of Asia that had not yet been evangelized. All kinds of spirits could be addressed in this area, binding and loosing them, including familiar spirits, spirits of idols, generational spirits, territorial spirits, and so on.

Paul's account shows that their only source of deliverance was in praying to God. "This happened that we might not rely on ourselves but on God, who raises the dead. He has delivered us from such a deadly peril, and he will deliver us. On him we have set our hope that he will continue to deliver us, as you help us by your prayers. Then many will give thanks on our behalf for the gracious favor granted us in answer to the prayers of many,' 2 Corinthians 1: 9-11. Prayer was their 911 call or relief call to God. It was their only form of spiritual warfare prayer or deliverance prayer in time of need.

More Scriptural Objection for Direct Confrontation

After covering on all these major biblical cases of indirect confrontation as our avenue of spiritual warfare and deliverance some may still argue about our authority to bind and loose demonic powers. Please read Chapter 2: Our Territory and Nature of Our Spiritual Authority. It explains what binding and loosing is according to the bible.

Others may say, we have the authority to directly confront evil spirits by casting them out of people. True and this is one exceptional area that scripture allows us to directly confront evil spirits. Chapter 5: Exception for Direct Confrontation covers on this topic. A single exception on direct confrontation does not justify other practices as means of directly confronting evil spirits.

Such teachings may sound great and empowering but their consequences (fruits) end up showing their true worth. They are extra-biblical teachings that have grown through misinterpretation of scripture. Sincere Christians end up being preoccupied with the evil spirit world much to their own peril. Teachings advocating for direct confrontation against demonic spirits invite what we call demonic ministry.

Demonic ministry is not the worship of Satan, at least when applied to fellow believers in the body of Christ. It simply means giving legal access for demons to attack us. Believers who unknowingly summon demons are heaven destined just as any of us, saved by grace.

However, they end up tying their lives down in perpetual problems in one area or another, spiritually, socially, materially, physically or any combination. They give demons access to hinder their lives in such a way that demons have a special ministry in their lives.

Churches that promote the false teachings on deliverance ministry end up being avenues through which demons use to perpetuate their evil ministry against believers. Instead of being free, believers remain bound in one area or another, as if their salvation through Christ was a false biblical promise. "**My people** are destroyed from lack of knowledge," Hosea 4.6 (emphasis added).

Weapons of Spiritual Warfare –Part 1

The spiritual amour in the Ephesians passage is composed of Truth, Righteousness, Gospel of Peace, Faith, Salvation, and the Word of God. All these are aspects of consecration, obedience to and fellowship with God.

The Lord uses our consecration and obedience to overturn Satan's legal hold over matters in our lives and the lives of those we've been assigned to minister to –spiritually, socially, materially and physically. "We will be ready to punish every act of disobedience *once* (when) your obedience is complete," 2 Corinthians 10:6 (emphasis added).

God stands as the highest Judge who takes up our cases as we submit them to him to bring justice. Our cases are already in our favor because we use the work of Christ and his blood atonement (sacrifice) for all humanity and matters in life to justify our cases. Our consecration and obedience to God enables the Holy Spirit to effectively work through us in punishing all the disobedience the enemy brings or attempts to, in our lives and the lives we're commissioned to serve.

The term spiritual warfare itself is not in the Bible. It is still relevant since it distinguishes between spiritual and physical warfare. Its closest association is the passage in Ephesians 6:11-18. Unfortunately the enemy has used it to deceive us that we have the right to *directly* fight his set-up in the heavenly realms. The lie is not new since Satan has throughout history used scripture to justify ungodly acts such as gender abuses, slavery, colonialism, persecution of non-Christians and so on.

The passage in Ephesians says, "For our struggle is not against flesh and blood, but against the rulers, against the authorities, against the powers of this dark world and against the spiritual forces of evil in the spiritual or heavenly realms.

"Therefore put on the full armor of God, so that when the day of evil comes, you may be able to stand your ground, and after you have done everything, to stand. Stand firm then, with the belt of *truth* buckled around your waist, with the breastplate of *righteousness* in place, and with your feet fitted with the readiness that comes from the *gospel of peace*.

"In addition to all this, take up the shield of *faith*, with which you can extinguish all the flaming arrows of the evil one. Take the helmet of *salvation* and the sword of the Spirit, which is the *word of God*. And pray in the Spirit on all occasions with all kinds of *prayers* and requests. With this in mind, be alert and always keep on praying for all the saints," Ephesians 6:11-18.

You'll notice that the entire armor of God is a call to a life of consecration, obedience and fellowship with God - *truth*, *righteousness*, *gospel of peace*, *faith*, *salvation*, *word of God*, *prayers*.

It is not meant for us to go out and start bombarding the spiritual forces of evil in the spiritual or heavenly realms. Paul used the metaphor of an armed Roman soldier, in showing how we can be prepared for spiritual warfare. In his time, a well-armed soldier wore a belt, breastplate, shoes, shield, helmet and carried a sword.

What a difference with our time when a few individuals can destroy the world many times over just by pressing buttons for nuclear and biochemical weapons. God forbid, though the battle of Armageddon is more than likely to feature this. If God placed no limits on Satan we'd all be cooked up by now. Satan would have quickly worked on his schemes to destroy God's creation. Our God still reigns and has his final say over matters on earth. Wheew!

The same mighty God has placed spiritual weapons in our spiritual hands that he says are mightier than human weapons. We have access to spiritual buttons that can devastate the devil's work against humanity.

Their indirect nature may look so simple but as we apply them they set the stage for our mighty God to directly overcome the devil's work against us and against all humanity. The following outlines our primary spiritual armor that has so much power in the realm of the spirit. Appendix 1: Weapons of Spiritual Warfare lists more of our spiritual weapons.

1) The belt of truth

We are to walk in truth in our motives, desires and conduct. Truth has scripture as its foundation. The scripture enables us not to live in error, deception, and sin if we apply it in our lives.

Truth is not relative or circumstantial but unchanging. It is based on the unbreakable scripture. It cannot be used for selfish motives such as to gain material wealth, influence and so on. There is also no room for "white lies," deception or exaggerations.

Walking in truth works as a weapon against Satan's deceptions, appeal to selfish desires and the flesh. It enables us to walk according to the will of God. No direct confrontation against Satan required yet his legal entry attempts are overcome as we walk in truth. The belt of truth is among our major indirect weapons of spiritual warfare and deliverance ministry.

2) The breastplate of righteousness

Righteousness is a state of living that enables us to be approved before God. He is holy and desires holiness as his standard of approval. Any lukewarmness is unacceptable, like the church in Laodicea. "Because you are lukewarm--neither hot nor cold -I am about to spit you out of my mouth," Revelation 3:16.

Although it is the righteousness of Christ (2 Corinthians 5:21) that makes us acceptable to God scripture is clear that we are expected to walk in holiness. It is a way of fulfilling our part in the call to righteousness. "Those who belong to Christ Jesus have crucified the sinful nature with its passions and desires. Since we live by the Spirit, let us keep in step with the Spirit," Galatians 5: 22-25.

The sinful nature crucified in our lives is what enables the righteousness of Christ to compensate for all the areas we may unwillfully fall short. Without doing our part the righteousness of Christ is in vain. It is degrading the grace of God as a license to sin.

On the other hand, when the sinful nature is crucified in our lives it enables the righteousness of Christ to overcome the legal grounds of Satan against us. God becomes our defender in Satan's accusations against us. He finds us blameless for Satan to have any claim to attack us. No direct confrontation against Satan required yet his legal entry attempts are overcome as we live righteousness lives. The breastplate of righteousness is among our major indirect weapons of spiritual warfare and deliverance ministry.

3) The shoes of the gospel of peace

Inner peace is not found among those living outside the will of God. They are very poor in this area regardless of whatever some may have achieved. "The wicked are like the tossing sea, which cannot rest, whose waves cast up mire and mud. 'There is no peace,' says my God, 'for the wicked.'" Isaiah 57:20-21.

Because their eyes are still blind they look in all the wrong areas trying to find it –worldly pleasures, entertainment, alcohol, pursuit of riches, fame, power and influence. Many of us were once there, constantly running from something or towards something all in pursuit of peace. Now we have the Prince of Peace living in us without resorting to alcohol, worldly pleasures and so on, to look for peace.

God has now given us the shoes of the gospel of peace to "walk" to people without peace. We reveal to them the gospel of peace that brings true peace in their lives.

The shoes of the gospel of peace also protect us from the rough ground that we walk on. The ground we walk on is the earth with all its problems that resulted from sin since Adam and Eve fell. There is much poverty, disease, greed, crime, immorality, wars, conflicts and so on. Without wearing our shoes we will have no peace walking in such territory. We will have no peace with ourselves, with God and with others.

With our shoes on we will have peace with ourselves, with God and with others in the midst of all kinds of problems. Satan's attacks will have no effect on our walk in proclaiming the gospel of peace. The rough ground he has created on earth will have no effect on us. The shoes enable us to trample on snakes and scorpions that come in form of the problems Satan has influenced. We can speak like Jesus, "The prince of this world is coming. He has no hold on me," John 14:30.

In the midst of conflicts in families, between different groups, different ethnic groups, nations, and so on we become peace makers. We secure peace with others. Even those who persecute us do not rob us of the peace we have with God. There is no anger or bitterness against them since we walk on their attacks with our shoes worn.

Anger, bitterness, unforgiveness, hatred, conflict and so on do not only rob us the peace with people at odds with but also with God. Without the peace of God our lives are as poor in peace as unbelievers.

Some believers live fruitless lives because they are not wearing their shoes of peace. They are unable to advance into territory that they could easily walk in if they had shoes on. So they remain on the same spot hoping that people will somehow change and become easier to deal with. We need the shoes of peace to effectively deal with their peculiarities. The shoes alone, not their way of conduct will make all the difference.

The shoes enable us to firmly stand against Satan's attacks and advance into territory full of snakes and scorpions (Satan's attacks and demonic influence). No direct confrontation against Satan required yet his legal entry attempts are overcome as we walk in peace. The shoes of the gospel of peace are among our major indirect weapons of spiritual warfare and deliverance ministry.

Walking with shoes of the gospel of peace comes through our relationship with Christ. He is the Prince of Peace (Isaiah 9:6). He is the peace Giver in the midst of life's storms, persecutions and unpleasant experiences. "Peace I leave with you; my peace I give you. I do not give to you as the world gives. Do not let your hearts be troubled and do not be afraid," John 14:27.

4) The shield of faith
Faith is critical in five major situations in life:
a) When we desire or seek something we are unable to have through our own strength and wisdom,
b) When storms and trials in life strike us,
c) When obeying God's word is being challenged by certain respected secular beliefs – e.g. where it's popularly said that saving money instead of giving is more important in increasing financial security. Though necessary it's not more important than giving,
d) When the temptation is strongest to have certain desires through biblically forbidden ways – e.g. the temptation of marrying a respectable non-believer, or seeking financial matters through non-biblical ways,
e) When believing in matters one may find difficult to understand or difficult to draw much sense out of them – e.g. the God of love in a troubled world, bad things happening to God's people, the trinity, etc.

Faith is probably the most important area that Satan targets most among believers. He knows that once we stop trusting God in a particular area he can easily offer us his deceptive solutions. He did that to Adam and Eve. The whole creation is still paying the price. The whole earth is still groaning from what it is being subjected to after Adam and Eve surrendered their inheritance to Satan.

In our own lives most of us succumbed to Satan's lies at one point or another. We knew what God's word says. However we still believed the lies were more worthwhile to follow. Satan may not have come in a serpent form yet he still came into our thoughts directly or through the media, through a person or through circumstances.

The moment we stopped trusting scripture our faith in God's word in the area of concern ended. The consequences are always the same – negative. Walking by sight or according to the flesh is costly in the long run.

On the other hand walking by faith enables us to receive rewarding results in the long run. In the short-run it may seem costly, slow and unconventional. However the rewards are worth the wait if we are willing to trust God for as long as it takes.

Walking by faith extinguishes "all the flaming arrows of the evil one," (verse 16). The flaming arrows include Satan's temptations, doubt, fear, despair and confusion. He will try to bring them through all sorts of ways – directly into our thoughts or through the media, through a person or through circumstances. We refuse to compromise for anything that is contrary to God's word.

We trust his word even when the shortcut appears rewarding or when we cannot see how it will work out. In this way we are lifting up the shield of faith against Satan's attacks. There is no direct confrontation yet Satan is overcome as we fulfill our indirect role God has assigned us.

Faith is a conviction, a resolve, to trust God based on what we know in his word. It is not a feeling, an impression or an imagination. Sometimes we may receive convictions or even clear voices in our hearts to endeavor on certain matters. Without examining these convictions or voices through scripture we will merely be acting out of presumption. Faith is not a blind leap in the dark. We would not need the scriptures if it operated this way.

The banner or shield of faith is maintained through what we know and believe in God's word. It is therefore important that we constantly feed on his word to maintain or increase our faith level. "Faith comes from hearing the message, and the message is heard through the word of Christ," Romans 10:17.

Faith in what we continue hearing from the word of God overcomes all the contrary words from Satan that he brings against us through different avenues. No direct confrontation against Satan required yet his legal entry attempts are overcome as we walk by faith. The shield of faith is among our major indirect weapons of spiritual warfare and deliverance ministry.

Having faith in God and his word does not imply having pleasant feelings. Unpleasant situations we may encounter may bring some level of fear.

However we still move on to trust in God's word more than in what the circumstances are saying. We may not have all the good feelings in our hearts yet we obey God's word in spite of the feelings. Using emotions to determine our level of faith in God is misleading and dangerous.

Before his crucifixion Jesus had such dreadful feelings that his body began to react. He began to sweat to the point that "his sweat was like drops of blood falling to the ground," Luke 22:44. Yet his faith in God was completely intact. He trusted God to even send hundreds of angels to his rescue.

God just had another plan by allowing his crucifixion. Jesus knew the plan though he began to find its final process unbearable. He chose to obey God's plan regardless of how painful it felt to follow it.

Faith is therefore demonstrated by our act of obedience to God rather than by how we feel. We may not even like what God's word says is required of us. Yet we exercise faith and trust in God if we choose to obey his word rather than our preference.

We choose not to trust in horses and chariots and all the alternative ways that promise a solution. We choose God's way because he requires it and we trust him that his ways are always right and good. Other ways only lead to destruction. No feelings required to walk by faith. Just obedience in God and his ways.

5) The helmet of salvation
Our salvation through Christ is the only treasure we will take with us after we die. Without it we would be heading for hell. It is the only treasure that the devil cannot take away from us. Like with Job, the Lord may allow him to take everything from us. Yet for as long as we remain trusting and having faith in God our salvation remains intact. Even if all fails we know the place God has prepared for us is better than the brief experiences on earth.

Like with the physical Israelites our salvation denotes deliverance by God from an oppressive ruler. In our case the oppressive ruler is Satan. They had a physical ruler named Pharaoh who enslaved them. We, spiritual Israelites, had Satan who is the ultimate oppressive ruler of all creation. Our acceptance of Jesus as our Lord and Savior freed us from the rule of Satan.

Now we are children of God living under a new government that is founded on love and eternal life rather than sin, destruction and hell. We have been saved from living hopeless lives.

"Who shall separate us from the love of Christ? Shall trouble or hardship or persecution or famine or nakedness or danger or sword? ...No, in all these things we are more than conquerors through him who loved us. For I am convinced that neither death nor life, neither angels nor demons, neither the present nor the future, nor any powers, neither height nor depth, nor anything else in all creation, will be able to separate us from the love of God that is in Christ Jesus our Lord," Romans 8:35,37-39.

We have confidence that eternity, our most important future, is secure. It is our "hope of salvation" (1 Thessalonians 5:8). This hope of salvation is able to protect us from losing our faith during severe moments of persecution, negative circumstances, discouragement or problems that Satan may use to strike at us.

No direct confrontation against Satan required yet his legal entry attempts are overcome by our hope of salvation. Our hope of salvation is among our major indirect weapons of spiritual warfare and deliverance ministry.

6) The sword of the Spirit

When Jesus "was led by the Spirit into the desert to be tempted by the devil," (Matthew 4:1) he used scripture to overcome Satan's temptations. Scripture is our best offensive weapon against the devil, over our lives and the lives of others. Notice in the temptation passage (Matthew 4:1-11) that Satan also used scripture in trying to deceive Jesus.

The passage where Jesus quoted scripture to overcome Satan's temptations has sometimes been used to justify verbal confrontation. It is often used as an example of verbal confrontation where Jesus exercised the word, the Sword of the spirit realm, against Satan.

A closer look shows that scripture does not support this. Satan appeared physically to Jesus in the wilderness (Matthew 4:1-11). It is fitting that he would talk to a being that appeared physically. The devil even took Jesus on a "tour," first to the temple, then to a high mountain.

After this experience there is no other account of Jesus quoting scripture to Satan as a way of fighting him. Yet throughout his ministry he was busy confronting and overcoming the enemy in the lives of people. Thus unless the enemy appears to any one of us physically (God forbid) we have no business talking to him verbally.

Even if he were to physically appear to any one of us God may require us to do something else –like just saying, "Away from me, Satan," (Matthew 4:10). No long verbal confrontations. Quoting any scripture may not be necessary. Our Lord was not setting a formula of using scripture in having conversations with the enemy. What we learn from his experience is that the enemy can use scripture that God gave us to live by. It's only that he twists it in order to deceive us.

The way this deception works is by him planting thoughts in our minds rather than appearing physically. We have more than enough experiences throughout history where God's people have fallen to lies through misinterpreted scripture. Satan used scripture to justify ungodly acts such as gender abuses, slavery, colonialism, persecution of non-Christians and so on.

Our recent accounts include the erroneous spiritual warfare and deliverance teachings. None of the people that fell to the lies throughout history had any outward conversation or physical encounter with Satan quoting scripture.

Most historical lies have lasted longer and have had more consequences on more lives than the spiritual warfare deception. Entire nations and peoples are still experiencing the bondage to the deception even after many generations have passed since it was exposed. The bondage includes material poverty and psycho-social humiliation of inferiority complexes.

Thankfully the Lord has been revealing the enemy's devises in his own time and still turning the evil to work for the good for all "who love him, who have been called according to his purpose," Romans 8:28. The evil may not work to everyone's good, but, as the Bible says, it certainly does for God's children. How it does is another lengthy topic.

If the scripture is rightly placed in our hearts the Holy Spirit enables us to discern these lies and counters them with the right scripture. The Holy Spirit living in us will "lift up" or wield the right scripture to fight the lies. The enemy's schemes are immediately resisted and the enemy flees for a season. Only to return with another lie. We keep confronting his schemes against us without any outward conversations or proclamations. The battle is lost or won from within. It's a tragedy when it's lost, particularly when it's a big lie that affects the lives of others.

We therefore always need the Holy Spirit to guide us "into all truth," (John 16:13). Quoting scripture does not imply wielding the sword. Memorizing the scripture as a defense against the devil's temptations is not enough. He has memorized it more than any one us can in our lifetime. The enemy has been around the earth ever since Adam and Eve fell, over six thousand years ago.

However the Holy Spirit, who is part of God himself, has been around for eternity. He knows how to deal with Satan's attempts against us. All we need to do is effectively submit to God in order to enable him to work in and through us.

As we walk right with God the Holy Spirit will lift up the right scripture in moments of battle in the mind and the battle in preaching the gospel. "Do not worry about what to say or how to say it. At that time you will be given what to say, for it will not be you speaking, but the Spirit of your Father speaking through you," Matthew 10:19-20.

Thus even the word of God, which is the sword of the Spirit, is intended to overcome the deception of Satan in the lives of people in an indirect way. As the word is preached it penetrates these spiritual strongholds of deception in the lives of people and sets them free from his bondage.

In our lives, as believers, the word overcomes Satan's temptations and the appeal of the flesh by enabling us to walk in truth. Scripture does not direct us to be quoting scripture against Satan in verbal confrontations and assuming that we're wielding the sword of the spirit. The battle is within not outside. God's word hidden in our hearts and minds surfaces whenever we're confronted with opposing beliefs and matters. God's word in our hearts and minds is among our major indirect weapons of spiritual warfare and deliverance ministry.

7) All kinds of prayers

After he described the various elements of the spiritual armor, Paul said that we are to be in constant prayer. Prayer is part of our spiritual warfare. "Pray in the Spirit on all occasions with all kinds of prayers and requests." Praying implies talking to God, not to Satan. All kinds of prayers and requests include:

1) Prayers of deliverance and protection (spiritually, socially, physically or materially),
2) Prayers of agreement,
3) Prayers of intercession,
4) Prayers of inquiry,
5) Prayers of importunity, supplication, appeal or petition,
6) Prayers of consecration/dedication/commitment,
7) Prayers of repentance,
8) Prayers in the word (praying with the scriptures),
9) Prayers of worship/adoration and thanksgiving,

All kinds of prayers and requests also include prayers for different groups of people. These include:
1. FAMILY NETWORK
a) Immediate Family
b) Relatives
c) Friends
d) Other beloved (e.g. local church pastor)

2. THE BODY OF CHRIST
a) Spiritual Leaders
b) Other Believers
c) Ministries

3. THE WORLD – THE HARVEST FIELD
a) Specific individuals
b) Political Leaders
c) Organizations
d) Geographic Communities (neighborhood, suburbs, villages, towns, cities, countries and continents)

4. PERSONAL MATTERS
a) Spiritual
b) Social
c) Physical health
d) Material

5. GENERAL MATTERS
Everything else. E.g. Global warming, wildlife, natural resources, etc.

Making proclamations to Satan and his forces cannot therefore be referred to as prayer. There is no scriptural reference where such an activity would be categorized as prayer. The admonition to make "all kinds of prayers and requests" does not therefore include making proclamations to Satan and his forces. Herein lies the deception that we fell for on this scripture. Prayer to God is among our major indirect weapons of spiritual warfare and deliverance ministry.

Weapons of Spiritual Warfare –Part 2

Other passages that cover on the armor for spiritual battle include 1 Thessalonians 5:8 and Isaiah 59:17. In 1 Thessalonians 5:8 faith and love comprise the breastplate. Associating the weapons of spiritual warfare to specific areas of the Roman armor is therefore less important than knowing the weapons and using them.

1 Thessalonians 5:8 shows that love is among the major weapons of spiritual warfare. Like the rest, it is an indirect weapon. The article on the "weapons of spiritual warfare" given in Appendix 1 also shows how the matters we exercise in our fellowship with God act as indirect weapons against Satan.

As the scriptures say, these weapons of spiritual warfare look simple but are powerful in overcoming the enemy. Please note the focus of the 20 "weapons" listed. All, except one, focus on God and us doing our part. There is only one exceptional "weapon" that directly targets the devil - weapon #4 -Exercising authority over unclean spirits. This involves casting out evil spirits dwelling in people (please read the next chapter: Exception for Direct Confrontation).

The rest of the 19 weapons focus on God and us doing our part. They are by no means exhaustive. Other "weapons" can be found in the scriptures and be added to them. However they all focus on God or us doing our part.

This is not to say we fight God. It implies that God takes care of any obstacles in our lives as we abide in him. Our spiritual weapons are therefore "weapons of righteousness" (2 Corinthians 6:7) that the Lord uses to confront the enemy and set captives free.

This may come as a surprise since we expect weapons of war to be used directly against enemy forces and territory. The case is a bit complex in the realm of the spirit because there is one group of forces in the natural realm and another in the spiritual.

In the natural realm there is us, God's servants on one side and on the other there are people knowingly or unknowingly being used by the devil, our main enemy. In the spiritual realm there is God almighty and his entire government of angels in their various roles and ranks. On the other spiritual realm side is the devil and his entire alliance of fallen angels in their various roles and ranks.

Explaining how and why the war rages may be another lengthy topic with its own limitations. The only important matter to note is that we have the entire heavenly government on our side including our Lord Jesus who stands as our intercessor (Romans 8:34) and our advocate in heaven's highest court (1 John 2:1, Job 16: 19-20). Our main concern here is the part we, as God's servants, play in this war. The scripture has laid this out quite clearly.

What we see from the scripture is that the battle is his and our concern is to focus on him rather than on Satan. In fact, Satan's influence over the outcome of any battle is so insignificant that he's the one to be pitied for having started any attack – if only we do our part. That's why the scripture says we're more than conquerors in any battle we may encounter.

"In all these things we are more than conquerors through him who loved us. For I am convinced that neither death nor life, neither angels nor demons, neither the present nor the future, nor any powers, neither height nor depth, nor anything else in all creation, will be able to separate us from the love of God that is in Christ Jesus our Lord," Rom 8:37-39.

Christian spiritual warfare is therefore not making proclamations against Satan and his forces. Such "warfare" is merely presumption and portrays that there are two powerful forces to talk to in the spirit realm –God and Satan. We have no business socializing or having some form of fellowship with Satan, even when we know he's the source of all troubles. God, the only heavenly being we fellowship with deals with Satan as we bring the issues Satan is causing.

Spiritual warfare Vs spiritual slander
Deliverance ministry Vs demonic ministry

Direct confrontation with Satan takes us into forbidden territory in the realm of the spirit. It is not spiritual warfare. It is what scripture calls spiritual slander of "celestial (heavenly) beings," and which it says brings trouble on the slanderers (Jude 1:8-10, 2 Peter 2:10-12). *Neither is direct confrontation a form of deliverance ministry. It is demonic ministry.*

We fight demons in a way that scripture forbids us by getting into unauthorized territory of the spirit realm. In this area Satan and his agents gain legal access to attack us for as long as we keep penetrating this territory of principalities.

It is like going to fight an enemy at his house while he has all the power and authority to retaliate. He has bodyguards and all the needed defense. I go with the assumption that Jesus is backing me. However Jesus, who is more powerful than the enemy, is nowhere to be seen. The enemy not only knows this, he is the one who influenced me to believe that scripture supports direct confrontation. With all my zeal and conviction I charge towards the enemy in the name of Jesus Christ, issuing all kinds of commands, which only amount to slander.

What follows is unfortunate for me over what was assumed to be spiritual warfare. Instead of being spiritual warfare it was actually spiritual slander. The demons take their position to begin their ministry. The enemy's bodyguards (the demons) end up beating me up in every way they can. I may not die but they cause quite a mess in my life.

The extent of the mess may depend on how long and how deep I got involved in the direct confrontation that gave them legal access into my life. The mess may be spiritual, social, material, physical or any combination. It is also possible that merely being in a congregation that practices the erroneous spiritual warfare and deliverance teachings can constitute being in agreement to also face the consequences of spiritual slander.

Some of the demonic attacks in believers' lives are so sadly severe that they seem like cases of demonic possession. Other demonic attacks resemble demonic experiences of people in the occult. These include sensing, seeing, smelling, and hearing evil spirit beings.

The extreme experiences of demonic attacks may seem like aspects of demonic possession to the victim. However as long as it's a Christian, who is now a child of God, they are merely aspects of demonic influence. The chapters that follow cover on such matters.

Direct confrontation therefore gives demons access to hinder believers' lives in such ways that demons have a special ministry in their lives. Churches that promote the false teachings on spiritual warfare and deliverance end up being avenues through which demons use to perpetuate their ministry against believers.

Churches embracing false teachings help bring more bondage instead of deliverance on believers' lives. Instead of being free believers remain bound in one area or another, as if their salvation through Christ was a false biblical promise.

Once they know the source of their strange experiences and apply what is required they close the door that kept bringing in the experiences. This book shows these doors of entry and how easily to close them. You'll get there by the time you start reading Part 1 of chapter 9, Christian Deliverance and Healing.

5. Exception for Direct Confrontation

CHAPTER 5 SUB-TOPICS:

-The One Exception
-Authority for Dealing with Demonic Possession
-Demonic Possession Vs Demonic Influence
-Nature of Demonic Influence and Possession
-Deliverance from Demonic Influence
-False Doctrine and Demonic Influence
-Deliverance from Demonic Possession
-Some level of Discernment
-Destiny of Evil Spirits
-Deliverance Methods in the New Testament
-Jesus our Example
-Scope of Deliverance from Demonic Possession

The One Exception

The only exception where we have been given the authority to directly confront evil spirits is when they are to be cast out of people. This is part of true deliverance ministry that is biblical. It is however, only one of other areas of deliverance ministry. It's also a deliverance ministry area that evangelicals differ on its present day relevance.

Casting out demons out of people is part of what Jesus did in his earthly ministry. Outside the realm of people possessed by demons Jesus had no business confronting demons in thin air, in territories, nor in the spirit world. Neither did the apostles. That did not imply there were no territorial spirits and principalities in their time. It only meant directly confronting the demons in their various ranks was not Jesus' assignment while in his earthly physical body.

Christ in his spiritual form, after ascending to heaven, is now able to directly confront them. He does it on our behalf as we fulfill our indirect roles over the conflicts raging in the heavenly (spiritual) realm. Christ being a Spirit, is able to engage the enemy spirits. He has hosts of angels under him that battle the evil spirits. The direct confrontation is therefore between spirits. It is a spirit to spirit confrontation.

"Praise the Lord, all his heavenly hosts, you his servants who do his will," Psalms 103:21. Angels do not just sing songs. They are God's mighty army or hosts against Satan's kingdom. In the book of Revelations they're fierce spiritual warriors in almost the entire book.

Our only role, as important as it may be, is indirect in nature (prayer to God (i.e. seeking for his intervention), submission to God, walking in love, forgiveness, charity, etc). It's challenging enough in fulfilling our clearly spelled out indirect roles, what more having to go after vague and unseen spirits! This is Christ's business, the Lord of hosts, who clearly sees and has power over them. Making it our assignment of directly confronting demons in the unseen spiritual realm is only fooling ourselves that principalities living outside people will bow to our demands.

It is also disobedience to God's spiritual laws by taking on responsibilities that God's spiritual army is assigned for. Many are unknowingly walking in disobedience to God's spiritual laws and calling it deliverance and spiritual warfare. The consequences on their lives are not pleasant as they enter spiritual realms that are forbidden territory.

The exception comes only when evil spirits occupy or possess human beings. When they enter a person(s) they leave their assigned spirit realm and enter a realm that Jesus died for - human beings. This is also a realm that God's angels do not have access to. In very rear cases, as we see in scripture, God allows angelic beings to come on earth in physical bodies. Angels do not have physical bodies like us to physically operate on earth. Their jurisdiction is in the unseen spiritual realm where in normal circumstances we cannot hear, see, nor touch them.

Demons that posses people are occupying bodies that are in the physical realm. In such territory Jesus said we, not the angels, are to confront them. We're authorized to liberate or deliver fellow human beings from being owned or possessed by demons. Just like Christ did while on earth we have his authority to directly confront demons that take up residence in people.

In such situations Jesus gave us the authority to cast them out or evict them from human bodies. We command the spirit(s), in the name of Jesus, to come out of an individual. This is very different from making proclamations and commands in thin air, all in the name of exercising authority over spiritual beings. Like prayer, such acts take us into spiritual realms, though in this case, the forbidden areas.

Needless to say that deliverance ministry of casting out demons dwelling in people is an area of controversy in the body of Christ. Some believe its scriptural relevance no longer applies to our time. Others believe such forms of deliverance ministry still apply today until Jesus returns.

My assertion is that there is no harm as long as it's done the way scripture prescribes. Praise the Lord if through such deliverance ministry people are truly delivered from demonic attacks that cause them unnecessary heartache mentally, emotionally, physically and so on. Praise the Lord too if people are truly delivered from demonic attacks through modern medicine, alternative medicine, psychology, psychotherapy, etc.

Authority for Dealing with Demonic Possession

Regarding deliverance ministry in dealing with demonic possession major passages that show where our authority over evil spirits lies are in Matthew and Luke.

"He called his twelve disciples to him and gave them authority to drive out evil spirits and to heal every disease and sickness," Matthew 10:1.

It says in Luke, "When Jesus had called the Twelve together, he gave them power and authority to drive out all demons and to cure diseases, and he sent them out to preach the kingdom of God and to heal the sick," Luke 9:1-2.

In both references the term "drive out" is used. Other bible versions may have "cast out." This is self explanatory. Driving out refers to moving something from one place to another. The same with "cast out," which implies expelling or evicting something.

Examples in scripture show us how and where the driving out or casting out of demons is to be exercised. "How" is through the name of Jesus. "Where" is casting them out of people. Confronting the evil spirits anywhere outside people is an act that is not in line with scripture. It comes with its negative consequences since we confront evil spirits in territorial spheres that we are powerless. We were never empowered to deal directly with them outside their presence in people.

The authority of directly confronting evil spirits was therefore in the area of demonic possession. On the passage in Luke *The International Standard Bible Encyclopedia* says, "In Lk 9:1 the terms 'authority' and 'power' are used in such a way as to show the belief of the evangelists that to cure demon-possession an actual power from God, together with the right to use it, was necessary. This group of passages gives the New Testament philosophy of this dread mystery and its cure.

"The demons are personal evil powers afflicting human life in their opposition to God. It is beyond man unaided to obtain deliverance from them. It is the function of Christ as the redeemer of mankind to deliver men from this as well as other ills due to sin. Miraculous cures of the same kind as those performed by Christ Himself were accomplished by His disciples in His name (Mk 16:17). The power attributed to "His name" supplies us with the opportunity for a most enlightening comparison and contrast."

As covered in the chapter on "Our Territory and Nature of Our Christian Authority," Jesus returned to us the authority we previously lost on the earthly realm. In addition to this he gave us authority over evil spirits living in people, not in geographical areas nor in the heavens were they are positioned in ranks. We ought to be aware of its nature and limits. Outside the limits is illegal territory that we are not authorized to trespass. Satan knows that and that could be why he has enticed us into confronting him in territory where he legally has power over us.

Demonic Possession Vs Demonic Influence

Baker's Evangelical Dictionary says, "Believers are not immune from demonic attack. Demons seek to influence Christians through false doctrines and teachings (1 Tim 4:1; 1 John 4:1-4) as well as false miracles and wonders (2 Thess 2:7-11; Rev 16:14). Paul was buffeted (2 Col 12:7; see Matt 26:67; 1 Col 4:11; 1 Peter 2:20; for the physical aspect). Though there can be no certainty as to how this buffeting was manifested, we do know that an "angel of Satan" caused it and that Paul could not remove it through prayer."

Paul therefore faced some form of demonic influence in his ministry, one of which God allowed over his life. His situation was demonic influence and not demonic possession. These two are completely different spiritual realms of demonic activity.

Demonic *influence* is interference from an external point. It is not internal. It is from an external position in the spirit realm where evil spirits can freely operate among believers and non-believers. In this spiritual realm they have no ownership over anyone yet constantly operate to influence people through temptation.

Demonic *possession*, on the other hand, is interference from within an individual. It is from an internal position where the evil spirits occupy and exercise some level of control over an individual. A single demon or more occupy an individual. He/she is said to be owned by demons. The individual is also said to be bound, demon possessed or demonized.

In such a case he/she has less free will in the area the demon(s) control. Demonic possession is more severe than demonic influence because the person is hindered from leading a normal life.

Nature of Demonic Influence and Possession

Demonic influence in people may be among areas such as physical health (some illnesses), social behavior (some behavioral problems like stealing, drugs and alcohol, violence, promiscuity and other sexual sins), emotional behavior (like recurring depression, suicidal tendencies, uncontrollable anger), mental behavior (like insanity), material matters (compulsive gambling, greed, extreme materialism, poverty (though poverty also comes through greed and exploitation)), spiritual behavior (like unbelief, atheism, witchcraft, the occult, hallucinations), and so on. All these are signs of demonic influence. Some can easily be confused with demonic possession, which is a higher form of demonic activity.

Signs of demonic possession, a higher form of demonic activity in which demons occupy or possess an individual, can be seen through extremes of involuntary behavior that can be medically categorized as insanity. Scripture also shows some illnesses are a result of demonic possession. For instance the woman who Jesus healed of an illness was said to be "bound for eighteen long years" by Satan (Luke 13:15). She was bound from within, that is, possessed.

However, cases of demonic possession are very rare. This includes most illnesses. Some may be a result of demonic influence but certainly not due to demonic possession. Demons can influence diseases in people from an external point without entering them. For example Job was smitten with painful sores from head to toe by Satan (Job 2:7). But it did not happen by Satan or Satan's fellow demons entering him. It was external, an aspect of demonic influence.

Most of what some fellow evangelicals rush to categorize as demonic possession is merely demonic influence. For example some have said an alcoholic or drug addict is possessed by a demon of alcohol or drug addiction. They operate deliverance ministries that do more harm than good in the so called possessed people.

Jesus said, "The whole world is under the control of the evil one," (1 John 5:19). He does not control the world by entering the lives of people. It's all done from an external point by influencing people to follow his ways. The influence has been from an external point starting from the Garden of Eden. He did not have to possess Adam and Eve to influence them in rebelling. We can tell who is ruling by the way things are worldwide –spiritually, socially, politically, materially and physically. It's primarily as a result of demonic influence, not demonic possession.

However, it is important to maintain that God is sovereign. He reigns over his entire creation, including over principalities and powers of darkness. He allows Satan only to operate within his limited boundaries. The boundaries go all the way back to the temptation and fall of Adam and Eve. Deliverance and healing primarily lies in walking outside those legal boundaries (discussed in the book). Christ came to rescue us from Satan's boundaries and to equip us from not falling back.

Believers are not immune from demonic influence. He keeps trying to win us back into his traps. Even our Lord Jesus endured temptation throughout his life. Scripture says he was, "tempted in every way, just as we are--yet was without sin." Hebrews 4:15. He overcame every form of influence from the devil, the Tempter.

Demonic *influence* is therefore possible over believers. It goes on a regular basis as demons try to entice us to fall to sinful ways. How about demonic *possession*? Can sincere believers be demonized, that is, possessed or owned by evil spirits? The next chapter - Chapter 6: Can a Christian Be Demon Possessed? answers this question.

Deliverance from Demonic Influence

Both demonic influence and demonic possession require God's deliverance because we deal with evil spirits that are more powerful and wiser than us. "Lead us not into temptation, but *deliver us from the evil one*," Matthew 6:12-13 (NIV, ASV, NKJV, BBE).

We're commissioned to pray for ourselves, fellow believers and unbelievers to be delivered from the evil one on a regular basis. Deliverance from demonic influence is a lifetime activity that God carries out in our lives. For as long as we're in this life the enemy will continue seeking to influence our lives spiritually, socially, materially, physically and so on.

Deliverance from demonic influence does not require casting out demons. The demons are already operating from an external point. Unfortunately some believers among fellow evangelicals rush to cast out demons from people that do not have a demonic possession problem. They operate deliverance ministries that do more harm than good in the so called possessed people.

The people end up having perpetual problems that need deliverance. They live to be unfruitful Christians because of being deceived that they have a demonic possession problem. Much to the devil's advantage because they are of no threat to his evil kingdom.

If they knew they had a demonic influence problem they would know how to effectively deal with matters that come through demonic influence. They would overcome such problems without hands being laid on them, being anointed with oil, demons being cast out, making deliverance prayers, spiritual warfare prayers and so on, all to no effect. They would move on from attending perpetual deliverance seminars to helping others in being delivered. No super spiritual event would be required for their deliverance.

Deliverance from demonic influence comes through fighting the true spiritual warfare. It comes through putting on the full armor of God. The armor of God protects us and equips us in rescuing others from demonic influence. As we do our indirect part over the battle that rages in the spirit realm God directly overcomes our spiritual adversaries. He sends his angels to our defense since he is too big to be having fights with Satan, a spirit being he created himself. Examples abound in the bible.

We therefore do not overcome demonic influence by being preoccupied with demons and evil spirits, familiar spirits, generational spirits, territorial spirits, spirits of this and that... We overcome demonic influence by being preoccupied with God and his Spirit, the Spirit of love, power, and a sound mind. Fulfilling our indirect part makes us more than conquerors against demonic influence over our lives and the lives of others. For an in-depth study on our indirect role please see the chapter on True Biblical Spiritual Warfare = Indirect Confrontation.

If we're liable to be influenced how much more are unbelievers? We even have to pray for ourselves regularly for protection. This means, unbelievers are in a worse off situation since they do not have the Holy Spirit living inside them.

"The whole world is under the control of the evil one," (1 John 5:19). This is because he can easily influence unbelievers to fulfill his schemes. His rule and control is indirect since he uses unbelievers to rule as his "open vessels," that is, being without the protection of the Holy Spirit. He doesn't have to be seen physically. We can tell who is ruling by the way things are worldwide –spiritually, socially, politically, materially and physically.

There is therefore a good reason why scripture warns us not to be "yoked together with unbelievers. For what do righteousness and wickedness have in common? Or what fellowship can light have with darkness? What harmony is there between Christ and Belial? What does a believer have in common with an unbeliever? What agreement is there between the temple of God and idols? For we are the temple of the living God," 2 Corinthians 6:14-16. Unbelievers are temples of idols (v.16). They can easily be used to bring us down spiritually, socially, materially and so on.

In our modern era of technology unbelievers do not just include people we meet physically but also those we "meet" through the multimedia. These include books, magazines, radio, television and the Internet. In his book, *Configuration with Christ*, James Alberione says, "Beware of false prophets who rise up on all sides - literature, friends, radio, and television programs, movies, shows of all kinds,... Whatever does not serve our last end is useless."

When we separate ourselves from such influences God says he will receive us as his children. "Therefore come out from them and be separate, says the Lord. Touch no unclean thing, and I will receive you. I will be a Father to you, and you will be my sons and daughters, says the Lord Almighty," 2 Corinthians 6:17-18.

This does not imply we associate only with fellow believers and avoid any contact with non-believers. It also does not mean we are to look down on them. We are their intercessors in seeking their salvation.

It means we're to choose to live not outside their physical world but outside their cultural world. Their cultural world is what shapes their values and understanding of life. Most of these beliefs are contrary to God's word. That is why we are to disassociate ourselves from such values.

Scripture calls it adulterous behavior when we associate ourselves with values that are contrary to God's word. It is like being in courtship with someone outside our marital union. "You adulterous people, don't you know that friendship with the world is hatred toward God? Anyone who chooses to be a friend of the world becomes an enemy of God. Or do you think Scripture says without reason that the spirit he caused to live in us envies intensely?" James 4:4-5.

False Doctrine and Demonic Influence

The problem believers have in various areas of their lives through false doctrine is due to demonic influence. It is not due to demonic possession. False doctrine also does not result in demonic possession. It only perpetuates demonic influence for as long as the believer continues to follow the wrong teachings.

False doctrine among believers has been around since the early church. "Command certain men not to teach false doctrines any longer nor to devote themselves to myths and endless genealogies," 1 Timothy 1:3-4. Since then every church body has had to be confronted over false doctrine it erroneously adopted. Some have accepted correction and changed. Others have remained stubborn to their false teachings up to this day. It's a never-ending job because no church is perfect or free from being liable to err.

All false doctrine results in some form of demonic influence among believers who follow it. Involvement in the false doctrine on spiritual warfare and deliverance ministry opens doors to severe demonic influence. Some of it may seem like demonic possession. The extent may depend on how long and how deep one got involved in the direct confrontation that gave demons legal access into his/her life. The demonic influence may be spiritual, social, material, physical or any combination. Many times merely being in a congregation that practices this kind of warfare is being in agreement to also face the consequences of spiritual slander.

The solution in receiving deliverance from all false doctrine consequences is the same in all cases. It is basically repentance (to God) and ceasing the practice. It also usually requires disassociating with groups that follow the false teachings. Healing from the deception may not be overnight but it certainly comes as the Lord enables. Deliverance is instant after repentance ending the legal access Satan gained into a believer's life through the false teaching. Please read the Chapter on Deliverance and Healing, particularly the sub-topics on repentance and ceasing the non-biblical practices.

Deliverance from Demonic Possession

Evil spirits could not live in people before Adam and Eve fell. When Satan rebelled against God he also came to tempt and deceive mankind into rebellion. When he succeeded he got the right (legality) to rule over mankind even to the point of possessing him with his fallen evil spirits. Fortunately the work of Christ on the cross liberated us from Satan's ownership and control.

Anyone who accepts Jesus as his/her Lord and Savior is free from legal demonic possession. Satan has no claim to possess anyone that accepts Jesus as his/her Lord and Savior. By casting the evil spirits out of a person we are simply announcing the illegal hold of the evil spirit(s) and proclaiming the liberty of the person. In and through the name of Jesus their authority over the person is removed. Christ is now the legal owner of the individual.

The delivered individual still has to do his part in walking out of sin in order to ensure the absence of Satan's legal grounds. Certain sins may open legal doors for the evil spirit(s) to return.

Jesus said, "When an evil spirit comes out of a man, it goes through arid places seeking rest and does not find it. Then it says, 'I will return to the house I left.' When it returns it finds the house *unoccupied* (i.e. empty, without the Holy Spirit in it), swept clean and put in order. Then it goes and takes with it seven other spirits more wicked than itself, and they go and live there. And the final condition of that man is worse than the first. That is how it will be with this *wicked* (sinful) generation," Matthew 12: 43-45.

The above scripture applies to those who once delivered continue in their wickedness.

Destiny of Evil Spirits

Once the spirit(s) leave the person we have no other business to deal with them. We do not have scriptural authority over them once they are outside the person. They are free to roam around the earth trying to influence people while God's angels fight them wherever they have no legal access. They are free to even attempt to influence believers into sin and deception but they cannot live inside us.

Our defense against their evil whispers and enticing offers to sin is putting on the full armor of God. This battle goes on in the mind not in the physical with verbal confrontations. With the armor the bible says we are able to demolish their "arguments and every pretension that sets itself up against the knowledge of God, and we take captive every thought to make it obedient to Christ," 2 Corinthians 10:4.

An area of misunderstanding involves the rebuking, binding, and "destruction" of the spirits. This is God's agenda not ours. Only God can bind these beings in their ranks and works. We can only ask him to do so rather than we. Our realm of authority of direct confrontation only involves casting them out of people. Number 4 in the chapter titled "Misinterpreted Scripture: The Source of False Teachings" elaborates on this.

Deliverance Methods in the New Testament

Baker's Evangelical Dictionary says, "The term most commonly used of the expulsion of demons in the New Testament is cast out (ekballo [ejk-bavllw]). In classical and Old Testament usage it had the sense of forcibly driving out an enemy. In the New Testament, it is typically used of a physical removal (John 9:34-35; see also Mark 1:12). Demons were cast out by the spirit of God (Matt 12:28; cf. Luke 11:20, ; "by the finger of God"), and this was done by verbal command rather than the elaborate rituals of the exorcists."

Apart from the word *"casting out"* there are other words used in the Gospels to describe Jesus' healing ministry among the demonized. *Baker's Evangelical Dictionary* says, "He *released* (luo [luvw]) the woman bound by demons for eighteen years (Luke 13:16). He *saved* (sozo [swvzw]) the Gerasene demoniac (Luke 8:36). He *healed* (therapeuo [qerapeuvw]) many (Matt 4:24; 10:22; 17:16; Luke 6:18; 7:21; 8:2; 13:14), a word used of healing the sick (lame, blind, mute, maimed, deaf) as well as the demonized and even of satanic healing.

"Its use implied that the restoration of demoniacs was on the same level of ministry as other types of healing, all of which showed Christ's mastery over Satan and sin. Jesus also healed (iaomai [ijavomai]) many who had spirits (Luke 6:19; under the power of Satan), including the Canaanite woman's daughter (Matt 15:28) and the young boy (Luke 9:42)."

There is no occasion in the ministry of Jesus where he goes to "bind" evil spirits, even in people. He simply cast them out of people. Binding and loosing have a totally different meaning that has nothing to do with evil spirits. Chapter 2: Our Territory and Nature of Our Christian Authority explains what binding and loosing mean in their purposed contextual meaning. "Casting out" is what has everything to do with evicting demons that occupy or possess in people.

Once cast out where the evil spirits went to was not Jesus' concern. Neither was he concerned about what would happen to them after they were cast out. Our Lord was never concerned about whether they were bound or were free to roam around. He once warned that demons can return to a person if the individual falls into sin. But he never said that they must be bound so that they do not return. It's up to the individual himself/ herself to insure that they do not return by not indulging in sin or falling from grace.

In one instance, after being cast out, demons asked him if they could go into a herd of pigs. Some have taken this to imply that we need to send them to a particular place like a desert, an ocean, in space, or in a lake of fire. Where they go to is God's business, not ours.

If we have an experience where the spirits ask us God may transfer this responsibility to us on that particular case. Even then we're to be discerning enough to receive his instructions on what to do and say. Other than that they're at liberty to roam the earth where they were cast down. They're even at liberty to try to influence believers, though believers have the final say over any of their deceptive attempts.

Jesus our Example

In one passage our Lord said "I have given you authority to trample on snakes and scorpions and to overcome all the power of the enemy; nothing will harm you," Luke 10:19.

Our area of authority in trampling on snakes and scorpions is seen in the way he dealt with evil forces. He did not literary trample on these unseen beings. Rather he exercised such authority over them by casting them out of people that they obeyed him.

Baker's Evangelical Dictionary says, "Jesus came to set Satan's captives free (Matt 12:22-29; Luke 4:18-21), and in all of his dealing with the demonized he demonstrated compassion for the people and authority over the spirits. He commanded the spirit in the Gerasene demoniac to come out (Luke 8:29) and ordered the demon out of the man in the synagogue (Mark 1:27) and the young boy (Mark 9:25).

Notice the context that Jesus granted this kind of authority to the disciples. It was soon after the "seventy-two returned with joy and said, 'Lord, even the demons submit to us in your name,'" (Luke 10:17). It was after they returned from casting out demons possessing people, not demons in territories, in geographic zones, in the spirit world, nor anywhere else. Jesus then replied, "I saw Satan fall like lightning from heaven," (v.18). Satan is overcome as evil spirits are cast out of people.

Jesus gave the disciples such authority when they returned from casting out evil spirits living in people. The context of authority constituted their work of casting out evil spirits living in people. Outside this context we are merely giving ourselves authority over the enemy that we were never granted. There is no scriptural reference were Jesus makes proclamations against the enemy in thin air as a way of exercising his authority. It was always when dealing directly with people oppressed by the enemy.

Our authority in directly confronting evil spirits therefore involves casting out demons living in people, not geographical locations, nor in the heavenly realm. Beyond this takes us outside our assigned realm of authority.

We simply cast them out. This is different from the binding that in our false assumption has meant arresting the evil spirit(s). The Greek word for "cast out" (Mark 16:18) means to throw out violently or to vomit. The evil spirit(s) are to be cast out of the person and once that is achieved the assignment ends. The person is free and wherever the spirits go we're not required to pursue them.

On a larger scale the preaching of the gospel did the most harm against Satan. As it was preached it penetrated Satan's spiritual strongholds of deception in the lives of people and set them free from his bondage. Evangelism is the most important form of deliverance ministry we've been commissioned to fulfill. Many that need deliverance can be set free by preaching the truth concerning their particular area of bondage.

For example, those that may want deliverance from financial or material "bondage" may have to follow the laws of giving and receiving. Their financial deliverance may take time yet it is scriptural. Casting out a demon of poverty is only at best an illusion, at worst putting an individual into a mental prison that deliverance will only come when a demon of poverty is cast out.

Another example may involve deliverance for someone in emotional or psychological trauma. Preaching the gospel truth about striving to help others in other kinds of problems such as poverty, sin and so on brings so much peace and fulfillment.

Some may even require to walk in forgiveness if they are hurting and being bitter with what others did. Must say such letting go is only possible with the help of God. Some people can hurt others so bad resulting in serious psycho-social ailments in the victim. Unfortunately unforgiveness only worsens it.

Our deliverance ministry ought to focus on seeking the Lord to bring healing through his word and directly through his Spirit. Casting out a demon of unforgiveness or a tormenting spirit can result in an individual assuming deliverance will only come when demons are cast out.

Many examples can be given were God's word brings the truth that sets us free. No demonic deliverance is required. An individual who regularly commits herself to God's word whether personally or in attending church services or bible study groups will at some point know the truth in particular areas of bondage. These may be in such areas as spiritual, social, material, physical or any combination. God said those who diligently seek him will eventually find him.

He wants us to seek him and his ways with all our hearts (Deuteronomy 4:29, 6:5, 11:12-13, 26:16, Joshua 22:5, Matthew 22:37, Mark 12:30, Luke 10:37). "You will seek me and find me when you seek me with all your heart. 14 I will be found by you," declares the Lord, "and will bring you back from captivity," Jeremiah 29:13.

This may require among other disciplines a prayerful lifestyle, occasional fasting, helping those in need, walking by faith (shield), striving for righteousness (breastplate), learning God's word (sword), walking in peace and mercy (shoes), etc.

Eventually these disciplines bring freedom to an individual which may never be achieved by casting out demons out of him/her. The demons, whatever level of influence over the individual, eventually loose their power over him/her. The Holy Spirit does his inner work and cleans his house from filth. No demons cast out. Simply a truth encounter in God's word and abiding in Christ which allows the Holy Spirit to cleanse his temple from evil spirits. It is deliverance ministry under the inner working power of the Holy Spirit.

Scope of Deliverance from Demonic Possession

Deliverance from demonic possession is normally a one-time procedure. The procedure differs with different individuals. This is because God may have a different prescription for different people. For most people the mere preaching of the truth sets them free from demonic possession. They may even come across a Christian book or an audio message dealing with an area of their problem and find freedom.

Proclaiming the gospel has been minimized in its power of bringing deliverance from demonic possession. Yet it does the most extensive work in setting captives free. Evangelism is the most important form of deliverance ministry we've been commissioned to fulfill. Limiting deliverance ministry to verbal expulsion of demons in people reduces its scope and meaning.

The second most important level that brings deliverance in most people is through prayer and fasting. Being in deliverance ministry is therefore every believer's commission. We're all ordained by God to deliver others in one way or another, spiritually, socially, materially or physically. Some may never verbally expel a single demon in their lifetime but they can pray and fast for people.

Some may never preach to multitudes but they can pray and fast for God to "deliver us from the evil one," Matthew 6:13. We can also pray for others to be delivered from the evil one. Scriptures that show the power of prayer and fasting are many. Appendix 1: Weapons of Spiritual Warfare lists a few in the section on prayer and others on fasting. Please also see the section on prayer and fasting in the Christian Deliverance and Healing chapter.

For some bound by the enemy verbal expulsion of demons may be required. As said earlier, this requires sound discernment as to how the Lord wants the evil spirits to be expelled. If verbal expulsion of demons fails on the first attempt, it is not necessary to engage the evil spirits in a lengthy dialogue. It's more appropriate to withdraw and seek the Lord in prayer.

The Lord may require praying and fasting for the individual. "His disciples asked him privately, 'Why could we not cast it (the demon) out' And he said to them, 'This kind cannot be driven out by anything but prayer and fasting,'" Mark 9:28-29, Matthew 17:21 (KJV, ISV).

He may require a simple word of health being proclaimed on the individual or laying on of hands. "A woman was there who had been crippled by a spirit for eighteen years. She was bent over and could not straighten up at all. When Jesus saw her, he called her forward and said to her, 'Woman, you are set free from your infirmity.' Then he put his hands on her, and immediately she straightened up and praised God," Luke 13:11-13.

Or he may require the use of anointing oil combined with prayer. "Is any one of you sick? He should call the elders of the church to pray over him and anoint him with oil in the name of the Lord," (James 5:14). And so on.

If it is Jesus who is working through us by the Holy Spirit to be burdened for certain people and matters that are in the enemy's hands then rest assured that no force has any power to defeat his mission. He will give us the necessary strategy and weapons of war to use on each unique matter. "Praise be to the Lord my Rock, who trains my hands for war, my fingers for battle," Psalm 144:1. All the enemy's tactics of resistance will be temporary.

In a way we are God's weapons of war on the earthly realm against the enemy. "You (Israel) are my war club, my weapon for battle with you I shatter nations, with you I destroy kingdoms," Jeremiah 51:20.

However, our roles in the cosmic (heavenly) battles are indirect in nature as continually emphasized in this book. God's role is direct as he uses his angles to directly confront Satan and his forces.

His angels do their part in the heavenly realm as we fulfill our indirect roles down here. "Praise the Lord, you his angels, you mighty ones who do his bidding, who obey his word. Praise the Lord, all his heavenly hosts, you his servants who do his will," Psalm 103:20-21. "Are not all angels ministering spirits sent to serve those who will inherit salvation?" Hebrews 1:14.

Deliverance from demonic possession is therefore an assignment that focuses on the demon possessed unbelievers turning to Christ for salvation and deliverance. It is also normally a one-time procedure in a particular area of oppression.

6. Can a Christian be Demon Possessed?

CHAPTER 6. SUB-TOPICS:

-Can a Christian Be Demon Possessed?
-Deception in the House
-Summoning Spirits -Occult Vs Church Practices
-Our Belief Systems Influence Our Outcomes
-If the Son Sets You free... (John 8:36)

Can a Christian Be Demon Possessed?

What some believers and ministries easily classify as demonic possession is actually demonic influence. Demonic *possession* and demonic *influence* are two completely different realms of demonic activity. Possession is ownership of demons from within. The unclean spirits possess, occupy or own an individual that is categorized as possessed. He/she is a prisoner to the demons that live inside him/her.

Demonic *influence* is interference of demons from an external position. It is not internal. It is from an external position in the spirit realm where evil spirits can freely operate among believers and non-believers. In this spiritual realm they have no ownership over anyone yet constantly operate to influence people through temptation. Please read the previous chapter which clarifies the distinction between demonic possession and demonic influence.

Can a Christian be demon *possessed*? A few evangelicals recently began to believe it is possible. A deeper scrutiny of scripture shows believers cannot be possessed or owned by evil spirits. As long as one is born again there cannot be any evil spirit living inside of him/her.

How could the Holy Spirit, from the Jealous God, be sharing a bed with demons? We are temples of the Holy Spirit. Can we be at the same time temples of demons? So the doctrine of Christians having demons is false. It is also dangerous doctrine.

"Don't you know that you yourself are God's temple and that God's Spirit lives in you? If anyone destroys God's temple, God will destroy him; God's temple is sacred, and you are that temple," (1 Corinthians 3: 16-17).

There is nowhere in scripture where evil spirits are cast out of believers. Secondly demon possessed people never went round looking for Jesus hoping to be delivered from evils spirits. The demon possessed were so out of their mind or so bound that they had no control of themselves. The demons owned or possessed them. So either people who knew them sought Jesus or Jesus and his disciples came across such people as they went about preaching the gospel.

Recently (from the late 1970s and early 80s) some believers began to categorize certain problems they found among other believers as aspects of demonic possession. Church history of over 2,000 has had its share of false teachings resulting from scriptural misinterpretation. Many of our recent waves of false teachings among fellow evangelicals have come from the spiritual warfare and deliverance movement.

For example if a believer had a serious temper problem he/she was said to have a spirit of anger. If he had a problem with lust he was said to have a spirit of lust or spirit of fornication. If it was woman disputing with her husband she was said to have a Jezebel spirit. And so on.

The categorization of evil spirits went out of hand and so did casting out these spirits. And many strategies were developed to get rid of the evil spirits out of Christians. Some included coughing them out, cursing them, rebuking them, stomping on them, and son on. Whether or not scripture had any backing to such practices did not matter. No wonder they continue to fail in bringing any lasting deliverance on those seeking deliverance.

There're many problems sincere Christians may go through that we may never fully understand why nor have the grace to solve all of them. We've got to be humble before our sovereign Lord and seek his perfect will while acknowledging that our understanding is limited. We prescribe biblical prescriptions to problems but beyond that would be going outside what the bible says.

In the bible, demon spirits, also known as evil spirits or fallen angels, are characterized as having extreme control over people who are categorized as demon possessed. We have an account where Jesus' disciples failed to cast out an evil spirit from a demon possessed child. The evil spirit controlled him to the extent that it often threw him in the fire or tried to drown him whenever the opportunity came. When the boy was brought to Jesus he said, "You deaf and mute spirit, I command you, come out of him and never enter him again," Mark 9:25.

This is one of the biblical examples of those owned or possessed by demons -they had no control of themselves. The spirits living inside them were their masters, manifesting their will whenever it pleased them. Such are the people that need believers to go to them and cast demons out of them or preach the gospel which miraculously overcomes demonic strongholds. We meet such people in our towns and cities that we categorize as insane and deranged. They are helpless under heavy demonic strongholds. They are temples of demons or temples of idols, with demons referring to each of them as their house (Luke 11:24-26).

Contrast this with believers who are temples of the Holy Spirit. We're under God's ownership with God living in us. Each believer is a house of God where God lives through his Holy Spirit. We are therefore not vulnerable to demons living inside us. We cannot be temples of God and temples of idols at the same time. It is one spirit or the other, not both at the same time. One spirit is from God, the other from Satan thus personifying their respective sources.

While it is possible not to be possessed by either spirit (as is the case for many unbelievers) it is impossible for both spirits to live in (or possess) the same person. It is impossible for God and Satan to live in the same house. It is actually an insult to our holy God to assume that he is willing to possess and dwell in the same house as unclean spirits.

"What does a believer have in common with an unbeliever? What agreement is there between the temple of God and idols? For we are the temple of the living God," 2 Corinthians 6:15-16. A believer has nothing in common in his/her spiritual makeup with an unbeliever.

Secondly there is no agreement between the temple of God and idols. A person cannot be both. He/she is either a temple of God or is a temple of idols. The two are mutually exclusive.

Other cases of demonic possession are people who get involved in the extremes of Satanism and the occult. These are not insane and deranged people in our society. People in extremes of Satanism and the occult are among the most talented in our society. Through desire for more power, wealth, and other influences they find themselves caught up in occult practices.

Many of the individuals who find themselves in extreme occult practices willfully invite Satan to come in and possess them during their rituals. It is similar to us believers who willfully invite Jesus to be our Lord and Savior. We ask him to abide in us and we occasionally take communion to symbolize his indwelling or possession of our lives.

People in the extremes of Satanism and the occult do just the same, except to a different master -Satan. They drink each other's blood, blood of animals and at worst levels, blood of people in sacrifice to Satan, their god. A different spirit enters them as they willfully summon Satan to take over their lives. They become possessed from within. Evil spirits enter their lives and begin to exercise control over their lives. Needless to say that there is plenty of hope for such people to find salvation.

If we fully understood the implications of inviting Jesus into our lives to possess us and be Lord few believers would entertain the idea that a Christian can be demon possessed or evil spirit possessed. We become spiritually reborn (born again) into a new spiritual identity where we become God's owned and possessed vessels. A person who has received Christ as his/her Savior cannot have a demonic possession problem. She has willfully embraced Christ as her Savior and invited him to live inside her through the Holy Spirit. She is now the temple of the Holy Spirit, with God living INSIDE her.

"Do you not know that your body is a temple of the Holy Spirit, who is IN you, whom you have received from God?" (1 Corinthians 6:19). Can the Holy Spirit, who is holy, holy, holy, tolerate sharing his temple with evil spirits?

He does not tolerate our sinful tendencies, how much more will he tolerate living together with an evil spirit?

Deception in the House

A believer who assumes he/she is demon possessed because of certain problems being experienced is therefore only deceived. Seeking demons to be cast out of him/her only opens the door to consequences of following false teachings. Those who jump to cast out demons from born again Christians only end up making the lives of these innocent unpossessed souls worse.

Cases of Christians ending up with more mental and other problems after being subjected to casting out of demons are legion. Most of them were victims that fell into deliverance false teachings that treat demonic activity outside biblical teachings. Matters of demonic influence end up being mixed up with matters of demonic possession with unfortunate consequences. Demonic influence is very different from demonic possession as explained in this book.

The demons in many cases put up a show to deceive "deliverance ministers" and the victim that they are really occupying a born again believer. The whole truth is that the demons are summoned through the proclamations of the "deliverance minister," being commanded to come out and sometimes summoned to a lengthy conversation.

This is not to mock ministers and believers caught up in false teachings in some deliverance ministries. Many are sincere in their motives. Bob DeWaay who was once a pastor that practiced deliverance ministry false teachings for more years than some of us says, "I do not doubt the motives of the spiritual technicians (deliverance ministers). When I was one I sincerely wanted to help people. I was working day and night, without salary or benefits. I wanted to serve God fully and advance His kingdom. I sincerely believed I was doing so. However, my deception caused me to put people in more bondage rather than to deliver them. I was unwittingly a bondage maker," (Bob DeWaay in his article "How Deliverance Ministries Lead People to Bondage").

Summoning Spirits -Occult Vs Church Practices

Some may still think the strange voices that come of a person are actually demons living inside of a person. You may need to ask some who were once in the occult at whatever level. When an evil spirit is summoned to manifest in a realm where our spiritual faculties can relate with spirits it shows up through whoever is made to act as its medium or vessel.

In some Asian and African countries like India, South Africa, Zambia and Zimbabwe, it is common among some subcultures to practice necromancy, the practice of communicating with the spirits of the dead.

The necromancers summon the spirits of the dead and sure enough they shows up. The spirits speak through a person who acts as its medium. In actual fact it is not the dead person but a demon that has been summoned. Demons can mimic voices of the dead or the living.

When evil spirits are summoned they show up through practices that invite them. The people that summon them or their companions working in agreement end up being vessels or mediums through which the spirits can express themselves.

Necromancy, transcendental meditation, horoscopes and other occult practices are fast returning to the Western world where Christianity had banished them for centuries. Harry Potter, Star Wars and much of the media make occult beliefs as harmless practices and invite people to try. Unfortunately many do with terrible consequences.

Children seem to have become the special target market in promoting occult beliefs. Jeff Harshbarger, a former Satanist now in Christ, says in his book, *From Darkness to Light*, "Parents, the occult is being marketed to your children at an unprecedented level through movies, television programs, books, games, toys, and trading cards. It's portrayed as innocent, fun, and entertaining. To see the newest or latest in occult items for kids, turn on the television, browse the children's department at the local bookstore, or walk the aisles of the toy store nearest to you," (*From Darkness to Light*, p.131-132).

However, as Harshbarger points out, the association of occult related content among children does not invite demonic activity. It nonetheless can pose as an invitation for children to experiment with higher level occult practices that summon demonic activity.

In the Christian camp, the calling forth of demons in the name of deliverance on born again Christians is one area believers summon demons to manifest. Demons receive a lot of attention in environments where such practices are common. They freely manifest themselves through people who seek demons to be cast out assuming they have a demonic possession problem.

The strange thing is that the same people keep coming back for deliverance. The demons keep playing games on them that they have a demonic possession problem. For as long as their focus is on demons living inside them the hide and seek game continues.

It is only when matters distinguishing between demonic possession and demonic influence are seen and addressed that deliverance and healing starts. Church ministers ought to stop blaming the innocent souls that they keep trying to cast demons out of and start focusing on revising their non-biblical teachings that keep people going in circles.

Our Belief Systems Influence Our Outcomes

In addition to directly summoning demons through non-biblical practices our belief systems also govern our outcomes. Our belief systems end up inviting what we strongly believe in.

That is why the positive thinking movement has gained a lot of adoration in the secular world. They have taken what the bible confirms and twisted it to seem like a newly discovered spiritual law. Many secular positive thinking "preachers" believe in spiritual laws but not in the bible. It is the bible where God shows us about these spiritual laws that he, himself set up.

Our belief systems govern our outcomes. A Christian with a worldview of Satan living inside him/her (in spite of being born again) ends up creating an opportunity for Satan to act as if he possesses him/her.

Ask Perry Stone, a prominent evangelist, in his early Christian stages who got so preoccupied with the demonic world and its assumed power. And sure enough demonic experiences showed up in his life. He began to see, hear, and experience these ugly beings from the dark world. "According to your faith will it be done to you," Matthew 9:29.

After the Lord rescued him from being preoccupied with the demonic world he says, "Focus on the devil and he shows up, focus on Christ and he shows up," (3:00 in the Morning: Tapping into the Spirit World). Summoning demons to manifest in a realm where our spiritual faculties can relate with them is easier than most people assume. Ask some who were once in the occult at whatever level.

We are therefore admonished to align our beliefs systems along the bible in order to receive the right outcomes in life. Applying these biblical truths or laws of spirit is what brings freedom into our lives. "If you hold to my teaching, you are really my disciples. Then you will know the truth, and the *truth will set you free*," John 8:31-32.

If the Son Sets You free... (John 8:36)

Once delivered from Satan by accepting Jesus as our Lord and Savior we have no business with demons. The exception is given only when casting demons out of people who are not saved and are in such bondage that demons need to be cast out.

Against us believers they can longer possess nor own us. They are powerless against us in terms of entering our human faculties. Christ set us free indeed, not halfway or some spiritual chains left. It's total freedom from any aspect of demonic possession or demonic enslavement. "So if the Son sets you free, you will be free indeed," (John 8:36).

Assuming that demons still have power over us is a dangerous doctrine that only invites them to play games on us that they really are inside. "According to your faith will it be done to you," Matthew 9:29.

So a born again Christian who may have some form of strange problem (spiritual, social, material or physical) cannot be said to be demon possessed. It can be from severe demonic influence but not from any level of demonic possession. Paul, the apostle was tormented by Satan throughout much of his ministry life. He received a thorn in the flesh from Satan that brought much pain and discomfort in his life. "There was given me a thorn in my flesh, a messenger of Satan, to torment me," 2 Corinthians 12:7.

What was Paul's solution? He kept pleading with God to deliver him. He did not address some demons to come out of him or cough them out. We do not hear any names of evil spirits being mentioned. He turned to God to remove the demonic influence that was illegally operating over his life. "Three times I pleaded with the Lord to take it away from me," (verse 8).

And God, not demon spirits, had the final say over Paul's torment. "He said to me, 'My grace is sufficient for you, for my power is made perfect in weakness.' Therefore I will boast all the more gladly about my weaknesses, so that Christ's power may rest on me," (verse 9). God delivered him in a non-traditional way, by giving him the grace to endure his affliction.

Each of us already born again are to seek God's deliverance from various obstacles we may have -spiritual, social, material, physical and so on. God will have his final say. The final say for breakthrough is not with some demonic beings who have only received God's permission to hinder us.

Without God's permission they'd have no door of entry into our lives - unless we legally open one. They illegally operate over our lives once all their legal doorways are closed: doors of deception, ignorance, sin and storms of life (when responded to in a wrong way).

The only one to answer for their illegal influence over our lives is God. He is the one we're to approach, not the demons. In his sovereign will he may allow strange demonic influence for a season, for a situation or for an entire lifetime like Paul.

Why God may allow such a high level of demonic influence (not demonic possession) on his children, the born again spiritual saints, can be another lengthy subject with its own limitations. The good news is that God always works all unpleasant matters we may experience to our good. Whatever he allows us to encounter (good or bad) eventually works to our good.

Our focus throughout whatever experiences should be on the Deliverer not the oppressor. We end up creating an atmosphere of faith in God and not fear for the devil. Faith as we know is God's spiritual license that he uses to work matters in our favor.

In terms of spiritual laws faith is our indirect spiritual weapon or spiritual positive energy that ends up pleasing God to create suitable circumstances for our victory. "Without faith it is impossible to please God, because anyone who comes to him must believe that he exists and that he rewards those who earnestly seek him," Hebrews 11:6.

Having a mindset or belief system that is focused on God is faith in motion and it is one of our indirect spiritual weapons for ultimate victory. "Take up the shield of faith, with which you can extinguish all the flaming arrows of the evil one," Ephesians 6:16.

7. Misinterpreted Scripture: The Source of False Teachings

CHAPTER 7. MISINTERPRETED SCRIPTURE SUB-TOPICS:

- Background to Misinterpreted Scripture
- Misinterpreted Scripture on Spiritual Warfare and Deliverance

Background to Misinterpreted Scripture

Misinterpreted scriptures are the source of false teachings and doctrines. When scripture is taken out of its context its original meaning changes. Its meaning and purpose ends up being inaccurate or being in err. Once this takes place those who are taught the inaccurate or erroneous interpretation are said to be receiving false teachings and doctrines.

Misinterpreted scriptures which result in false teachings do not arise because God's servants deliberately want to twist the scriptures or feel like deceiving people. They arise because we are human and limited in our understanding. We are liable to err as Chapter 1: Fallibility of the Church explains.

At the root of most scriptural misinterpretation is Satan trying to take advantage of our fallibility (being liable to err). While we have the Holy Spirit in us who guides us "into all truth," (John 16:13) God does sometimes allow us to fall under certain errors for a season before revealing the truth to us. How else can we explain the extreme blunders throughout church history done in God's name by sincere Christians?

The way this deception works is by Satan planting thoughts in our minds rather than appearing physically. We have more than enough experiences throughout history where God's people have fallen to lies through misinterpreted scripture. Satan used scripture to justify ungodly acts such as gender abuses, slavery, colonialism, persecution of non-Christians and so on.

Our recent accounts include the erroneous spiritual warfare and deliverance teachings. None of the people that fell to the lies throughout history had any outward conversation or physical encounter with Satan quoting scripture.

In regard to gender abuses, some even in the body of Christ, are still holding on to historical role modeling that have no real scriptural backing. Most of what is advocated that women are supposed to be this or that and men are supposed to be the other are merely molding of roles born from traditions of men.

Jesus was such an opponent of traditions that had nothing to do with the scripture. "You have a fine way of setting aside the commands of God in order to observe your own traditions," Mark 7:9.

Many gender traditions have no biblical basis. For example, the assumption that women are not "supposed" to have strong assertive traits, nor be intellectual. Men are "supposed" to be aggressive not soft nor have feelings.

Role modeling throughout history has rewarded those fitting their "gender roles" while punishing those not fitting. Few ever bothered to challenge these man-made roles until recently, from the 1960's onwards.

In our era of increased understanding these roles are only serving to create marital and workplace distress. It's largely men, not women, that need to wake up to many gender roles that have no biblical basis.

Yes some in the secular world are pursuing militant and non-biblical gender ideologies. However, this does not invalidate the fact that we have to remove traditions of men that have no biblical basis and are a stumbling block to the body of Christ.

Have you ever wondered why the body of Christ, God's mighty army in the earthly realm, has far more women than men? Could God be saying something in between the lines - being the fact that he's the one who saves us and grafts us to the body of Christ? Does God want women to be benchwarmers in a sphere they are the majority?

Does being predominantly physically weaker vessels also translate to being spiritually weaker vessels? Are women not meant to play a key role in their area of strength?

Think about it, without running to the bible for some historically famous scriptures that have largely been taken out of context to justify certain gender interests. Scripture can be used to justify almost any matter but it does not necessarily imply it is being applied or interpreted correctly. Didn't Satan also use the bible in trying to tempt and deceive Jesus? Wasn't the bible used for centuries to justify subjugation of certain ethnic groups and non-Christians?

Misinterpreted Scripture on Spiritual Warfare and Deliverance Principles

The following are among misinterpreted scripture that have been used to justify direct confrontation with evil spirits in territories and the spirit world. Some have already been covered in the book and thus did not merit being repeated.

1. "They overcame him by the blood of the Lamb and by the word of their testimony; they did not love their lives so much as to shrink from death," Rev. 12:11

The above scripture has been presumed, among those advocating for the erroneous spiritual warfare and deliverance teachings, to refer to believers going to Satan and confronting him with or invoking the blood of Jesus. However, the preceding verse (v.10) talks about "the Accuser," who is Satan, going before God and making accusations against us. The scripture says he does this "day and night" (v.10) trying to gain legal ground to attack us spiritually, physically, socially, materially and so on.

It doesn't say he goes to believers. Since he approaches God it is God himself who looks into the accusations made against us. And he, being the ultimate Judge, God considers our side of the case that we have presented before him. The blood of Jesus that covers our sins and our testimony which is God's word and our conduct of living upright lives disqualify the accusations Satan has made against us.

The blood of the Lamb and our testimony overcomes him in the court of heaven. We have access to heaven, God's kingdom, so we can always plead our side of the case against Satan, our Accuser.

The scripture therefore does not imply direct confrontation with our Accuser. We cannot afford putting it out of context to justify direct confrontation. After all, in every court of law, each side presents its case before a judge. They do not directly argue against each other to win a case.

Matthew Henry's Concise Commentary says, "The conquered enemy hates the presence of God, yet he is willing to appear there, to accuse the people of God. Let us take heed that we give him no cause to accuse us; and that, when we have sinned, we go before the Lord, condemn ourselves, and commit our cause to Christ as our Advocate."

In their book, *Unbroken Curses*, Rebecca Brown and her husband, Daniel Yoder, discuss how after all the "spiritual warfare" of direct confrontation failed they decided to approach God as the Supreme Judge. All their attempts to directly confront and bombard the evil spirit world failed until the strategy was changed to indirect confrontation. They decided to approach God to act on her behalf.

In the last chapter of *Unbroken Curses* titled "The Final Court of Appeal," she says, "There just isn't enough time or space for me to tell you all the wonderful things the Lord has performed in our lives since the night I visited the courtroom of the Judge of the Universe. Daniel 7:21-22 has truly been fulfilled in our lives. (In this chapter, Daniel was given a vision of the nations and rulers to come. The rulers were represented by horns. The last ruler was represented by a horn, which is Satan.)"

Daniel 7:21-22: "As I watched, this horn was waging war against the saints and defeating them, until the Ancient of Days came and pronounced judgment in favor of the saints of the Most High, and the time came when they possessed the kingdom,"

Dr. Brown says, "Dear reader, are you struggling just as we were? Do you know that God has called you to do a specific task for him, but Satan has been blocking you from doing it? If you have no legal grounds (i.e. legal doorways) in your life for Satan to attack you, then I would suggest that you consider going before the Judge of the Universe." (p. 171).

She says, "In the time since we have learned this very powerful tool of spiritual warfare, we have met a number of people who have been in the same position of discouragement we were. God does not want His people to live a life of defeat and discouragement! He placed us here on planet earth to possess and control it. We are to be owners, not renters!...

"When you, the reader have done everything you know to do...perhaps you need to go before the Judge of the Universe...He has made provision for us so that we can walk in victory and bring the glorious Gospel of Jesus Christ to the lost and dying world," (p173-174).

What Brown did not realize is that approaching God to judge every case in our favor is how we're intended to deal with the enemy. It is indirect spiritual warfare, yet powerful and fully backed by scripture. That is why it worked in her case and continues to work in all of us who go before God's throne of grace through Christ. She tried all the direct confrontation attempts to no avail then only to find her victory through indirect confrontation. That says on its own what works and what doesn't, what's biblical and what's not.

Brown's narration of a prayer of appeal has been a great inspiration to me in seeking God to intervene in moments of crisis. Earnestly appealing to God, sometimes with fasting, during times of need has time and again proved to be the only solution. Prayers of appeal have proved to be true spiritual warfare prayers and deliverance prayers.

The rest of her book advocates for the erroneous spiritual warfare and deliverance teachings that call for direct confrontation with Satan. I followed them to my peril before the Lord rescued me from the scriptural misinterpretation on spiritual warfare and deliverance principles.

The other forms of direct warfare are our invention that came through the enemy misquoting scripture to us. That's why they do not work and if they ever do, they have no lasting results. They open doors for worse problems in other areas of our lives.

In her book, Brown narrates her appeal to God in a chapter titled, "The Final Court of Appeal." It is a petition to God for his intervention against the works of the enemy. The victories that followed resolved matters that all her "spiritual warfare" of direct confrontation failed to bring.

No need to buy her book just to read her prayer of appeal. Most of the book focuses on directly bombarding evil spirits which scripture forbids. An example of a prayer of appeal is covered in this book. See Appendix 2: Deliverance, Healing and Restoration Prayer.

Besides, reading a prayer made by someone else is not what makes the difference. It's applying the required biblical principles in one's area of concern. The chapter series on deliverance and healing (Chapter 9) cover on principles in many of these areas. It is walking with God in such a way that having done our part of applying his will enables him to fight our battles.

We would have had more victories in the body of Christ if we knew true spiritual warfare to be from the indirect perspective. *Matthew Henry's Concise Commentary* says, "If Christians had continued to fight with these weapons (the blood of Jesus and the word of their testimony), and such as these, their victories would have been more numerous and glorious, and the effects more lasting."

This is not going after the enemy but by ensuring that, "we give him no cause to accuse us; and that, when we have sinned, we go before the Lord, condemn ourselves (through repentance to God), and commit our cause to Christ as our Advocate."

2. "Put on the full armor of God so that you can take your stand against the devil's schemes. For our struggle is not against flesh and blood, but against the rulers, against the authorities, against the powers of this dark world and against the spiritual forces of evil in the heavenly realms," Ephesians 6:11-12.

The above scripture has been presumed, among those advocating for the erroneous spiritual warfare and deliverance teachings, to imply that since we do not fight against our fellow flesh and blood we're to directly confront our real enemies who are the rulers, the authorities, the powers of this dark world and the spiritual forces of evil in the heavenly realms.

The scripture is talking about persecution from people. Instead of trying to overcome their persecution of us with worldly methods (weapons) like arguments, lawsuits, physical confrontation, war, and so on, we're to primarily ignore their attacks. We focus on overcoming the one using them. It's the enemy fighting us through them. With our spiritual weapons we overcome his works against us and against them.

Our spiritual weapons, as covered in this book, have nothing to do with directly confronting Satan. Please read Chapter 4. True Biblical Spiritual Warfare = Indirect Confrontation. Our spiritual weapons are "weapons of righteousness" (2 Corinthians 6:7) that the Lord uses to confront the enemy and set captives free.

This may come as a surprise since we expect weapons of war to be used directly against enemy forces and territory. There is no scriptural example of Jesus or any members of the early church directly confronting evil spirits by making proclamations against them in thin air nor in territories in order to overcome their influence.

What has made us assume we can do otherwise is quite a puzzle. And the consequences among many applying the erroneous spiritual warfare and deliverance teachings are unfortunate.

3. *"(Verse 4) The weapons we fight with are not the weapons of the world. On the contrary, they have divine power to demolish strongholds. (v.5) We demolish arguments and every pretension that sets itself up against the knowledge of God, and we take captive every thought to make it obedient to Christ. (v.6) And we will be ready to punish every act of disobedience, once your obedience is complete," 2 Cori. 10:4-6*

In the *New International Version* (NIV) bible this verse is in a chapter titled "Paul's Defense of His Ministry." Paul maintains that we're not to live by the standards of this world. He said we should not be like "some people who think that we live by the standards of this world (v.2)." These were among believers. Some were stirring up believers against him.

Matthew Henry Complete Commentary on the Whole Bible notes that, "There was no place in which the apostle Paul met with more opposition from false apostles than at Corinth; he had many enemies there…Though he was so blameless and inoffensive in all his carriage."

Paul was therefore referring to punishing "every act of disobedience" among believers who were not walking right with God. It does not imply punishing the disobedience of Satan by directly confronting him. It meant confronting the disobedience among believers. This disobedience would be punished not by weapons of this world (e.g. arguments, lawsuits, physical confrontation, war, and so on) but by our spiritual weapons that "have divine power to demolish strongholds" (v.4).

Spiritual strongholds are strongly established sinful ways and false beliefs that have gained a strong influence over a person to the extent that each stronghold "sets itself up against the knowledge of God" (v.5). The individual is unable to accept or follow God's word because these spiritual strongholds have an excessive influence on him.

Strongholds are high levels of demonic influence (not possession) in the mental faculties of an individual. Think of people caught up in some sinful behavior like atheism, unbelief, stealing, greed, alcohol addiction, drugs, sexual sins, promiscuity, pornography, homosexuality, uncontrollable anger (temper tantrums), compulsive gambling, etc. They feel easily pulled to or controlled by whatever matter that is entrenched into their lifestyle.

Concerning homosexuality some readers in Western nations who're not in mainline evangelical circles may claim it's a biological makeup that some are born with, thus divinely destined for the lifestyle and therefore unjustified to be called a sin. Since it'd be going out of the context of this book to discuss this matter in detail I urge such readers to visit GotQuestions.org for plenty of bible based answers. You can type in your query in the search bar.

It's a helpful bible-based website covering even on matters central to this book: biblical spiritual warfare, can Christians be demon possessed, tongues, praying to Mary, yoga, etc. Please make use of such resources, including resources at our websites (JesusW.com and SpiritualWarfareDeliverance.com) and public or church library resources for questions unanswered in this book. Feel free to email us a question to consider answering in the next edition or adding to the website. However the volume of email received makes it unbearable to reply to every person that writes.

The bible does refer to homosexuality as a sin. Those of us who are obligated to follow the bible to qualify as true Christians, as followers of Christ, have no choice but to accept its do's and don'ts. The bible takes strong positions on many issues and we've no choice but to follow its dictates.

It's true some matters have been misused in church history to take positions that the bible never intended, such on slavery, gender abuses, and subjugation of non-Christians. This does not invalidate positions the bible takes that are clear and in conclusive black and white terms (as opposed to grey unclear issues - e.g. speaking in tongues (true tongues), Sunday worship, trinity, etc).

What if the bible said people of a certain ethnic group, race or gender were not acceptable even if biologically they just found themselves in such a makeup? If I found myself to be in the ethnic or gender category that the bible denies I would not waste my time trying to change what it says in clear black and white terms. I would move on and join a religion or belief that welcomes me. I'd make no protests because the bible like any script has a right to say what it wants as long as those who believe in it do not come to trespass over my own basic freedoms.

This is not what is happening among some embracing homosexuality – particularly among some in Western countries. Some of them deny what the bible clearly says and are furious with those that say the bible condemns the behavior. They want to be recognized as Christians without changing the behavior the bible categorizes as sin. To me it seems more sensible, dignifying and respectful of other people's beliefs to seek another belief that's accepting rather than trying to forcefully change their beliefs so that I can be accepted.

For anyone in homosexual behavior it's worth considering what the bible clearly says -see GotQuestions.org. You are free to accept or reject its stand. If you accept its stand feel free to make use of the biblical deliverance and healing principles covered in this book. Fortunately from a biblical perspective deliverance and healing is not a genetic or biological matter but a spiritual one.

And you don't have to change political parties. None of them in the real sense represent God's agenda on earth (even if they claim). But the church (body of Christ) does. Set aside ten Christians that can pray and fast for twenty one or forty days, they would accomplish ANY agenda regardless of which political party is in charge. The body of Christ seems to have lost its leadership mantle by assuming politicians play a central role in God's agenda on earth.

It's important to vote but let's not quarrel over minor issues on who's worth voting for. Let's not be deceived into leaving the major issues of how much we're willing to carry burdens in prayer and fasting to make a difference as a unified church. See what'd happen if together we labor in taking God's agenda to his throne room, not before politicians. We lobby or petition him not with money or signatures but with our sacrificial lives for his cause.

Strongholds are divinely demolishable through our indirect weapons of spiritual warfare and deliverance. They are not demolished by directly confronting certain assumed spirits in geographical territories, familiar spirits, generational spirits, Jezebel spirits, spirits of division, spirits of unforgiveness, spirits of addiction, spirits of this and that. Neither are they demolished by petitioning politicians. God was not joking when he gave us our indirect weapons. Let's aggressively use them and it'll make all the difference in the world.

Believers are not immune from extreme forms of demonic influence that constitute strongholds -e.g. sexual sins, pornography, compulsive gambling, alcohol addiction, etc. Just not to be misunderstood, alcohol addiction is not the same thing as a believer who consents to taking some wine at a special occasion. The addict is controlled by the bottle while a believer that opts to take some does it out of practical reasons suitable for that occasion –e.g. to loosen up (there're some scary serious and unsociable believers out there). One side is bondage, unhealthy, and sinful while the other side scripture does not condemn.

Paul says with our spiritual weapons (that are indirect in nature) we're able to "demolish arguments and every pretension that sets itself up against the knowledge of God, and we take captive every thought to make it obedient to Christ" (v.5). He then says our obedience to God enables us to "punish every act of disobedience, once your (our) obedience (to God) is complete" (v.6).

One way that our obedience to God has punishing effects on the works of Satan on earth is through prayer. Our obedient lives are weapons of righteousness that enable our prayers not to be hindered. This is indirect spiritual warfare. No direct confrontation with Satan or his evil spirits is required.

No scripture even advocates direct confrontation with Satan as a way of punishing his acts of disobedience to God among people or matters in our lives. Yet there are plenty of scriptures showing that our prayers to God combined with our obedience to him accomplish the impossible. For some major examples of scriptures on prayer please see Appendix 1: Weapons of Spiritual Warfare, weapon number 1 – prayer. It's astonishing how powerful prayer is.

On directly confronting spirits, G. Richard Fisher says, "Biblically taking cities for God by crippling and disarming the demons of the city is nowhere taught in Scripture. Paul preached the Gospel in each city without dramatics or evasive claims. We do not find Paul doing "prayer walks" and spiritual stakeouts. Logic tells us that for all the time the "demon busters" have been at it, they should have had these cities all under control by now and demon free.

"In the new theatrics of demon busting, one word, "stronghold," has been taken out of 2 Corinthians 10 and used to create an entire theology. The context of chapter 10 is confronting false belief. If anyone is tearing down strongholds, it is the counter cult and apologetic movement (the counter cult and apologetic movement are the people that expose false teachings in and outside the body of Christ). Dualistic demonism is in itself a stronghold of error and false teaching," (G. Richard Fisher, Walking in the Shadow of the Walk).

4. *"When a strong man, fully armed, guards his own house, his possessions are safe. But when someone stronger attacks and overpowers him, he takes away the armor in which the man trusted and divides up the spoils," Luke 11:21-22.*

"How can anyone enter a strong man's house and carry off his possessions unless he first ties up the strong man? Then he can rob his house," Matthew 12:29 (NIV)

This passage is used, among those advocating for the erroneous spiritual warfare and deliverance teachings, to justify that we have the authority to bind or tie up evil spirits in people, geographic territories or even spiritual forces of evil in the heavenly realms. Unless we bind him we would not be able to overcome him, as it is advocated among those advocating for direct confrontation against Satan, the strong man.

However, the one with the binding or arresting assignment is Jesus, not us, his disciples. He is the one that is stronger than the strong man. Unless we begin to assume that we're stronger than him. That's not what the bible says. "Bold and arrogant, these men are not afraid to slander celestial beings; yet even angels, although they are stronger and more powerful, do not bring slanderous accusations against such beings in the presence of the Lord. But these men blaspheme in matters they do not understand," 2 Peter 2:10-12.

About the "strong man" passage *Matthew Henry Complete Commentary on the Whole Bible* says, "The world, that sat in darkness, and lay in wickedness, was in Satan's possession, and under his power, as a house in the possession and under the power of a strong man; so is every unregenerate soul; there Satan resides, there he rules.

"Now, the design of Christ's gospel was to spoil the devil's house, which, as a strong man, he kept in the world; to turn the people from darkness to light, from sin to holiness, from this world to a better, from the power of Satan unto God (Acts 26:18); to alter the property of souls....When nations were turned from the service of idols to serve the living God, when some of the worst of sinners were sanctified and justified, and became the best of saints, then Christ spoiled the devil's house, and will spoil it more and more."

John Wesley's Explanatory Notes on the Whole Bible also say, "How can one enter into the strong one's house, unless he first bind the strong one - So Christ coming into the world, which was then eminently the strong one's, Satan's house, first bound him, and then took his spoils."

The one who does the binding is therefore Jesus. His work on the cross took away Satan's authority over the earth, which became his house after Adam fell. He destroyed the legal grounds that Satan gained authority over us who had become his goods in his house. The legal claim came through sin.

About the work of Jesus scripture says, "He forgave us all our sins, having canceled the written code, with its regulations, that was against us and that stood opposed to us; he took it away, nailing it to the cross. And having disarmed the powers and authorities, he made a public spectacle of them, triumphing over them by the cross," Colossians 2:13-15.

The strong man can only be bound only by "someone stronger" who "attacks and overpowers him" (v.22). That stronger person is Jesus. We have no strength of our own to bind him. If we did Jesus was not necessary to come to our aid. Christ continues to spoil Satan's house in people as we preach the word and the Holy Spirit convicts sinners. He spoils his goods as evil spirits are cast out of people.

This is an ongoing work as Christ labors to overcome the works of Satan on earth. "I will build my church, and the gates of Hades will not overcome it," Matthew 16:18. In the spirit realm he overcomes Satan and his forces as we preach the gospel, heal the sick and cast out demons. We focus on our work on earth while he does his in the spirit realm.

5. "And God raised us up with Christ and seated us with him in the heavenly realms in Christ Jesus, in order that in the coming ages he might show the incomparable riches of his grace, expressed in his kindness to us in Christ Jesus," Ephesians 2:6-7.

The above scripture is obvious to many. Only a few have assumed it refers to our authority over principalities in the heavenly realms. Being seated with Christ in the heavenly realms has made some to assume that we can now rule over evil spirits that were cast down to the lower heavens and to earth.

Although the passage shows us our present standing with Christ in the heavenly realms it says nothing about our authority over principalities. However it does show what we will have "in the coming ages," that is, in eternity. Christ will "show the incomparable riches of his grace." Scripture says in the coming ages, "we will judge angels," 1 Corinthians 6:3.

Not only will we have authority over principalities, but we "will judge the world," (v.2). In this present age we remain in our realm of authority -over the earth. Assuming the passage is giving us a license to judge fallen angels is merely taking it out of its context.

It is a great privilege to be "raised us up with Christ and seated us with him in the heavenly realms in Christ Jesus." We can be at peace that we have the entire heavenly government on our side on matters that God has ordained to fulfill in and through us.

As we approach God in prayer we are entering these heavenly realms of God's kingdom. We are appealing for his grace, anointing, protection, provision and all that will enable us to overcome the works of the devil in our lives and those we're commissioned to serve.

8. Scripture Against Direct Confrontation

CHAPTER 8. SCRIPTURE AGAINST

*1. "Then the Lord spoke to Job out of the storm: .... 'Can you pull in the leviathan with a fishhook or tie down his tongue with a rope? Can you put a cord through his nose or pierce his jaw with a hook? Will he keep begging you for mercy? Will he speak to you with gentle words? Will he make an agreement with you for you to take him as your slave for life? Can you make a pet of him like a bird or put him on a leash for your girls? Will traders barter for him? Will they divide him up among the merchants? Can you fill his hide with harpoons or his head with fishing spears? **If you lay a hand on him, you will remember the struggle and never do it again! Any hope of subduing him is false; the mere sight of him is overpowering. No one is fierce enough to rouse him.** Who then is able to stand against me? Who has a claim against me that I must pay? Everything under heaven belongs to me, '" Job 40:6, Job 41:1-11.*

Easton's Bible Dictionary says Leviathan means in Hebrew, "'twisted,' 'coiled.' In Job 3:8, Revised Version, and marg. of Authorized Version, it denotes the dragon which, according to Eastern tradition, is an enemy of light; in (Job) 41:1 the crocodile is meant; in Psalms 104:26 it 'denotes any large animal that moves by writhing or wriggling the body, the whale, the monsters of the deep.'"

It denotes a serpent like animal. No other spiritual being apart from Satan represents the serpent. Beginning from Genesis to Revelation the serpent and dragon represent Satan or his agents. In the passage above the Lord says, "If you lay a hand on him, you will remember the struggle and never do it again! Any hope of subduing him is false; the mere sight of him is overpowering. No one is fierce enough to rouse him."

The Lord concludes this long imagery of Satan saying, "Nothing on earth is his equal- a creature without fear. He looks down on all that are haughty; he is king over all that are proud," Job 41:33-34.

Satan is therefore not our equal even though "God raised us up with Christ and seated us with him in the heavenly realms in Christ Jesus," (Ephesians 2:6-7). He is God's enemy yet God did not assign us to rule over him. Otherwise we would be contradicting this scripture. In this life we remain "a little lower than the angels," Hebrews 2:7. This includes fallen angels.

Only God deals directly with Leviathan. He will completely slay Leviathan on Judgment day. "In that day, the Lord will punish with his sword, his fierce, great and powerful sword, Leviathan the gliding serpent, Leviathan the coiling serpent; he will slay the monster of the sea," Isaiah 27:1.

Our realm of authority assigns us to deal indirectly with Leviathan. We see this in the way Christ exercised his authority and dealt against the works of

Leviathan in people. He preached the gospel that made the deception and false beliefs in people to be cast out by the truth.

The only exception is when casting out or expelling evil spirits living in people. Here we have the authority to speak directly to them and command them to come out of people.

This is the realm of authority where our Lord said, "I have given you authority to trample on snakes and scorpions and to overcome all the power of the enemy; nothing will harm you," Luke 10:19. Notice that Jesus said these words soon after the seventy-two disciples "returned with joy and said, 'Lord, even the demons submit to us in your name,'" (v.17). He then replied to them, "I saw Satan fall like lightning from heaven," (v.18).

He said the famous words when they returned from casting out evil spirits living in people. The context of authority constituted their work of casting out evil spirits living in people.

Outside this context we are merely giving ourselves authority over the enemy that we were never granted. The consequences are severe as the book of Job says: "If you lay a hand on him, you will remember the struggle and never do it again! Any hope of subduing him is false; the mere sight of him is overpowering. No one is fierce enough to rouse him," Job 41:8-10.

Even our Lord Jesus used indirect principles assigned to us during his time on the earthly realm (when he came in human form). He was made a little lower than the angels and thus had to follow the authority structure. The story changed after his resurrection.

He now has full authority over Satan in both the heavenly and earthly realms. "We see Jesus, who was made a little lower than the angels, now crowned with glory and honor ..." Hebrews 2:9.

2. *"These dreamers pollute their own bodies, reject authority and slander celestial beings. But even the archangel Michael, when he was disputing with the devil about the body of Moses, did not dare to bring a slanderous accusation against him, but said, "The Lord rebuke you!" Yet these men speak abusively against whatever they do not understand; and what things they do understand by instinct, like unreasoning animals--**these are the very things that destroy them**," Jude 1:8-10.*

This passage has been explained in the chapter on "Our Territory and Nature of Our Christian Authority."

3. *"Bold and arrogant, these men are not afraid to slander celestial beings; yet even angels, although they are stronger and more powerful, do not bring slanderous accusations against such beings in the presence of the Lord. But these men blaspheme in matters they do not understand. They are like brute beasts, creatures of instinct, born **only to be caught and destroyed**, and like beasts they too will perish," 2 Peter 2:10-12*

This passage has been explained in the chapter on "Our Territory and Nature of Our Christian Authority."

9. Christian Deliverance and Healing Parts 1 to 7 (Book 2)

This section on Christian deliverance and healing could have been another book altogether. Many people are put off by big books, perhaps by life's demands. Plus production costs are higher for larger books.

For this book it seemed worthwhile to combine spiritual warfare and deliverance principles because they're inseparable when applied. Spiritual warfare is a component of deliverance principles while deliverance principles depend on spiritual warfare disciplines of indirect confrontation at every level.

Deliverance means rescuing from bondage, oppression, hardship, or domination by evil.

Deliverance ministry is carrying out Christian principles that that lead to freedom from bondage, oppression, hardship, or domination by evil. It is a recent term that has mainly been associated with deliverance from demonic possession. In our context its broader meaning is adopted where demonic *possession* is only a small part of deliverance ministry. Much of deliverance ministry deals with demonic *influence* which Christians are liable to.

Deliverance ministry principles are also part and parcel of the Christian life, thus a responsibility of every Christian. They're Christian deliverance disciplines beneficial for oneself, for loved ones, and for those burdened with.

CHAPTER 9. PART 1: FUNDAMENTALS 1 - SUB-TOPICS:
- **Biblical Deliverance and Healing 101**
- **The Jealous God on Christ-Centered Deliverance**
- **Biblical Deliverance = Truth Encounter**
- **Connecting with Christ the Deliverer –Ministry Role**
- **Doorways of Satan's Legal Entry and Demonic Influence**
- **Overcoming Life's Battles like Christ Jesus**

CHAPTER 9. PART 2: FUNDAMENTALS 2 - SUB-TOPICS:
- **Understanding Deliverance and Healing Differences**
- **Repentance, Including Over Sins of Ignorance**
- **Ceasing to Associate with the Sin**
- **Deliverance = Instant**
- **Healing is a Process**
- **Continual Search for Unknown Doorways**
- **Other Battles to Overcome**
- **The Danger of Blind Faith**
- **The Body of Christ and its Spiritual Growth**
- **Note on Prayer Group and Fellowship**

- Note Concerning Signs and Wonders

CHAPTER 9. PART 3: PRAYER AND FASTING - SUB-TOPICS:
- Prayer and Fasting -Sowing to the Spirit
- Seed time and Harvest time -No neutral ground
- Nature, Role and Purpose of Fasting
- How to Fast
- The Power of Fasting
- Carrying Cross of Self-denial on Desires of the Flesh
- Major Prayer and Fasting Scriptures

CHAPTER 9. PART 4: SPIRITUAL HEALTH AREAS - SUB-TOPICS:
- The Wounded spirit
- Sources of Spiritual Wounds (spiritual illness)
- Effects of a Wounded Spirit (broken spirit, crushed spirit)
- Healing the Wounded Spirit: the Christian Approach
- Healing the Wounded Spirit: the Secular Approach
- God's "Plan B" and Maintaining a Healthy Spirit
- Deliverance from Hearing Voices, Seeing Demons, etc
- Deliverance and Healing from Spiritual attacks through Dreams
- Deliverance and Healing from the Occult, Witchcraft or Satanism

CHAPTER 9. PART 5: SOCIAL HEALTH AREAS - SUB-TOPICS:
- Deliverance from Unforgiveness Curses
- Deliverance from Generational Curses
- Deliverance from other Curses
- Deliverance from Family Curses

CHAPTER 9. PART 6: FINANCIAL HEALTH AREAS - SUB-TOPICS:
- Same Principles, Different Limits
- Obedience is the Key
- Still Under Manna or in Canaan?
- Financial Curse (Wilderness) -A Father's Discipline
- Breaking the Curse of Poverty Through Obedience
- How God Opens the Floodgates of Heaven
- How God Prevents Satan from Destroying the Blessings
- Where to sow
- How to Start

CHAPTER 9. PART 7: PHYSICAL HEALTH AREAS - SUB-TOPICS:
- Natural Physical Health
- Food as Medicine and other Natural Cures for Natural Health
- Supernatural Physical Health

9.1 Christian Deliverance and Healing, Part 1: Fundamentals 1

CHAPTER 9. PART 1: FUNDAMENTALS 1 - SUB-TOPICS
- Biblical Deliverance and Healing 101
- The Jealous God on Christ-Centered Deliverance
- Biblical Deliverance = Truth Encounter
- Connecting with Christ the Deliverer –Ministry Role
- Doorways of Satan's Legal Entry and Demonic Attacks
- Overcoming Life's Battles like Christ Jesus

Biblical Deliverance and Healing 101

This chapter deals with deliverance and healing in major areas of biblical spiritual warfare and deliverance ministry. The primary difference with non-biblical spiritual warfare and deliverance principles is on scriptural interpretation. The non-biblical principles use a handful of misinterpreted scriptures to back up their resolve for recent practices.

The biblical principles have stood their ground for 2000 years since the earthly ministry of our Lord Jesus. Why a massive change occurred among some fellow evangelicals as recently as the early 1980s confirms Christ's end-time prophesy: "For false Christs and false prophets will appear and perform signs and miracles to deceive the elect - if that were possible. So be on your guard; I have told you everything ahead of time," Mark 13:22-23.

We're in an era of increased deception that Christ foretold. The apostles followed up on the same warning. "*For the time will come when men will not put up with sound doctrine*. Instead, to suit their own desires, they will gather around them a great number of teachers to say what their *itching ears want* to hear. They will turn their ears away from the truth and turn aside to myths," 2 Timothy 4:3-4.

Since false doctrines sometimes sound more itchy and pleasant how does one stay on guard against them? We're instructed to grow in the knowledge of God's word through our own study, fellowship with believers embracing biblical doctrine and to avoid worldly pleasures.

Our maturity and walk with God will be our defense. "Then we will no longer be infants, tossed back and forth by the waves, and blown here and there by every wind of teaching and by the cunning and craftiness of men in their deceitful scheming," Ephesians 4:14.

The following deliverance and healing principles embrace what we've always followed as biblical doctrine. There is no shade of recent teachings of bombarding evil spirits, performing certain rituals and so on. No special mountain was climbed to receive these biblical principles. Maybe the mountain of vast experience in the false teachings can be said to be one.

Years of personal experience and counseling of other believers has confirmed what works and what doesn't, what's biblical and what's not, what brings deliverance and what invites bondage. The principles shared will save you from avoidable torment some of us went through.

The only thing new here is the increased awareness on the role of deliverance and healing ministry in the body of Christ. Being saved is not an end in itself. It's a beginning of a new life of deliverance and healing from the effects of the old life.

It's also a new life that can be vulnerable to and hindered by destructive teachings, deception and sin. It's a journey from darkness to light, from ignorance to knowledge of God's word, from bondage to deliverance, in all areas of life - spiritually, socially, materially and so on.

A key point to note is that there is no drama needed in biblical deliverance and healing. Some assume deliverance will come after a powerful prayer or in some super-spiritual way with demons screaming all over, as God comes down in glorious thunder and lightning. Christian Hollywood, not the bible, has taught some that it's got to be dramatic.

They feel something is missing when you tell them deliverance is as simple as applying the following steps of faith:

1) prayer of repentance for walking outside God's will,
2) ceasing all known association and practice of matters that bring bondage through a) deception (false teachings), b) through ignorance (lack of knowledge), c) through sin, and d) through storms of life (when responded to in a wrong way),
3) being familiar with and applying biblical requirements in areas were deliverance and healing is sought (most biblical requirements in different areas are covered in this book), and
4) a simple prayer to ask God for continued guidance, equipping and grace in opening one's eyes to true biblical living.

Some believe identifying and listing all curses and spirits affecting their lives is necessary. Others expect the blood of Jesus pleaded on their lives and a prayed for bottle of anointing oil sent to them. Some believe they have demons that need to be cast out. The new sensational teachings have misled some in the body of Christ into such beliefs.

The Jealous God on Christ-Centered Deliverance

God in his wisdom has made deliverance a simple act of faith and will. We're the ones who have complicated it. We've turned deliverance ministry into a religious ritual involving a specialized deliverance ministry or deliverance church who focus on supposed deliverance ministry activities.

If you believe there's a powerful deliverance church or deliverance ministry out there that'll bring deliverance you may search forever. And God forbid that anyone ends up with a "deliverance ministry" that only increases the demonic attacks. Especially after coming across books like this that distinguish between bible based and non-biblical deliverance ministry.

The Lord is so jealous that he does not want to share his glory with no man, no woman, and no ministry when bringing your deliverance. It's true that levels of anointing may differ among believers.

But it's also true that many believers have sought deliverance and prayer from prominent names only to return empty. And some who refused to give up went on to petition God for their breakthrough. The breakthrough came in moments of their personal devotion and supplication. This increased their faith and direct relationship with God.

Maybe you have sought deliverance from all sorts of people and churches, including the wrong ones. God could be waiting for your direct connection with him. Remember that among God's numerous names is the name Jealous. "Do not worship any other god, for the Lord, whose name is Jealous, is a jealous God," Exodus 34:14. We hardly use this name but it's one of his. It describes his nature just as well as the others do (e.g. Healer, Provider, Fortress, Shepherd, etc.).

God, the Jealous One, is seeking our focus on him, not on fellow men, women or ministries. To him this is a form of idolatry, worship of another god. And he is willing to wait until an individual begins to focus on him. He responds to obedience not to levels of need. If his response was based on need he'd have come long ago because human needs continue to get more desperate every succeeding period. Human needs are worse off now than ever before in spite of technological advances.

Biblical deliverance and healing leads a person to Christ to do the deliverance work in her and for her. It is not centered on a deliverance ministry nor deliverance church. Rather it is truth-centered and Christ-centered. It is centered on bringing biblical truths that set captives free by drawing them closer to God and deliverance principles in his word. It is not centered on a deliverance ministry or deliverance church performing certain rituals and calling it deliverance ministry.

When you learn these biblical truths you're better able to deal with matters that were root causes of problems in your life or the lives of others. No demons need to be cast out of a born again, blood of Jesus purchased and heaven-bound Christian. Biblical deliverance and healing empowers you to walk with and abide in Christ, your personal Lord and Savior. It does not empower a deliverance ministry or deliverance church to continue having you under some constant dose of "deliverance medication."

Biblical Deliverance = Truth Encounter

Biblical deliverance ministry focuses on a truth encounter in God's word. It is the truth that sets us free in whatever area we may be under attack. Receiving the truth in God's word in an area of concern is what brings deliverance and healing. When the truth comes and is applied all the legal doorways that demons entered through are closed.

There is no binding and loosing of demons involved, no special anointing oil, no laying on of hands, no powerful deliverance prayers and so on. And no special emotions either to feel the deliverance experience. It is simple a simple act of faith and the will to apply required biblical deliverance principles. God's angels then go ahead to overcome the demonic forces in the spirit realm that before had legal entry once the truth comes and is applied.

This entire book shares these biblical truths on spiritual warfare and deliverance. The Lord inspired it to help you personally connect with him and his word. The truths enable you to receive what some call self-deliverance. It is actually not self-deliverance but truth deliverance. The biblical truths one learns are the ones that bring freedom. "Then you will know the truth, and the truth will set you free," John 8:32.

Prior to the above sentence Jesus said, "If you hold to my teaching, you are really my disciples," John 8:31. Holding to his teaching, his word, and applying it is what brings freedom. It is abiding in him. He wants a one to one relationship with each of us.

Through such an intimate connection with him we're able to receive and understand truths that others are blind to. He's able to remove the veil or covering of ignorance that blinds us from many matters that create hard to solve problems. This is liberating. It is true deliverance.

Please note that the freedom that comes with walking in truth does not imply having everything the way we desire or pray. It is having the right understanding to life and whatever comes our way. It is knowing how to navigate through trials of life, being made better instead of bitter through them.

It is understanding the sovereignty, power and love of God rather than being preoccupied with people, evil spirits or circumstances in determining the course of our lives. It is being empowered to walk with God in such an intimate way that he becomes our focus, not people or circumstances, and certainly not Satan.

Connecting with Christ the Deliverer –Ministry Role

A ministry's role is to help people draw closer to Christ, the actual Shepherd and head of the church. It is to equip fellow believers in intimately connecting with his work and his role in their lives. A relationship consolidated with Christ is what brings lasting deliverance work in believers' lives. Taking Christ off the center and putting a ministry as the main avenue that Jesus works through only hinders Christ's deeper work.

This arises when believers are led to assume that a pastor, like myself, has some special VIP honor in relating to God. It's been there since Christ's time with the Pharisees and it's still with us today.

Many pastors prefer to preserve this Pharisee tradition because it gives them some power and influence. Unfortunately believers end up being deprived of their own empowerment that comes through their direct relationship with Christ.

Ultimately the entire body of Christ is deprived from much fruit empowered believers can bear. There would be no centralized deliverance ministries if believers understood their direct connection to Christ.

We may, as pastors, have certain gifts and knowledge more than average believers. However this does not imply we have any special position in relating with Christ. It only implies we've been entrusted to share matters we know so that others can better connect with their Lord and Savior.

Being called into a sensitive area like deliverance ministry makes it a big sin to play on people's ignorance. Yet many ministries, including prominent ones are doing this. They take people's attention away from Jesus and place it onto themselves claiming some special anointing is on them that works through them, and them only. Association with their ministry, not with Jesus, is claimed to release this yoke breaking anointing upon people.

You're probably familiar with what I'm saying. I spent years serving in and sowing to ministries that linked deliverance and breakthrough to financial contributions or other commitments to their ministries. Scriptures were skillfully used to back up their claims.

During my own devotional time I'd all kinds of prayer sessions. Apart from the right prayers which are addressed to God there were also some bombarding evil spirits. Others were prayers in tongues in their various assumed types –praise tongues, spiritual warfare tongues, intercessory tongues, self edification tongues, worship tongues, etc. I was an expert in speaking in tongues. And my list of rituals was endless, including sprinkling the assumed blood of Jesus around my surroundings. You name it I've probably fallen for it.

(In case you need detailed info on modern versions of speaking in tongues, etc, please visit GotQuestions.org. It's a Christian website that answers questions from a biblical perspective. They do not dispute all modern day versions but caution on going into non-biblical practices (some of us learnt of it the hard way). You can type in your query in the search bar. It's a helpful bible-based website covering even on matters central to this book: biblical spiritual warfare, can Christians be demon possessed, tongues, praying to Mary, yoga, etc. Please make use of such resources, including resources at our website and public or church library resources for questions unanswered in this book. Feel free to email us a question to consider answering in the next edition or adding to the website. However the volume of email received makes it unbearable to reply to every person that writes).

With all my personal rituals and church obsessed programs my Christian life was still worse off compared to some close colleagues who happened to be non-Charismatics. They were Baptist and Presbyterian. When I tried to "preach" to them about the wonderful Charismatic devotionals they had my life as evidence enough to close their ears. I still couldn't get it.

Only the Lord knows why I was blind for so long. But I'm so thankful for being delivered from such blindness and manipulation. Having academic degrees could not take away the blindness. Only the Spirit of God did.

When the truth came I realized that even sincere Christians can be very blind spiritually. We can be so blind to the extent that fellow believers who're not misled over some matters shake their heads in embarrassment. They can't believe what's being followed in God's name. Even non-believers can point out certain major logs jammed in our eyes. History bears lots of such records.

I attended all sorts of "deliverance seminars," "breakthrough seminars," "breakthrough crusades" and so on. In between them were church special days according to Jewish traditions, Christian calendar months, special church programs, and so on. Nothing wrong with any of them when used in their context.

It's when they are used to manipulate people that their deliverance is tied to observing these ministry-centered programs which also mostly seek "special seed offerings." People give not only their money but time, loyalty and even sanity to these ministries to a level of ministry worship, a form of idolatry.

Such ministries are not necessarily charismatic or Pentecostal. It just happens that my experience was from a radical charismatic church. So I'm not trying to characterize any particular denomination as having lost its Christian and bible campus. You yourself will be able to identify churches that fall in this group after having read this book. They can be from any denomination or non-denomination.

This book takes you away from this needless and fruitless ministry-centered religion. God allowed some of us to go through it so that you don't have to. The focus is on God, following deliverance principles in his word and developing a closer walk with him.

There is no special offering sought for your breakthrough. Any donation made to our ministry is merely because you desire to partner with us in helping others to understand empowering biblical principles for their lives.

Please visit us online for more resources and updates, at JesusW.com and SpiritualWarfareDeliverance.com (the two websites for Jesus Work Ministry are interlinked through easy navigation).

The Lord will respond to your obedience in fulfilling whatever he biblically requires of you in your area of need. It will not come through a special seed offering to a ministry that will be prayed for and anointed with oil for your breakthrough.

Using deceit and manipulation is a sin even though certain blessings come through faithful giving. It's God that blesses the giver for obeying his word on sowing to his kingdom (the body of Christ), not because it was given to a certain ministry. It's true ministries like ours need funding to prevail in outreach programs, but it's a sin as witchcraft to use manipulation.

And neither respond to any ministry online, on television, other media, or in your neighborhood if they said God told them if you sowed a certain seed he will answer your needs. Why couldn't he directly relate to you? He desires to connect with you directly more than through some individual who thinks he/she is closer to God because of being called to pastoral ministry.

Our pastoral role is to lead you closer to him and his ways in the bible so that you can develop the same direct connection with him. Then you'll be more empowered to deal with matters in your life according to his word, not according to a certain seed offering.

May you find in this book all the required areas of biblical deliverance principles and apply them in all your areas of concern. Where you need more assistance do contact us or browse through our various spiritual resources online at JesusW.com and SpiritualWarfareDeliverance.com (the two websites for Jesus Work Ministry are interlinked through easy navigation). Do contact us even on matters concerning this book such as on typographical errors, grammatical errors, etc.

You certainly won't find ministry-centered initiations but Christ-centered material. Prayer requests are most welcome but with emphasis on personal input in connecting with God. No idol worship, no ministry worship, only Jesus worship and worship of our heavenly Father.

Doorways of Satan's Legal Entry and Demonic Influence

Just not to be misunderstood: Satan's entry into one's life implies influence into one's life from an external position. It does not imply possession of one's faculties, an aspect of demonic possession. His entry is therefore an aspect of external demonic attack and not demonic possession. Please read the chapter on Exception for Direct Confrontation if you are not familiar with differences between demonic *possession* and demonic *influence*.

Satan operates *within* the boundaries that God allows, that God has set-up as spiritual laws. Outside these boundaries he has NO means, authority nor power to enforce his wishes. Our God remains almighty and all sovereign. This makes God in charge of everything, including over Satan. He thus has not left his throne to Satan to do whatever he pleases. Satan only operates within the limits God has set-up.

That is why Satan uses traps to bring people into his boundaries -so that he can attack them. Within his boundaries he gains legal access to attack in whatever way he has access to –spiritually, socially, materially, physically, etc. The methods he uses to gain legal access to people are through:
1) Deception,
2) Ignorance,
3) Sin, and
4) Storms of life (when responded to in a wrong way)

1) Deception

Deception is deliberately misleading someone to believe something that is not true. Satan successfully deceived Adam and Eve in the Garden of Eden. He tried to deceive Jesus in the wilderness by twisting scriptures but failed. Most deception goes unnoticed when one has little or no foundation on scripture. Highly concealed deception includes glorification of earthly riches, worldly pleasures, power, fame, beauty, and knowledge.

Such deception is as close as the secular media channels around us. All one needs to do to fall under the spell of deception is to turn one of these secular channels on. That's why television is sometimes called the devilvision in Christian circles. But it depends which programs and channels one watches.

Alternatives exist like Sky Angel which provides exclusively Christian friendly programming with as many as 36 channels. It currently (Dec. 2006) broadcasts to US and Caribbean residents. Residents along the boarder with USA, i.e. Canada and Mexico, have access to its satellite signal.

Readers in the US you have Sky Angel at your doorstep that provides diverse programs including world news and family friendly movies for Christian families and communities. And it's cheaper than devil vision channels through its satellite broadcasting (see SkyAngel.com to request for a free brochure).

I bought a lifetime subscription offer that remains till death do us part with Sky Angel. No excuse to watch devil vision when a better alternative exists. Even were no Christian channels exist falling for most (not all) secular media is as good as dancing with the devil.

2) Ignorance

Ignorance is lack of knowledge. There was a real-estate advert I heard on radio where someone says, "I don't even know enough to know that I don't know." The words stuck but the ad has been forgotten.

Many believers settle down quickly in their Christian lives assuming that being saved and going to church is enough. They don't even know enough to know that they need to continue growing. This can open bad doors to adopting all kinds of dangerous beliefs and doctrines with the assumption that they are biblical. "*My people* are destroyed from lack of knowledge," Hosea 4.6.

3) Sin

Sin is transgressing, violating or trespassing God's laws in the bible. It is going outside his prescription for our lives. Whether done knowingly or out of ignorance sin has the same consequences. No excuses for breaking spiritual laws.

The only matter that saves us from reaping bad fruits from every bad seed is God's grace. None of us would make it all in life without God's grace. "The Lord is compassionate and gracious, slow to anger, abounding in love... he does not treat us as our sins deserve or repay us according to our iniquities," Psalms 103:8,10.

Thanks be to God for his grace, many of us would be drowning in self inflicted sorrows. At the same time it is not wise to assume we'd be rescued by God's grace when we violate his spiritual laws.

Sin gives the devil legal entry and God may not allow his grace to stop him. The chaotic state of affairs the world is in shows how much legal entry humanity has given Satan.

4) Storms of life

Storms of life are unpleasant experiences that befall us out of no fault of our own. They are the Joseph experiences. God allows them to happen but does not plot them against us. He only does not stop them. Depending on how we handle such matters storms of life can be our stepping stones to our promotion (like with Joseph) or they can be our downfall. They can be assets the Holy Spirit can use to our good or they can be assets Satan can use to block us from moving forward.

For example, Joni Eareckson Tada a professional diver got severely injured and unable to use her hands and legs at a young age. Such an experience might as well have been the end of her beautiful life. Heaven said no.

There is not much space here to chronicle what God has been doing through her global ministry. She is our modern day example of Joseph (Genesis 50:20). What the devil intended to use for destruction God has used it to lift the lives of millions of people.

Whatever storms of life one may have faced or maybe facing - spiritually, socially, materially or physically they are not intended to be obstacles. At least from God's point of view. The devil wants them to be obstacles and destiny killers. But they cannot stop God from fulfilling all that he purposed to accomplish through each of us. God is able to transform the experiences to eventually work to our good if our focus is on him rather than our limitations.

The evil may not work to everyone's good, but, as the Bible says, it certainly does for God's children. How God does it could be another book. Please read through the following passage. It's an awesome passage on God's sovereignty, love, and power in the midst of all experiences in our lives:

"And we know that in all things God works for the good of those who love him, who have been called according to his purpose. For those God foreknew he also predestined to be conformed to the likeness of his Son, that he might be the firstborn among many brothers. And those he predestined, he also called; those he called, he also justified; those he justified, he also glorified.

"What, then, shall we say in response to this? If God is for us, who can be against us? He who did not spare his own Son, but gave him up for us all-- how will he not also, along with him, graciously give us all things? Who will bring any charge against those whom God has chosen?

"It is God who justifies. Who is he that condemns? Christ Jesus, who died--more than that, who was raised to life--is at the right hand of God and is also interceding for us. Who shall separate us from the love of Christ? Shall trouble or hardship or persecution or famine or nakedness or danger or sword? As it is written: 'For your sake we face death all day long; we are considered as sheep to be slaughtered.'

"No, in all these things we are more than conquerors through him who loved us. For I am convinced that neither death nor life, neither angels nor demons, neither the present nor the future, nor any powers, neither height nor depth, nor anything else in all creation, will be able to separate us from the love of God that is in Christ Jesus our Lord," Romans 8:28-39.

Deception, Ignorance, Sin, and Storms of Life Vicious Circle

The four traps are largely interrelated with one resulting into another. For example deception eventually leads to acts of ignorance which have some level of sin that end up inviting more avoidable storms of life. They create a vicious circle (or cycle).

A deception such one on spiritual warfare leads to believers directly confronting evil spirits, a practice scripture calls slander of "celestial (heavenly) beings," and which it says brings trouble on the slanderers (Jude 1:8-10, 2 Peter

2:10-12). The trouble on believers comes because the demons gain legal access into their lives as they violate spiritual laws. These traps end up bringing believers into sins and non-biblical practices that open legal grounds for demonic attacks.

How does one get out of a vicious circle that invites demonic attacks? He/she needs to be open to searching for areas that may not be according to the bible. Some could be beliefs embraced by certain churches. These include erroneous teachings on spiritual warfare, spiritual warfare prayers, deliverance prayers, binding and loosing demons, most of modern day speaking in tongues, pleading the blood or sprinkling the blood of Jesus (instead of taking holy communion like Jesus instructed us), the Rosary and praying to Mary (instead of to God, our heavenly Father), and so on.

(In case you need detailed info on modern versions of speaking in tongues, etc, please visit GotQuestions.org. It's a Christian website that answers questions from a biblical perspective. They do not dispute all modern day versions but caution on going into non-biblical practices (some of us learnt of it the hard way). You can type in your query in the search bar. It's a helpful bible-based website covering even on matters central to this book: biblical spiritual warfare, can Christians be demon possessed, tongues, praying to Mary, yoga, etc. Please make use of such resources, including resources at our website and public or church library resources for questions unanswered in this book. Feel free to email us a question to consider answering in the next edition or adding to the website. However the volume of email received makes it unbearable to reply to every person that writes).

Overcoming Life's Battles like Christ Jesus

Please remember that Satan is not the problem of concern in ALL matters we face in life. Far from it. If he was the problem then Christians would have two Gods to fear – one good God and another evil god. Some deliverance ministries have given Satan so much power as to believe he can do whatever he pleases while a sovereign God helplessly looks on.

Others say God has given us authority to rule a spiritual being we cannot see nor fully understand how he operates. Either assumption gives Satan and his demons a lot of focus that scripture does not support. Satan is not the problem in ALL matters we face in life.

Jesus said, "The ruler of this world is coming. He has no power over me," John 14:30 (International Standard Version). King James version also gives its accurate meaning "the prince of this world cometh, and hath nothing in me." Jesus was saying this at the height when all hell was about to break loose in the mission to have him crucified. Satan was coming in full force on a mission to have Jesus crucified yet Jesus said he had no power over him.

Satan was not his major problem or concern. He was not his problem even if he was the one who would infiltrate the minds and hearts of all those who would work to crucify him.

Why would Satan not be a problem to Jesus? Because Jesus understood how Satan operates and how to overcome him. Once you know how your enemy operates and how to overcome him the enemy becomes powerless. That's why nations spend billions gathering "intelligence" about their potential enemies. Jesus understood that Satan gets his source of power over people through legal entry.

The major problem to deal with was therefore not Satan but the doorways to his entry. These are through ignorance, deceit, sin or storms of life. Once all these doors are closed or effectively dealt with Satan has no access. The battle is won.

The problem is therefore not in endeavoring to fight Satan but in endeavoring to understand and close all the avenues Satan attempts to gain entry. The matters that give Satan access to interfere with our lives are the problem. Once these matters are taken care of Satan becomes of no concern. He is rendered powerless. We can say like Jesus on any attempt from hell that, "the ruler of this world is coming but he has no power over me."

In the case of Jesus the only access Satan could have was outside any legal entry. All legal entry was closed for he lived an upright life. In other ways it could only happen if and only if God gave Satan permission outside the boundaries Satan has legal influence. God would allow his angels not to stop Satan on matters he gave permission. Jesus knew this. He told his disciples not to fight what God had already allowed to come to pass.

He said to the one who confronted a servant of the high priest, cutting off his ear: "Do you think I cannot call on my Father, and he will at once put at my disposal more than twelve legions of angels? But how then would the Scriptures be fulfilled that say it must happen in this way?" Matthew 26:53-54.

Even storms of life through circumstances, people or whatever have no power over a believer. Circumstances or people should therefore not be our concern when matters may not be going in ways we believe they should. Before his crucifixion Pilate boasted about how much influence he had. If Jesus cooperated Pilate would make all the difference. "Do you refuse to speak to me?' Pilate said. "Don't you realize I have power either to free you or to crucify you?" John 19:10.

Jesus responded, "You would have no power over me if it were not given to you from above. Therefore the one who handed me over to you is guilty of a greater sin," John 19:11.

In other ways the One from above is the one who has the final say on matters in our lives. The circumstances or people have no power over us except that which is given to them from above. In the case of Jesus the One from above had permitted a righteous man with no crime to die on the cross, the worst punishment any criminal could face. The One from above who gave such permission, was the one to blame. It was not the people for they only had such power given to them to do it.

That is why Jesus said the One from above "is guilty of a greater sin." He did not imply that God sinned. He meant that God, the one who allowed such a storm to happen would be the one to account for all that was happening. God would account for his decision to forsake a sinless person. Without God's permission none of this would have taken place. Why not?

Because under normal circumstances of spiritual laws that God set up it could only happen to those who violated his laws. God could not forsake those who lived according to his will. Their obedience was their defense and covering.

Violators of his laws on the other hand, gave legal access to Satan to attack them to whatever levels they had given him entry. For instance criminals who faced crucifixion where among the biggest transgressors through murder and all kinds of crimes. Jesus was classified among these criminals not because he was one. It was because God allowed circumstances that would classify him as one.

Under normal circumstances God could not allow this. In God's eyes he was sinless and Satan had no legal right to interfere with his life. Satan was powerless over him. There was no entry through ignorance, deception or sin that Satan could attack Jesus.

Yet God who could give Satan permission over anything allowed him to operate outside his boundaries. This is the wisdom of God that is beyond our comprehension. Every time God allows such an illegal entry the ultimate outcome always benefits his kingdom. It does not mean he has forsaken us.

God ultimately upholds his faithfulness and righteousness. In the case of our Lord Jesus we know the final outcome. For dying as a sinless person he took all our sins upon himself. And the awesome outcome of this sacrifice can be another book. He now is able to say to all humanity, "I am the way and the truth and the life. No one comes to the Father except through me," John 14:6.

Therefore not all unpleasant experiences imply there is legal entry of demonic attacks. God can permit Satan to operate outside his boundary, e.g. in the case of Christ and Job. Satan had to first obtain permission from God because all avenues of legal access were closed. The same applies to all believers who walk in truth and are under the righteousness of Christ. Satan can only gain entry only after getting permission from God.

However God granting permission is an exception rather than a rule. He doesn't easily grant the Accuser to break the rules. The ultimate outcome always leads to victory rather not defeat for the believer and God's kingdom. We know how Job ended up with more than he lost. Christ's unrighteous death ended up being a price paid for the sins of all who accept him as Lord and Savior.

God ultimately upholds his faithfulness and righteousness when he allows storms outside any legal grounds of Satan's entry. There is always victory over such experiences if our focus remains on him, his power, love and sovereignty.

We cannot afford to allow storms of life to be the devil's legal entry to hinder us. This comes if we allow the storms to seem as if God has forsaken us and to doubt that there could be any way out. Persecution is one area God seems to give Satan a lot of permission. Please read the chapter: Christian Persecution - a Deliverance Exception.

In our lives our approach to life should be the way Jesus approached it. Instead of being preoccupied with Satan, people or circumstances we're to be preoccupied with God. He's the only one who has power over us. We endeavor to live according to his ways in all the areas of our lives. This enables us to overcome any areas that may try to give entry to Satan. With all the areas overcome anything that God allows in his sovereignty will eventually work to our good and the good of the body of Christ.

Endeavoring to overcome any areas that may try to give entry to Satan is our main battle. It is part of our spiritual warfare. Under the power of God we are enabled to win the constant attempts of Satan to create legal grounds for him to attack. We do not focus on Satan. We focus on God in enabling us to overcome these doorways. Once the doorways are closed Satan has no access, excerpt by special permission from God.

The problem therefore lies in the matters that give Satan access to interfere with our lives. The major problem is these doorways not Satan himself. The battle is won once we deal with these matters that give Satan access into our lives. As said in this book Satan enters through any of the four doorways: ignorance, deception, sin and storms of life. So the search can be made easier by endeavoring to find what's coming through lack of knowledge (ignorance), through false beliefs (deception) and through sin, and through storms of life.

Fulfilling our Areas of Responsibility in the Deliverance Process

Deliverance ministries that focus on Satan and casting out demons from Christians wounded in life's battles do not understand spiritual laws that God instituted for our good. Yet the entire history of the Israelites from the Old Testament shows us how these laws worked.

In times of distress and need of deliverance they did not focus on their problem or finding out what kind of spirits were behind it. They always asked themselves, "what has made God to allow this to come upon us." They knew God was sovereign, so he had the final say on whatever occurred in their lives, good or bad.

In their search for answers and deliverance they sought prophets. Sometimes false prophets came forward and gave oracles (revelations) they cooked up. The real prophets always came forward with more challenging words. They included admonitions like "get your house in order, there is sin in the camp, you have adopted the ways of the heathens which have provoked God to anger, etc."

No one wants to hear such critical words when they think there're not the source of the problem. They're convinced the problem or fault lies outside their own input or sphere of responsibility. That is why most real prophets were eventually killed by those who could not handle their statements. But they were only proclaiming the prescription for deliverance and warning against matters that invite bondage.

All these statements had at least one element that pointed to lack of knowledge (ignorance), practice of false beliefs (deception) or involvement in sin. The dice pointed to the people doing their part of closing the doorways.

There was no preoccupation with Satan or some evil spirits that needed a deliverance minister to make some strong deliverance prayers. Going after evil spirits, binding and loosing them and calling it spiritual warfare only worsens the problem. It only increases the violations to God's spiritual laws.

Without us doing our part of closing the doorways heaven continues to wait. God's angels remain out of bounds on areas they're commissioned to protect us. Which gives demons unrestrained access to believers, God's people.

Deliverance ministries that focus on Satan and demons are therefore modern day false prophets that make statements not supported by scripture. If statistics could be kept on how many people come out worse off after undergoing deliverance sessions from these ministries there would be a national outcry to stop them.

Stopping them infringes on separation of church and state. However where evidence is available to show that their practices harm innocent people may prove to be worthy. Can you imagine sincere people, mostly heaven destined believers going to these deliverance ministries and later ending up in worse off emotional, spiritual, psychological, social and other related problems? Some end up in mental institutions. The so-called deliverance ministries only worsen their problems.

That said I'm still in favor of separation of church and state that prohibits involvement of the government in religious affairs. If government is given more control over religious affairs in the name of protection we will likely end up with a government sanctioned Christianity. European church history tells us more than enough on this. Many Protestants were martyred because of a government controlled Christianity.

So the challenge is on us believers to clean up on our own and seek the Lord's intervention. We ask him to enlighten the ministers about the errors or close the ministries before many fall to needless bondage.

We also ought to warn believers about wolves in sheep's clothing around us. Apart from the wolves there're also sincere believers who for lack of knowledge have fallen into the spiritual warfare and deliverance false teachings (deception). They have deliverance ministries that are only breeding grounds for demons to afflict innocent believers.

Please support us in this work or continue doing your part in sounding the alarm. (Please visit our websites: JesusW.com and SpiritualWarfareDeliverance.com (the two websites for Jesus Work Ministry are interlinked through easy navigation)). "Snatch others from the fire and save them; to others show mercy, mixed with fear--hating even the clothing stained by corrupted flesh," Jude 1:23.

And there is hope for the victims as well. I was once trapped in such false beliefs (deception) so I have much to testify that there is plenty of hope. The doorway of false beliefs that give entry to demons can be closed just as easily as any other door they come through (lack of knowledge (ignorance), sin and storms of life (when responded to in a wrong way)).

Instead of focusing on demons and evil spirits believers need to focus on finding doorways of entry. The doorways are what give them access. Access is denied and fully guarded by God's angels once the doors of entry are closed. Without being closed God's angels remain out of bounds on areas they're commissioned to protect us. "Are not all angels ministering spirits sent to serve those who will inherit salvation?" Hebrews 1:14.

As said earlier the search can be made easier by endeavoring to find what's coming through lack of knowledge (ignorance), what's coming through false beliefs (deception), through sin and through storms of life. It can also be made easier by narrowing down the area of the problem. It could be a spiritual area, a physical area, material, social and so on.

For example, the problem could be in a social area like family matters. You can narrow the search by looking at biblical family principles. You try to find out where there could be a lack of knowledge on biblical family principles, what could be coming through false beliefs on family principles and what could be coming through sin on biblical family principles.

There is no need to wait for some strange discernment or a supernatural word from God while searching. God gave us a mind to use. It is not evil to think. The only difference with unbelievers is that we have "the mind of Christ" (1 Corinthians 2:16) controlled by the Spirit of God. It is said that we use less than 10% of our brain power. This is not good news if we want to do exploits for God's glory. We ought to ask God to enable us to maximize our potential, including our mental faculties.

After praying for God to enable you to understand certain matters the next step is to apply your faith of believing that he has answered your prayers. You begin to think and think, read and read, on areas relating to your obstacle. You trust that he will reveal all the areas of biblical truths relating to matters you're dealing with. In that way you're exercising the mind of Christ instead of allowing the dictates of circumstances, other people or blind faith to control you.

9.2 Christian Deliverance and Healing, Part 2: Fundamentals 2

CHAPTER 9. PART 2: FUNDAMENTALS 2 - SUB-TOPICS:
- **Understanding Deliverance and Healing Differences**
- **Repentance, Including Over Sins of Ignorance**
- **Ceasing to Associate with the Sin**
- **Deliverance = Instant**
- **Healing is a Process**
- **Continual Search for Unknown Doorways**
- **Other Battles to Overcome**
- **The Danger of Blind Faith**
- **The Body of Christ and its Spiritual Growth**
- **Note on Prayer Group and Fellowship**
- **Note Concerning Signs and Wonders**

This section mainly covers on steps to deliverance and healing on matters that are found to originate from any of the four doorways Satan gains legal grounds: ignorance, deception, sin and storms of life (when responded to in a wrong way). The deception on spiritual warfare and deliverance is used as an example in steps to deliverance and healing.

In addition, a key distinction is made between deliverance and healing. Please note that deliverance is one thing while healing is another matter altogether. They are not the same. Each has its unique areas. Once one understands the distinction he/she is able to experience the healing process with much peace, faith and patience.

Understanding Deliverance and Healing Differences

An understanding of the difference between deliverance and healing will facilitate the growth of the fruit of the Holy Spirit. "The fruit of the Spirit is love, joy, peace, patience, kindness, goodness, faithfulness, gentleness and self-control. Against such things there is no law. Those who belong to Christ Jesus have crucified the sinful nature with its passions and desires. Since we live by the Spirit, let us keep in step with the Spirit," Galatians 5: 22-25.

It will also overcome matters that grow in the absence of the fruits of the Holy Spirit. These include doubt, fear, hurry for instant results, excessive demand for deliverance to come from other "super-spiritual" people instead of coming from within or from those burdened to intercede for an individual, and so on.

God's deliverance ends any further interference of Satan that came through the practice of the false spiritual warfare or whatever area that one was previously in ignorance, deception, sin or under storms of life (that were responded to in a wrong way).

Healing, on the other hand, enables us to recover from all the harm caused by the assumed spiritual warfare or whatever gave Satan access. The harm may have been spiritual, social, physical, material and so on. We seek God to bring healing in all the areas that have been wounded through ignorance, deception, sin or storms of life as we begin to begin to walk according to his biblical ways.

Healing may be instant or may be an ongoing process determined by the Healer, the Lord. Deliverance, on the other hand, is instant once one repents and ceases practices that are contrary to God's will. The legal grounds of Satan that he used to interfere with one's life are broken once old ways that brought legal grounds end and the biblical ways begin to be applied.

For instance, ending the practice of the erroneous spiritual warfare and applying true biblical spiritual warfare and deliverance principles closes all the doorways that brought problems through the erroneous spiritual warfare.

To illustrate the distinction between deliverance and healing suppose I have a dog named Ignorant. A neighbor has one named Trouble. Trouble continues to harass Ignorant because he is able to enter our yard. Ignorant has a habit of digging holes by the hedge of the yard.

These holes enable Trouble to enter the yard. Life is terrible for Ignorant after digging up these holes. He has constant wounds from Trouble that he keeps nursing. He is unable to lead a normal life because of Trouble's constant entry and beatings.

Then one day I decide to block the holes by the hedge around the yard in order to stop Trouble from entering. Since that day Ignorant has never had to worry about any further attack from Trouble. The hedge or covering around the yard is now properly sealed. Trouble is unable to enter.

Ignorant is now delivered from Trouble's attacks. Never will he have to worry about being attacked, unless he breaks the hedge in another area. Ignorant is now unhindered to enjoy and pursue his dreams around the yard. No more further beatings or fear of beatings anywhere around the yard. It is total deliverance from further beatings.

However, Ignorant remains with one problem to overcome. He still has wounds that Trouble inflicted on him before holes to the hedge were sealed. He needs healing from all these wounds. He needs to ensure he eats healthy food, avoid things that may slow or hinder the healing process, etc. If the wounds need extra treatment he would need a vet to care for him. Deliverance was instant but healing will have to be a process.

Repentance, Including Over Sins of Ignorance

Before asking the Lord to "***deliver us from evil (or from the evil one)***," (Matthew 6:12-13) we're required to repent to God for walking outside his will. Anything outside his will is sin regardless of whether it was willfully done or was out of ignorance. It was common in the Old Testament to confess all sins including those done through ignorance. Even sins of parents and ancestors were confessed. These were sins none of them had anything to do with.

The people that arranged, out of ignorance, for Christ to be killed also needed to repent although Christ had already forgiven them. He said, "Father, forgive them for they do not know what they are doing," (Luke 23:34).

Yet they still had to repent. "Now, brothers, I know that you acted in ignorance, as did your leaders. But this is how God fulfilled what he had foretold through all the prophets, saying that his Christ would suffer. Repent, then, and turn to God, so that your sins may be wiped out, that times of refreshing may come from the Lord," Acts 3:17-19

In the spiritual warfare and deliverance deception case, the sin involved going beyond our given authority that amounted to slander through our direct confrontation with celestial beings. We acknowledge it as sin, like the book of Jude puts it, for "speaking abusively" against whatever we did not understand and slandering celestial beings even if they are God's principle enemies:

"These dreamers pollute their own bodies, reject authority and slander celestial beings. But even the archangel Michael, when he was disputing with the devil about the body of Moses, did not dare to bring a slanderous accusation against him, but said, "The Lord rebuke you!" Yet these men speak abusively against whatever they do not understand; and what things they do understand by instinct, like unreasoning animals--***these are the very things that destroy them***," Jude 1:8-10.

We confess to God the sin of slander against celestial beings, acknowledge that we walked in ignorance, repent of the sin and ask God to deliver us from all its consequences. We also thank him for revealing such truths to us and ask him to continue revealing all truth that will set us free from Satan's influence.

For an example of a prayer of repentance, deliverance and healing please see Appendix 2: Deliverance, Healing and Restoration Prayer. It may help those who may need to understand scriptural backing on repentance, deliverance and healing. It is not intended to be a substitute for one's own devotions.

Ceasing to Associate with the Sin

Repentance also requires ceasing to associate with the sin. This includes throwing away any books, literature or multimedia that embrace non-biblical matters such as the erroneous spiritual warfare and deliverance. It was customary in the Old Testament to destroy all that was detestable in God's sight.

This did not change in the New Testament. Jesus violently cleansed the temple of traders who where using God's house for wrong purposes. We are temples of God's Spirit (1 Corinthians 3: 16-17). He has no comfort living with objects that do not please God.

Christian converts in Ephesus who had practiced sorcery and divination were asked to destroy the materials they used. They destroyed them publicly. "A number who had practiced sorcery brought their scrolls together and burned them publicly. When they calculated the value of the scrolls, the total came to fifty thousand drachmas. In this way the word of the Lord spread widely and grew in power," Acts 19:19-20.

The unscriptural spiritual warfare and deliverance may not fall in the core definition of sorcery or divination. However it is still in this category since it deals with the spirit world outside scriptural order. The practice invokes or arouses evil spirits to answer to our demands in a way that scripture forbids. Our interaction with them in the spirit world only opens doors for them to interfere with our lives.

This is not to say sincere believers who advocated this type of spiritual warfare willfully misled people into forbidden activities. The deception flood of the erroneous spiritual warfare and deliverance teachings got so high that many of us easily found scripture to back up our resolve for direct confrontation. Believers were zealous in their resolve to directly confront demonic spirits that scripture was easily taken out of context without even realizing it. Some are still zealous in such false teachings.

Our ministry (Jesus Work Ministry) has an outreach to such believers. Part of our calling is in overcoming the false teachings by revealing biblical principles on spiritual warfare and deliverance ministry areas. Deception can be conquered just as it has throughout church history in various areas. (Please visit our websites: JesusW.com and SpiritualWarfareDeliverance.com (the two websites are interlinked through easy navigation)).

Wherever the deception started on spiritual warfare and deliverance has not been a key concern of this book. The introduction covers on Peter Wagner as one of the likely pioneers.

However it was only to identify the big names that endorsed the false teachings in their 1980s early stages. Sincere believers found themselves embracing the wrong doctrine. The result has been a flood of books, literature, other multimedia and online ministries on these false doctrines. In true repentance we're required to clean up on any books, literature and other multimedia that embrace practices that God forbids.

Other books and multimedia that do not deal with the erroneous spiritual warfare teachings by the same authors need not be destroyed. Some of the authors are true believers who have in fact been used greatly by God. They just never had the truth revealed in this area – for reasons only God can explain. If you are not sure about the credibility of an author please consult other evangelical believers. Normally the content of what they write will speak for itself.

Repentance may also include separating from prayer groups that continue embracing the false spiritual warfare and deliverance teachings. It may not require moving to another church if one's local church rarely brings up such false doctrine.

One also needs to avoid being in agreement during any moments that the erroneous spiritual warfare and deliverance teachings are exercised. Moving to another church may be appropriate if the erroneous spiritual warfare and deliverance teachings are such a heavy preoccupation of a local church. Many charismatic churches only bring them up once in a while.

However, it's worthwhile to remain prayerful for the sincere believers that do not understand. "Snatch others from the fire and save them; to others show mercy, mixed with fear--hating even the clothing stained by corrupted flesh," Jude 1:23.

Prayer will enable their eyes to be opened to the truth instead of learning from fiery experiences. The believers to mainly pray for are church leaders that are able to share the truth on spiritual warfare with more people. If you're able to reach the church leaders it may be worthwhile to share this book with them or any book that challenges the false teachings.

Deliverance = Instant

Deliverance comes once we have embraced the truth about spiritual warfare or whatever area that we were previously in ignorance, deception, sin, or under storms of life (when responding to storms in a wrong way). Our Lord said, "If you hold to my teaching, you are really my disciples. *Then you will know the truth, and the truth will set you free*," John 8:31-32.

Any area where truth is revealed therefore brings freedom. We're to expect complete freedom from manipulations and attacks of the enemy. Deliverance ends all that came from our involvement in deceptive spiritual warfare and deliverance or whatever area that we were previously in ignorance, deception, sin or under storms of life (that were responded to in a wrong way).

Deliverance is instant once the required biblical principles are applied. Deliverance ends any further attacks. The wounds may appear as if deliverance has not occurred but that's if one does not understand what has taken place in the spirit realm.

The enemy's legal grounds of using the erroneous spiritual warfare and deliverance teachings to steal and destroy any areas of our lives and those we're connected to are destroyed once we know and apply the truth. The Lord comes to our defense in this area where the enemy once used to bring defeat in our lives.

It implies we will never receive another attack from hell using the door of false teachings on spiritual warfare and deliverance. Such a door or whatever door that we were previously vulnerable through ignorance, deception, sin or through storms of life is shut forever once the truth is embraced.

While deliverance is instant healing is a process. For example, a believer can be delivered from the yoke of debt and financial chaos. His/her debt and financial problems do not disappear instantly at the moment of deliverance. The effects or consequences still have to go of having been previously vulnerable on biblical financial principles through ignorance, deception, sin or under storms of life. They are the financial wounds that need healing.

However a believer will not face any further attacks that could continue increasing his debts or financial problems. The doors of entry for such attacks are closed once a believer begins to apply the biblical financial principles of seed-time and harvest-time. The spiritual pockets with spiritual holes have now been sealed.

He will be able to service his debts until being debt free. Between the period of paying off debts and being debt free God will be opening strange doors to enable him to continue settling the debts. For some he may wipe them out instantly or in a very short period. This is his supernatural strategy that defies natural conditions, limitations, and circumstances. For instance lenders may cancel the debt or a strange opportunity may surface that enables paying off debts, and so on.

However to be preoccupied with waiting for his supernatural strategy while neglecting the day to day opportunities he provides is as good as having blind faith. There is nothing wrong with praying for quick fixes.

It is when we assume it is the only way God can better heal the wounds that came through being previously vulnerable through ignorance, deception, sin, or through storms of life in whatever area. Deliverance has already taken place. Our remaining challenge is to cooperate with God on his healing strategy. It may be instant – which is his rare strategy. It may be a process – which is his usual strategy.

With a sigh of relief we can identify with the scripture in Daniel: "As I watched, this horn was waging war against the saints and defeating them, until the Ancient of Days (God) came and pronounced judgment in favor of the saints of the Most High, and the time came when they possessed the kingdom," Daniel 7:21-22.

God has come to our rescue by revealing the root cause of whatever problem. He has also revealed the required biblical truths for freedom in the area of affliction. Applying required truths brings deliverance and closes all legal entry of further attacks.

We can now more effectively focus on matters related to advancing God's kingdom. Our preoccupation with nursing our own problems and those we're close to ought to greatly diminish. That's if we're also walking in obedience and truth in other areas.

Healing is a Process

"…Then your light will break forth like the dawn, and your *healing* will quickly appear; then your righteousness will go before you, and the glory of the Lord will be your rear guard. Then you will call, and the Lord will answer; you will cry for help, and he will say: Here am I," Isaiah 58:6-9

The Lord delivers us not just from further attacks but also from the consequences of the ignorance, deception, sin or storms of life (storms that were responded to in a wrong way). Deliverance from the consequences is what is called healing. The attacks brought wounds in our lives in one way or another – spiritually, physically, socially, materially, and so on.

The wounds are the consequences of the ignorance, deception, sin or storms of life. The Lord brings healing and restoration in our lives as we embrace his biblical ways and truths on the areas that we were previously in ignorance, deception, sin or under storms of life.

The healing and restoration may come in different ways than we may expect. It's not a return of the same matters that were lost, even though God may work it that way for some. It may be a double spiritual anointing to serve God. It may be a social healing in the family or church. It may be a career or financial breakthrough. It may be a physical healing from an illness. Or a combination of many factors.

The life of apostle Paul can be an example, though his experiences are not related to falling to the spiritual warfare deception. He was nevertheless deceived by the enemy that what he was doing (persecuting Christians) was right in the eyes of God. When God opened his eyes the Lord used him to do multiple times more damage to Satan's kingdom than what Satan had used him for. To this day we're still being edified by his divine inspired epistles.

The time of restoration will be different for each of us. In our era of modern technology which has increased the speed of getting things done it's tempting to desire quick fixes. Our patience has been declining even in the body of Christ.

God however, seems not to be "catching up" with our growing sense of urgency. He has a way of relating with us often outside our time frame. This can be difficult now and again if we're not submissive enough to have him lead us the way he pleases as a responsible Father.

It'll therefore be helpful to understand that God is still working according to his schedule in case we don't receive instant restoration. However, there's nothing wrong with expecting instant answers. "Will not God bring about justice for his chosen ones, who cry out to him day and night? Will he keep putting them off? I tell you, he will see that they get *justice*, and *quickly*," Luke 18:7-8.

"Is not this the kind of fasting I have chosen: to loose the chains of injustice… share your food with the hungry…Then your light will break forth like the dawn, and your *healing* will *quickly* appear…Then you will call, and the Lord will answer; you will cry for help, and he will say: Here am I," Isaiah 58:6-9.

God will also give you the grace in doing your part to facilitate the healing process. The following are some examples of healing processes in different areas – spiritually, socially, materially and physically.

A) Spiritual Healing

If healing is in a spiritual area God will give you the grace in doing your part to facilitate the healing process. This includes healing of the wounded spirit.

It also includes deliverance and healing of spiritual wounds that exposed one to the spirit realm. For example, one seeing and hearing demonic spirits will be able to stop fearing the appearance of these beings.

Seeing, hearing or sensing demon spirits implies one previously tapped or got access into the spirit world through whatever wrong practices. Prayer combined with fasting also helps in the healing process.

Until God completely closes your access into the spirit world your focus should be on him not the evil spirits being seen, heard, or sensed. In his time God will bring the required covering to your spiritual eyes and senses.

You will then be like the majority of us who are covered from seeing and hearing these evil beings. For more information on spiritual healing areas please see Part 4 in this chapter that focuses on deliverance and healing in spiritual areas.

B) Social Healing

If healing is in the social area God will also give you the grace in doing your part to facilitate the healing process. For example, in a family area on conflicts he will give you the grace to pray and fast for matters or individuals bringing problems.

If you're the problem he'll enable you to fix issues that cause problems. Do not expect a superhuman personality but a change in how you handle you weaknesses that cause problems. For more information on social healing areas please see Part 5 on deliverance and healing in social areas.

C) Material Healing

In the area of finances God will enable you to cultivate a generous heart. He'll also enable you to let go of expenses you can live without. These expenses not only hinder repaying of debts (if you have any) they also hinder you from giving, an avenue that God uses to release his material blessings. For more information on material healing areas please see Part 6 on deliverance and healing in material areas.

D) Physical Healing

If it's in the area of physical health God will enable you to know and apply physical health principles that are in your sphere of responsibility. These are natural health principles.

Where it's in God's sphere of responsibility or power he'll bring healing supernaturally. For more information on physical healing areas please see Part 7 on deliverance and healing in physical areas.

Continual Search for Unknown Doorways

A believer also needs to be open to continue searching for areas in his/her life that may still be giving access to seeing and hearing demonic spirits. Some could be beliefs embraced by certain churches that are not biblical.

These include erroneous teachings on spiritual warfare, spiritual warfare prayers, deliverance prayers, binding and loosing demons, most of modern day speaking in tongues, pleading the blood or sprinkling the blood of Jesus (instead of taking holy communion like Jesus instructed us), the Rosary and praying to Mary (instead of to God, our heavenly Father), and so on.

(In case you need detailed info on modern versions of speaking in tongues, etc, please visit GotQuestions.org. It's a Christian website that answers questions from a biblical perspective. They do not dispute all modern day versions but caution on going into non-biblical practices (some of us learnt of it the hard way). You can type in your query in the search bar. Please make use of such resources, including resources at our website and public or church library resources for questions unanswered in this book. Do email us a question to consider answering in the next edition or adding to the website. The volume of email received makes it unbearable to reply to every person that writes).

Some of these non-biblical practices can open doors to seeing and sensing demonic forces. The beliefs and practices tap into the wrong spirit world, making Christians able to see or experience unpleasant demonic activities.

We need to continue seeking God for answers in other unpleasant matters in our lives not connected to involvement in any area we have been delivered and receiving healing from. We all have different journeys in life and the Lord relates to us in different ways in the course of the journeys. In his sovereign will he may allow unpleasant experiences. Again the book of Job illustrates this.

However we need to ensure they are not as a result of ignorance, disobedience or plain robbery that the enemy is entering our lives through. We need to be alert for his attempts against us and against those we're commissioned to serve.

Phillip Keller, author of *Power! The Challenge of Elijah*, says, "It is surprising how few, even within the church, are acutely aware of this battle that is fought unceasingly. Evil cannot tolerate righteousness. Darkness is opposed to light. Death attempts to destroy life. Hatred is against love. Deception is determined to obliterate truth... In the end God always has the last word... Though temporarily they may appear to succeed, in the end it is God who will triumph. It is he who shall have the final word as to the destiny of men and nations."

Other Battles to Overcome

The freedom that is granted only applies to the area of the enemy's previous oppression that biblical truth is now applied. It does not carry over into other areas where another light of truth is required. For instance, one may be oppressed financially due to not knowing the truth about the biblical principles of seed-time and harvest-time. Being free from Satan's manipulations that came from involvement in false teachings on spiritual warfare and deliverance may do nothing in bringing financial freedom.

It'll only come once the individual knows and applies the principles of seed-time and harvest-time. It's therefore important to be submissive to God and allowing him to lead us by his Spirit. His Holy Spirit is the one who guides us to all necessary truth for living a fruitful life. Biblical truth does not come by our own intellect and reasoning. If it did all university graduates and professors would be born again and applying the most biblical principles in their lives.

The Holy Spirit is the one who reveals God's truths into our minds. Scripture says we have "the mind of Christ" (1 Corinthians 2:16) controlled by the Spirit of God. Being able to discern and understand these truths therefore does not mean we're better thinkers than unbelievers.

It only means the Holy Spirit is able to relate God's principles to us in a way that unbelievers do not yet have access. Being submissive to God in prayer, fulfilling his word and applying other biblical devotions allows him to lead us by his Spirit.

Submission to his will enables our minds to be closer to his counsel and voice. As we think and think, read and read, on areas relating to whatever matters the Holy Spirit is able to show us the biblical solutions. Biblical truth comes as we hold (embrace) and follow (obey) the biblical teachings of Christ from Genesis to Revelation.

"If you hold to my teaching, you are really my disciples. Then you will know the truth, and the truth will set you free," John 8:31-32.

Holding to his teaching includes thinking, reading and searching for God's truths. His teachings do not come by blind faith that assumes God will just work things out without our input.

Thinking is therefore important, together with other disciplines like prayer, charitable giving, fasting and so on. It is not a sin to think. The only difference with unbelievers is that we have "the mind of Christ" (1 Corinthians 2:16) controlled by the Spirit of God.

Thinking, reading and searching for God's truths is a way of exercising the mind of Christ. But it is only fruitful when our submission to God is sufficient enough to enable the work of the Holy Spirit. Our Christian lives and walking in truth depend on him.

Otherwise the void where there is ignorance may give place to the enemy to deceive and oppress us in that area. Blind faith will not overcome areas of ignorance. Only God's truth does.

The Danger of Blind Faith

Blind faith is not a spiritual weapon against ignorance, deception, sin or storms of life. Only the truth is and applying it. If blind faith was a weapon against ignorance or deception all Christians would have almost no problems. All we would need is to believe God that somehow he would drop the answers to our various obstacles. I wish this was the case. But it's not.

For instance, many believers are trusting God to bless them materially and to miraculously overcome their financial obstacles. But few aggressively apply God's biblical principles to financial freedom. Having faith in God does not enable him to make short-cuts to his laws of seed-time and harvest-time. Having faith in him and obeying his ways is what pleases him. It is fulfilling all our required areas of responsibility that pleases him.

Faith is actually inevitable when applying God's principles to financial freedom. The less resources one has to sacrifice the more he/she would need to believe that whatever she gives up will bring a reward in future.

A believer who is not sure making needed sacrifices would later solve financial problems would be less willing to make sacrifices. Such a believer assumes making sacrifices is as good as playing the lottery, gambling her scarce resources and counting on some strange statistical luck.

Few would want to make sacrifices of scarce resources on matters that have little or no guarantee of having any reward. So a believer who obeys God's word in applying his biblical principles to financial freedom has faith in God to fulfill what he's promised in his word. Faith leads to application of God's principles. It should not lead to mere belief in God to solving whatever obstacles. Such is blind faith.

There are many sincere believers that through blind faith are facing avoidable afflictions. "My people are destroyed from lack of knowledge," Hosea 4.6. God's people, not those whose father is the devil (John 8:44) are destroyed from lack of knowledge. God's people are destroyed not because Satan is strong and furious. It is because they lack knowledge in areas Satan has gained access.

Neither are they destroyed because they have no faith in God. It is because they are missing the knowledge that needs to be combined with the faith. May this never be the case over any one of us who are have settled not to live by blind faith. Please see what real faith is, covered in the chapter: True Biblical Spiritual Warfare = Indirect Confrontation. True faith is discussed among the weapons of spiritual warfare. It is a shield.

The Body of Christ and its Spiritual Growth

There're other areas of truth that have not yet been revealed to the Body of Christ. The Bible says we do not yet have perfect knowledge of everything, until this present world passes away. "For we know in part and we prophesy in part, but when perfection comes, the imperfect disappears," 1 Corinthians 13:9-10. The imperfect knowledge we have will be replaced by the perfect.

We therefore only know in part, according to the level the Lord chooses to reveal. More revelation brings more freedom and more empowerment in the body of Christ against Satan's works on earth. "If you hold to my teaching, you are really my disciples. Then you will know the truth, and the truth will set you free," John 8:31-32.

We only effectively learnt recently that the Body of Christ is one big network of believers. This network consists of believers in different denominations operating under different levels of grace, revelation, anointing, and callings. It has brought more freedom to associate with one another across denominations.

The increasing unity is enabling us to put our resources together, thereby accomplish more in fulfilling the Great Commission. Previously we were bound by thick denominational walls that divided us even over minor differences. In each of our denominations our spiritual arrogance made us think we were the only ones that got the scriptures right. Thank God for the increasing unity.

Needless to say that there are plenty of wolves in sheep's clothing around us. We ought to be watchful for them by observing their fruits. Most of the bad fruit boarders on compromise with ways of the sinful nature. For instance some churches are embracing what the bible forbids - homosexuality.

The enemy attempts to bring new attacks to the new freedom the church has received. Scripture says we will know the impostors by their fruits (Matthew 7:20-23). Their fruits are contrary to the fruits of the Holy Spirit. Only the Holy Spirit can produce good fruit in and through vessels he has effectively occupied.

His fruit cannot be counterfeited or falsified by any other spirit, including the human spirit and the evil spirits. His fruit includes love, joy, peace, patience, kindness, goodness, faithfulness, gentleness and self-control," Galatians 5:22-23.

New revelations in the body of Christ therefore bring new battles. Our increasing unity has now given us a new battle of knowing and avoiding mixing with impostors. Perry Stone, in his book *Dealing with Hindering Spirits*, says "New levels (of anointing), new devils (trying to fight the anointing)."

Our constant walk with God through prayer, his word and the leading by his Spirit will expose these new "devils." He'll also equip us with the appropriate spiritual weapons and strategy to overcome them. The enemy cannot cross the boundaries the Lord puts around us. He can only reach the extent the Lord allows. The book of Job illustrates this.

Our level of disobedience to God also defines the extent Satan can legally reach us. Each level of disobedience invites his attacks because it gives him legal grounds to attack. Obedience to God, on the other hand, overcomes his legal claim that he would use to attack. Obedience is therefore a weapon of righteousness that brings freedom from Satan's legal attacks. Attacks he wages outside any legal claims are insignificant because if God allows them, they in the long run, only end up working to our favor individually or corporately in the body of Christ.

The bible says, "We will be ready to punish every act of disobedience once (when) your obedience is complete," 2 Corinthians 10:6 (emphasis added). We're able to punish more illegal or disobedient acts of the enemy the stronger our obedience to God is.

Disobedient acts of the enemy in our callings, ministries, families, health, society, finances, and so on, are punishable through our high level of obedience to God. It's not that an easy life will result. Rather it's that obedience enables us to effectively deal with hindering matters in our callings, ministries, finances, health, society, finances, etc.

Note on Prayer Group and Fellowship

A note on church fellowship just not to be misunderstood. I've said in this chapter that repentance may also include separating from prayer groups that have chosen to continue embracing the erroneous spiritual warfare and deliverance teachings even after being informed about its deceptiveness. This is not a prescription for every believer.

The Lord may require you to remain associating with a group that may not embrace the true scriptural strategy on spiritual warfare and deliverance. In this case he'll protect you as you fulfill your role in the Body of Christ through that congregation. Interceding for the congregation is still important. It's therefore important that each individual seeks the plan that the Lord has for them.

The problem is not that the erroneous spiritual warfare and deliverance teachings may lead someone to hell. It is its destructive nature it brings on sincere believers in this life. The sincere believers are no less Christian than anyone outside this deception. Many are actually doing great exploits in their respective callings.

There is therefore to be no ill perceptions against fellow believers in evangelical congregations that advocate for the erroneous spiritual warfare and deliverance teachings. We are all members in the large body of Christ fulfilling his will in spite of our limitations, imperfections, liability to err and so on.

The books and other multimedia resources however have no basis being kept unless you have a scriptural justification or for academic purposes. Please do share the scriptural justification if you come across one.

Note Concerning Signs and Wonders

Miracles that come through the manifestation of the gifts of the Holy Spirit sometimes attract us to churches that manifest more of them. This has been so among some of us in the body of Christ.

Miracles seem to show that God is really at work in places where signs abound and the preaching is within evangelical beliefs. Unfortunately, the scripture has a different view. Our Lord said the fruit of his followers will be the determinant of whether or not God is at work in each congregation. The fruit not the gifts are the most important (Matthew 7:20-23), even if the gifts are necessary for doing God's work.

This being so then there ought to be no distinction in preference of a church whether Pentecostal, Baptist or other evangelical church as long as the fruit is evident in a particular church. The fruit is what is acceptable to God while the gifts are necessary for effectively doing God's work.

Jesus said, "By their fruit you will recognize them. Not everyone who says to me, 'Lord, Lord,' will enter the kingdom of heaven, but only he who does the will of my Father who is in heaven. Many will say to me on that day, 'Lord, Lord, did we not prophesy in your name, and in your name drive out demons and perform many miracles?' Then I will tell them plainly, 'I never knew you. Away from me, you evildoers!' Matthew 7:20-23.

Good fruit comes only from the Holy Spirit. It cannot be counterfeited or falsified by any other spirit, including the human spirit and the evil spirits. The gifts of the Holy Spirit, particularly miracles, however can be counterfeited by evil spirits.

Gifts of the Holy Spirit also remain active in Christians even when their walk with God is questionable. God does not withdraw his gifts because they are irrevocable. "God's gifts and his call are irrevocable," Romans 11:29. That is why the extreme importance of fruits cannot be compared to gifts.

The good fruit is produced among those who proclaim and apply the will of God in their lives. It comes as the Holy Spirit freely works in our lives as we submit our lives to be possessed and owned for the glory of God. The nature of the fruit that is produced in our lives is diverse.

Scripture says, "The fruit of the Spirit is love, joy, peace, patience, kindness, goodness, faithfulness, gentleness and self-control. Against such things there is no law. Those who belong to Christ Jesus have crucified the sinful nature with its passions and desires. Since we live by the Spirit, let us keep in step with the Spirit," Galatians 5: 22-25.

The greatest attribute in the fruit of the Spirit is love. "Now I will show you the most excellent way. If I speak in the tongues of men and of angels, but have not love, I am only a resounding gong or a clanging cymbal. If I have the gift of prophecy and can fathom all mysteries and all knowledge, and if I have a faith that can move mountains, but have not love, I am nothing. If I give all I possess to the poor and surrender my body to the flames, but have not love, I gain nothing," 1 Corinthians 12:31-13:1-3.

The verses that follow define what love is: "Love is patient, love is kind. It does not envy, it does not boast, it is not proud. It is not rude, it is not self-seeking, it is not easily angered, it keeps no record of wrongs. Love does not delight in evil but rejoices with the truth. It always protects, always trusts, always hopes, always perseveres. Love never fails,"1 Corinthians 13:4-8.

This kind of love goes beyond the boarders of our family network and local church members. Even the worst of sinners have some natural bonds of love towards their family and "inner circle."

As Christians our expression of love goes to all kinds of people regardless of their beliefs. We go to the extent of blessing those who curse us or wish the worst of us. We pray for their salvation. We overcome evil with good. "Bless those who persecute you; bless and do not curse…Do not be overcome

by evil, but overcome evil with good," Romans 12:14,21. It's very hard sometimes but we have no other option.

Matthew Henry Complete Commentary on the Whole Bible says, "A
man may be a preacher, may have gifts for the ministry, and an external call to
it, and perhaps some success in it, and yet be a wicked man; may help others to
heaven, and yet come short himself. That in thy name we have cast out devils?
That may be too; Judas cast out devils, and yet was a son of perdition."

It says about all Christians that do not bear good fruit: "They think they
shall go to heaven, because they have been of good repute among professors of
religion, have kept fasts, and given alms, and have been preferred in the church;
as if this would atone for their reigning pride, worldliness, and sensuality; and
want of love to God and man...Let us take heed of resting in external privileges
and performances, lest we deceive ourselves, and perish eternally, as multitudes
do, with a lie in our right hand.

"'Depart from me, ye that work iniquity'...Why, and upon what ground,
he rejects them and their plea—because they were workers for iniquity...Secret
haunts of sin, kept under the cloak of a visible profession, will be the ruin of the
hypocrites.

"Living in known sin nullifies men's pretensions, be they ever so spe-
cious...I never knew you; "I never owned you as my servants, no, not when you
prophesied in my name, when you were in the height of your profession, and
were most extolled...If a preacher, one that cast out devils, and wrought
miracles, be disowned of Christ for working iniquity; what will become of us, if
we be found such? And if we be such, we shall certainly be found such."

As Jesus said, his followers will be known by the fruit they produce. It
brings doubtful questions if the fruit attributes mentioned in Galatians are not
easily discernible in the lives of those that call Jesus, "Lord, Lord."

Matthew Henry Commentary says, "Those are not taught nor sent of the
holy God, whose lives evidence that they are led by the unclean spirit. God puts
the treasure into earthen vessels, but not into such corrupt vessels: they may
declare God's statutes, but what have they to do to declare them? ... What
affections and practices will they lead those into, that embrace them?

"If the doctrine be of God, it will tend to promote serious piety, humility, charity, holiness, and love, with other Christian graces; but if, on the
contrary, the doctrines these prophets preach have a manifest tendency to make
people proud, worldly, and contentious, to make them loose and careless in their
conversations, unjust or uncharitable, factious or disturbers of the public peace;
if it indulge carnal liberty, and take people off from governing themselves and
their families by the strict rules of the narrow way, we may conclude, that this
persuasion comes not of him that calleth us."

9.3 Christian Deliverance and Healing, Part 3: Prayer and Fasting

CHAPTER 9. PART 3: PRAYER AND FASTING - SUB-TOPICS:
- Prayer and Fasting -Sowing to the Spirit
- Nature, Role and Purpose of Fasting
- How to Fast
- The Power of Fasting
- Occasional Food Fasts and Permanent Worldly Fast
- Seed time and Harvest time -No neutral ground
- Carrying Cross of Self-denial on Desires of the Flesh
- Major Prayer and Fasting Scriptures

Prayer and Fasting -Sowing to the Spirit

Fasting is probably the greatest avenue for enabling us be sensitive and responsive to the Spirit of God. God is always speaking to us in one way or another. However, only those who are sensitive and responsive enough to him can effectively hear him.

Our Lord Jesus said fasting would be necessary for his disciples after he ascended. "The time will come when the bridegroom will be taken from them; then they will fast," (Matthew 9:15)

The early disciples remembered the words of their master and thus they made fasting vital. The outstanding work God accomplished through them speaks for itself. They could easily hear God speak to them in their moments of fasting. "While they were worshipping and *fasting*, the Holy Spirit said, 'Set a part for me Barnabas and Saul for the work to which I have called them,' " (Acts 13:2).

Thus the ministry of Paul started after a period of fasting and praying. "So after they fasted and prayed, they placed their hands on them and sent them off," (Verse 3).

Just not to be misunderstood, it is not a must to fast as in making it a sin if one does not. Jesus said "When you fast..." implying that it's an essential Christian discipline. People are not obligated to fast but they could be limited in experiencing matters that can be realized in their Christian lives only through both prayer and fasting.

For those with health limitations it's not wise to fast at all depending on the severity of the illness that can be worsened through fasting.

Nature, Role and Purpose of Fasting

Fasting, that of abstaining from food, can become legalistic and ritual oriented when taken out of context. It can become a religious activity performed in order to influence God. Fasting, is not a tool to win God's audience. God is always ready to speak to us and to help us. It is for our sake to tune ourselves to his wavelength in order to hear from him and effectively walk with him.

In his audio sermon on fasting, Ron Gartner makes an important point. He says fasting is not giving up meals and making a sacrifice so that God can speak to us or bless us. It is not an exchange of a sacrifice in order to obtain blessings.

He says, it is moving into a spiritual realm of faith and power by putting down (denying) our flesh desires. The Holy Spirit and the spirit part of us then take dominance in moving in an area of prayer (communion with God) that we cannot get into through any other way. It is moving into the spirit and walking in the spirit. This does not mean being foolish and turning our reasoning off. It is being wise with the mind of Christ while being submissive to the Holy Spirit.

Fasting may be unpleasant since our bodies are conditioned to be our masters. When they cry for food we quickly feed them. When they're denied food they scream louder and louder at us.

Common body reactions include extreme thirst and hunger (of course), weakness, fatigue, headaches, and occasional dizziness. In the early stages of attempting to fast these reactions are more intense. They fade and fasting becomes easier as the body becomes more conditioned.

With more regular fasting our bodies become less "unruly." God also helps us in our natural weakness of finding it difficult to fast. He always makes his grace abundant on his children that are sincerely willing to obey his word. "God is able to make all grace abound to you, so that in all times, having all that you need, you will abound in every good work," (2 Corinthians 9:8).

Regular fasting cannot kill the body. We may lose weight and strength during prolonged fasts but the spiritual breakthroughs in moving closer to God are too precious compared to anything we can lose.

How to Fast

There're no rules on fasting periods. One can set apart a day every week without food and water. Or she can set three days aside every month to recondition her sensitivity to God. Water can be taken in a three day fast though it's possible to do without it up to three days. Beyond three days water is essential for your body.

There is a story of one believer who fasted for 40 days without drinking water. He died on the fortieth day. He's no doubt heaven-destined and probably had victories over matters he fasted for. However he went too soon for lack of knowledge on appropriate fasting principles. A prolonged fast from 4 days to 40 days needs water and probably a slice or two of bread (or three) per day.

Fasting beyond 40 days is not biblical. It's not a sin to fast over 40 days but it's a health risk. There is no scriptural record of anyone fasting beyond 40 days. This should be a medical health alarm because beyond 40 days physical health is likely to start deteriorating. It can bring health complications that may be hard to reverse. On the other hand fasting within biblical limits has lasting health benefits – though it's the spiritual benefits that are more important.

After ending a 40 day fast I weighed 130 pounds (58.9 Kg) at 6 foot (1.83m). It was like coming out of a concentration camp with a chest showing all the bones of the ribcage. Only the Lord enabled this fast since I had a six-day full time job at the same time. Two to three slices of bread where taken every midnight. On two or three occasions a small portion of beans was taken after feeling completely weak.

Headaches can come once in while but this ought to be endured during the fast. Headaches only signal the cries of the body. They're to be ignored for as long as they don't worsen. The victories from the fast cannot be quantified to this day.

If there is any mountain for the Lord to move allow fasting to facilitate the work. Seek him to enable you rather than making all kinds of excuses. After all it's you that stands to gain over all the matters you're burdened with. It's such a privilege to give birth to these matters after much travail through fasting. And God's work goes beyond the matters of concern thus making the victories through fasting hard to quantify.

Prayer and fasting is like sowing in tears. It's a sacrifice yet a more than worthwhile one. "Those who sow in tears will reap with songs of joy. He who goes out weeping, carrying seed to sow, will return with songs of joy, carrying sheaves (bundles of crop harvest) with him," Psalm 126:5-6.

I believe a 40 day fast ought to be once in a lifetime –if one has the grace to even do it. It ought not to be done more than once if you are enabled to fast up to 40 days. Only Moses is said to have taken two 40 day fasts in the bible. If you want to be like Moses it's no sin. However note the health precautions. Our bodies have been designed to work in certain ways. Fasting helps them when it's done within limits that our bodies have been framed.

Outside these limits fasting becomes detrimental. Victories come but at health costs that were not even necessary. After one 40 day long fast it is advisable to stick to 2 to 3 day fasts afterwards. Besides 3 day fasts without food or water can be as overcoming as a 40 day fast when taken multiple times. For instance one can purpose to fast a total of at least 40 days in a year taking 2 to 3 day fasts.

How often one needs to take such fasts depends on the grace one has. Allow the Lord to equip you and enable you rather than use your own limitations as yardsticks. At one point he may enable you to take 3 day fasts three times in one month, at a later period once, and so on. His enabling rather than yours should win the day. But do your part in allowing him to work through you. Plan ahead when you sense his leading. When that day comes make no excuses. Commit yourself rather than flip flopping.

A fasting program ought to include prayer, intercession, reading of God's word (i.e. one way of listening to God), allowing God to speak from within. It can also include worshipping him with songs of praise on multimedia or personally. Listening to or watching sermons focusing on areas you are burdened with is also edifying.

Allowing God to speak from within is not waiting to hear a strange voice. It is God speaking from within. His Spirit dwells in you so he speaks from within. You will be able to grasp matters in your life and the lives of others in ways you never perceived them before. That is God speaking to you and revealing his ways to you. What he says is always supported by scripture.

If it's something contradicting scripture then it's the voice of a stranger, Satan. Satan also speaks to our hearts with his temptations and appeal to the flesh. His voice can be recognized by its appeal to the flesh, the fallen nature and contradiction of what God has told us in his word.

Scripture also tells us to move out of our comfort zones and stretch our hands to those who don't have whatever basic needs we have. We share whatever resources we have with them and with extended family members that may be underprivileged.

Many forget that charity is part of our Christian pillars and has its level of blessings or curses, depending on how we carry ourselves. See Isaiah 58:6-9 outlined below for the fast that God desires. Without engaging in most of these areas, fasting only becomes a form of dieting or hunger strike.

"Is not this the kind of fasting I have chosen: to loose the chains of injustice and untie the cords of the yoke, to set the oppressed free and break every yoke? Is it not to share your food with the hungry and to provide the poor wanderer with shelter-- when you see the naked, to clothe him, and not to turn away from your own flesh and blood?

"Then your light will break forth like the dawn, and your healing will quickly appear; then your righteousness will go before you, and the glory of the Lord will be your rear guard. Then you will call, and the Lord will answer; you will cry for help, and he will say: Here am I," Isaiah 58:6-9

In our New Testament (Covenant) era Jesus said we should make fasting a secret. It should not be like the Pharisees who blew the horn and covered their heads with oil to show everyone how holy they were. No one needs to know unless one has health ailments that fasting may affect. Particularly short fasts, fasting ought to be between you and God.

Anointing ones head may be necessary since Jesus said so. "**When** (not, if or in case) you fast, put oil on your head and wash your face, so that it will not be obvious to men that you are fasting, but only to your Father, who is unseen; and your Father, who sees what is done in secret, will reward you," Matthew 6:17-18.

Notice after saying "put oil on your head," he also said "wash your face, so that it will not be obvious to men that you are fasting." So you can anoint yourself and then wipe the oil out. It will not be a problem if you don't apply any oil. Application of oil when fasting was the Jewish custom. Jesus did not want to discredit the oil so he included its relevance but attacked the wrong motives for its application. Some anointed themselves to show everyone they were fasting instead.

One may be asking on how to use the anointing oil if one decides to use it. It's any oil that you have, even basic cooking oil. It does not have to be some special oil straight from Jerusalem.

God is more interested in our faith than in what kind of oil is being used. It can even be petroleum jelly like Vaseline if you cannot afford any oil. Jerusalem oil, Olive oil, cooking oil or Vaseline oil will all have the same effect if applied in faith.

You can pour some oil in a smaller bottle for future use. Take some oil and apply it on your forehead and pray that God uses it as a point of faith in anointing you and consecrating you.

Your consecration enables you to be under his agenda of fasting. Anointing oil is for consecration, being set apart as holy vessels for the Holy Spirit to work through. "He (Moses) poured some of the anointing oil on Aaron's head and anointed him to consecrate him," Leviticus 8:12

The oil is meant to be an act of faith in receiving the anointing of the Holy Spirit. The anointing of the Holy Spirit enables us to fast for the right reasons and to flow under the power and influence of God. He is also the one who moves into our lives to break yokes and overcome spiritual strongholds – spiritually, physically, materially, socially and so on.

The Power of Fasting

Richard LaFountain gives a good summary on the power of fasting. Detailed people like me would have written another book just to say the following:

What Is Fasting?
Fasting is going without food to pursue and/or focus on something more important.
1. Fasting helps subject our bodies to our spirits. (I Cor 9:27)
2. Fasting is disciplining the body, mind, and spirit. (Prov. 25:28)
3. Fasting is subordinating our flesh-desires to our spirit-desires. (Gal 5:17)
4. Fasting helps set the priorities in our lives. (Mt 6:33)

5. Fasting is longing after God. (Ps 63:1-2)

Why Should We Fast?
1. Honor God - Mt 6:16-18, Luke 2:37, Acts 13:2, Mt 5:6
2. Humble Yourself - 2 Chron 7:14-15
3. Discerning Healing - I Cor 11:30, James 5:13-18, Isaiah 59:1-2
4. Deliverance from Bondage - Mt 17:21, Is 58:6-9 (loose bands of wickedness)
5. Revelation - God's vision and will - Dan 9:3, 20-21, Dan 10:2-10, 12-13
6. Revival - personal and corporate - Acts 1:4, 14 / 2:16-21, Joel 2:12-18
7. Repentance - personal failures - Psalm 51: Jer. 29:11-14, James 4:8-10

LaFountain's summary above shows that fasting is so critical in our Christian lives. Unfortunately few Christians take fasting seriously. If we all did there would be great revivals world over, breaking of bondages (yokes) in our lives and other people's physical lives, spiritual areas, and loosing the bonds of Satan's wickedness in people's lives in their physical health, spiritual blindness and deafness to the gospel, marital, family, financial, mental and career bondages.

We would also be able to hear from God over most of our repetitive prayers. "Is not this the fast that I Choose: to loose the bonds of wickedness, to undo the things of the yoke, to let the oppressed go free, and to break every yoke? Is it not to share you bread with the hungry, and bring the homeless poor into your house...Then shall you call, and the Lord will answer; you shall cry, and he will say, here I am," (Isaiah 58:6-7, 9)

Few believers ever dream or attempt to fast for 40 days. Breakthroughs that would come after the 40 days can take an entire lifetime to realize, if at all. But let's focus on at least three days of fasting. It's good to start on an incremental level to reduce the cries of the body after starting a fast. The first time can last a day. Next can be two days. Then three days. Anyone who reaches three days can easily prolong the fast to even 40 days since the body stops crying and kicking after two to three days.

This is our one major discipline that moves mountains. Unfortunately it's a rarely practiced discipline in the body of Christ. Some have even assumed that breakthroughs come when we go after demon spirits in thin air and command them let go of our blessings as if they have any. They bombard these spirits, calling it spiritual warfare prayer or deliverance prayer only to come under more attacks.

God said when we humble ourselves through prayer and fasting he, himself takes care of these spirits that have gained legal access into our lives. Our consecration to him closes their legal entry and enables him to rebuke all the devourers and weeds around our lives. He rebukes them, not us. Our only role is to focus on him over what he requires of us, and not to focus on whatever demon spirits are up to.

Prayer and fasting constitute our true spiritual warfare prayers and deliverance prayers. We bring matters before God in humble submission and seek him to deal with them in his power and might.

The outcome is twofold: first is victory and deliverance over matters being submitted to him. Second, we draw closer to God, experiencing his grace, love and power. Going after demonic spirits in thin air and calling it spiritual warfare prayer or deliverance prayer is our invention that the bible does not support. No wonder it leads to more bondage instead of deliverance.

Occasional Food Fasts and Permanent Worldly Fast

Most people God greatly used began their calling in intense prayer accompanied with one type of fasting or another. Although fasting is basically abstaining from food, self-denial from other things of the flesh is also fasting. For instance, couples are advised to *mutually* deprive each other of intercourse whenever necessary for more effective prayer. "Do not deprive each other except by mutual consent and for a time, so that you may devote yourselves to prayer," (1 Corinthians 7:5).

There are many things of the flesh (of worldly value) that hinder sensitivity to the spirit of God. Some require occasional fasts like intercourse for couples, interaction with certain people. Some require frequent fasts like certain foods and quantities, certain books and multimedia, etc.

Others require permanent fasting. These constitute things that are either directly sinful or indirectly sinful. Anything that does not add to our closer walk with God the Father, the Son and the Holy Spirit is a seed of the flesh. It therefore requires a permanent fast. Otherwise, by partaking of it quenches the God's Spirit whom we desperately need in our daily walk with God. Each seed sown to please the flesh and sinful nature eventually adds up for its due level of harvest.

Seed time and Harvest time -No neutral ground

The law of sowing and reaping applies to whatever we think of, say or do. No neutral ground. "A man reaps whatever he sows. The one who sows to please his sinful nature, from that nature will reap destruction; the one who sows to please the Spirit will reap eternal life (Galatians 6:7-8)." Every thought, word, or act is a seed either to the flesh or to the Spirit.

Seed sown to please the sinful nature therefore eventually bring some level of destruction in our lives. Anything that brings destruction upon an individual is sinful. Thus a Christian who's serious about desiring to always grow in her walk with God, hearing from him and fulfilling his will is expected to guard against things that look innocent on the outside. Otherwise they'll bring destruction in one area or another in her walk with God.

We usually think of destruction as physical death. In that case all of us end our lives in destruction. In scripture, it is the isolation of the spirit part of us from God. It is alienation from the Spirit of God. A person engaging in thoughts or activities of the flesh is thus alienating himself/herself from God. The greater the intensity of involvement in activities of the flesh the wider the distance he/she separates herself from God. It therefore, becomes more difficult for her to hear from God.

That is a challenge to those of us who desire to walk with God and effectively hear from him. We're called to permanently fast over things of the flesh – things of worldly value. "Do not love the world or anything in the world. If anyone loves the world, the love of the Father is not in him. For everything in the world - the cravings of sinful man, the lust of his eyes and the boasting of what he has and does – comes not from the Father but from the world," (1 John 2:15-16).

Carrying Cross of Self-denial on Desires of the Flesh

Our Lord said we must carry our cross of self-denial from all worldly things if we desire to follow him (Luke 14:27). Paul, like the other early disciples did just that. He said, "May I never boast except in the cross of our Lord Jesus Christ, through which the world was crucified to me, and I to the world," (Galatians 6:14).

He said he was crucified and died to worldly desires, though like Christ, he also died to save the world. This too is our calling: "Set your minds on things above, not on earthly things. For you died and your life is now hidden with Christ in God," (Colossians 3: 2-3)

Setting our minds on things above demands forsaking things below. These include most secular programs, music, magazines, books, certain places, certain forms of entertainment and activities, and so on. One cannot partake of things below and expect to effectively hear from God and fulfill his will.

For instance, watching secular films only contributes to increased spiritual deafness. It only opens the individual's spirit to the many voices and images of the world which easily crowd out God's voice. Whatever we give our attention to takes charge of our hearts.

Not only do our hearts become increasingly impure to hear from God, we also partake of other people's sins in these programs. We share their sins. For instance, on sexual sins, our Lord said, "Anyone who looks at a woman lustfully has already committed adultery with her in his heart," (Matthew 5:28). The sin therefore does not have to be physically committed for the individual to account for it. That sounds harder than the Old Covenant law under Moses. But thank God we have the Holy Spirit and the grace of God to help us in the New Covenant under Christ.

And an avenue like fasting has been given to us to connect with the Holy Spirit who enables us to live lives worthy of our Christian calling. Try fasting over some sins and you'll see how easily they will drop off. No binding and loosing of demons and so called spiritual warfare prayers needed.

If the sinful tendencies return get back into fasting, for longer periods if necessary. And continue the fight for as long as you're here on earth. Fasting breaks demonic strongholds, demonic attacks and helps us to walk in the spirit, not the flesh, to sow to the Spirit, not to the sinful nature.

It's a mystery how fasting works in bringing such outcomes. Or shall we say it's a mystery how God works through fasting in bringing such outcomes. Why we're so keen to guard our flesh interests is also another mystery -a mystery of lawlessness (2 Thessalonians 2:7 (KJV)). May God enable us to overcome appetites that have nothing to do with our walk with him and the glorious promises lying ahead of us.

The issue of sowing to earthly verses spiritual things can be a long and controversial one. It's tempting to justify certain things of the flesh we're not willing to give up. In a nutshell, self-denial is a prerequisite to a closer walk with God. Many types of non-food fasts are required to silence the flesh and exalt the spirit.

Major Prayer and Fasting Scriptures

"*When* (not, if or in case) you fast, put oil on your head and wash your face, so that it will not be obvious to men that you are fasting, but only to your Father, who is unseen; and your Father, who sees what is done in secret, will reward you," Matthew 6:17-18

"Is not this the kind of fasting I have chosen: to loose the chains of injustice and untie the cords of the yoke, to set the oppressed free and break every yoke? Is it not to share your food with the hungry and to provide the poor wanderer with shelter-- when you see the naked, to clothe him, and not to turn away from your own flesh and blood? *Then* your light will break forth like the dawn, and your healing will quickly appear; then your righteousness will go before you, and the glory of the Lord will be your rear guard. Then you will call, and the Lord will answer; you will cry for help, and he will say: Here am I," Isaiah 58:6-9

"His disciples asked him privately, "Why could we not cast it (the demon) out" And he said to them, "This kind cannot be driven out by anything but *prayer and fasting*," Mark 9:28-29, Matthew 17: 21, (in KJV, ISV bibles)

"And I set my face unto the Lord God, to seek by prayer and supplications, *with fasting*, and sackcloth, and ashes: And I prayed unto the Lord my

God, and made my confession, and said, O Lord, the great and dreadful God, keeping the covenant and mercy to them that love him, and to them that keep his commandments…O Lord, listen! O Lord, forgive! O Lord, hear and act! For your sake, O my God, do not delay, because your city and your people bear your Name." Daniel 9:3, 19

Faced with great invasion king Jehoshaphat proclaimed a *fast* and prayed: "O Lord, God of our fathers, are you not the God who is in heaven? You rule over all the kingdoms of the nations. Power and might are in your hand, and no one can withstand you. O our God, did you not drive out the inhabitants of this land before your people Israel and give it forever to the descendants of Abraham your friend?.... But now here are men from Ammon, Moab and Mount Seir….O our God, will you not judge them? For we have no power to face this vast army that is attacking us. We do not know what to do, but our eyes are upon you," 2 Chronicles 20:6-7,10,12

"Even now," declares the Lord, "return to me with all your heart, *with fasting* and weeping and mourning. Rend your heart and not your garments. Return to the Lord your God, for he is gracious and compassionate, slow to anger and abounding in love, and he relents from sending calamity," Joel 2:12-13

"While they were worshipping the Lord and *fasting*, the Holy Spirit said, 'Set apart for me Barnabas and Saul for the work to which I have called them,'" Acts 13:2

"Paul and Barnabas appointed elders for them in each church and, with *prayer and fasting*, committed them to the Lord, in whom they had put their trust," Acts 14:23.

9.4 Christian Deliverance and Healing, Part 4: Spiritual Areas

CHAPTER 9. PART 4: SPIRITUAL HEALTH AREAS - SUB-TOPICS:
- **The Wounded spirit**
- **Sources of Spiritual Wounds (spiritual illness)**
- **Effects of a Wounded Spirit (broken spirit, crushed spirit)**
- **Healing the Wounded Spirit: the Christian Approach**
- **Healing the Wounded Spirit: the Secular Approach**
- **God's "Plan B" and Maintaining a Healthy Spirit**
- **Deliverance from Hearing Voices, Seeing Demons, etc**
- **Deliverance and Healing from Spiritual attacks through Dreams**
- **Deliverance and Healing from the Occult, Witchcraft or Satanism**

This section on deliverance and healing covers exclusively on spiritual areas. This is unlike social, physical or material areas. Spiritual areas include matters experienced in the unseen realm of the mind, emotions and will.

They cannot be observed by any of us whether in a counseling situation, as an intercessor, as a victim or as mere listener. For example we cannot see or hear the experiences of hearing demons or seeing them when someone describes his/her experiences.

Spiritual attacks, next to social and financial problems cause the worst afflictions to believers and non-believers. Some are so severe that the victims end up being ruined spiritually. You have probably heard of references such as nervous wretch, emotional wretch, maniac, etc. The ruin can be in any area or combination of our inner selves –mind, emotions and will areas.

Our make up as humans is triune. We exist is in three in parts – spirit, soul and body. The spirit part of us is what relates with the soul which in turn relates with the body. The body is what relates with the rest of the world. When it dies the spirit leaves it awaiting its final destination – heaven or hell.

The soul is what gives sense to the body. It consists of the mind, will and emotion faculties. A book titled Free Indeed by Tom Marshall gives an in-depth biblical analysis on the spirit, soul and body. It's a worthy read if you can find it among online stores.

The soul which connects with the spirit is sometimes referred inter-changeably with the spirit, even in the bible. We will consider them as one and the same thing here. This will simplify understanding while still being consis-tent with scripture. We will refer to the mind, will and emotion faculties as being part of the spirit as much as they are part of the soul.

The Wounded Spirit

What is a wounded spirit? It's also known as a broken spirit or crushed spirit.

The bible says, "A man's spirit sustains him in sickness, but a crushed spirit who can bear?" Proverbs 18:14

"A cheerful heart is good medicine, but a crushed spirit dries up the bones," Proverbs 17:22.

A wounded spirit is injury to any area of our soul or spirit faculties - mind, emotions and will. It is injury to the unseen areas of our being. The only way others can see the injury is how we behave and conduct ourselves. At least one area inside us may be more affected than the others. The deeper or more severe the wounds the greater the negative effect on an individual's life - spiritually, socially, materially and physically.

As the scripture says a wounded spirit is worse than physical sickness. Physical sickness can be sustained by a healthy spirit but a sick spirit cannot be sustained by anything. The spirit part of us is the engine to our lives. Life is broken without its performance no matter how beautiful, healthy and expensive the body may look. In fact the breakdown of the spirit eventually brings sickness to the body. It dries up the bones.

A wounded spirit is not a poor man's bread but affects all economic groups. You've probably heard this: A survey of 65 countries, published by *New Scientist* (1999-2001, UK), said that people in Nigeria are the happiest people on earth followed by people in Mexico, Venezuela, El Salvador and Puerto Rico respectively. Third world nations took the lead. The United States of America was 16th.

This confirms Christ's words: "Watch out! Be on your guard against all kinds of greed; a man's life does not consist in the abundance of his possessions," Luke 12:15. People have rephrased it as: "money cannot buy happiness." The researchers actually described the desire or longing for material wealth as "a happiness suppressant." So those longing for earthly possessions end up less happy and prone to spiritual wounds.

Sources of Spiritual Wounds (Spiritual Illness)

Sources of spiritual wounds are avenues through which spiritual wounds come from. They are doorways Satan gains legal entry in his mission or ministry to "steal and kill and destroy," John 10:7. There are four doorways Satan gains entry. These are through:
1) deception,
2) ignorance,
3) sin, and

4) storms of life (when responded to in a wrong way)

His entry through any of these doorways can bring spiritual wounds as much as it can bring other wounds - social, material and physical. But spiritual wounds are the worst because they affect the other areas of life more severely. The following gives examples of how each of the doorway can give access to Satan's attack against our human spirits.

1) Deception

Highly concealed deception includes glorification of earthly riches, worldly pleasures, power, fame, beauty, and knowledge. You have probably read on at least one pastor or prominent Christian who fell for the love of money. The results are terrible, including the loss of an individual's credibility among those he/she needed it most. Some have lost their faith altogether with the grief that comes from rejection and judgmentalism against them.

"Some people, eager for money, have wandered from the faith and pierced themselves with many griefs," 1 Timothy 6:10. Wrong perspectives on money brings "many griefs" – various problems that injure the mind, will or emotions. The situation is worse among unbelievers.

Other deceptive tactics of Satan are planting of false teachings in the body of Christ. He makes them appear to be biblical.

The false teachings on spiritual warfare and deliverance have caused (and still causing) terrible spiritual wounds among innocent believers who fall prey to them. The false teachings expose some believers to the dark spirit world and enable their human spirits to see and hear demonic forces.

The beliefs and practices tap into the wrong spirit world, making Christians able to see or experience unpleasant demonic activities.

2) Ignorance

Ignorance or lack of knowledge makes one vulnerable to fall victim to Satan's deception and false doctrines. It's an open door for deception. *"My people* are destroyed from lack of knowledge," Hosea 4.6. Lack of knowledge can be an open door to adopting all kinds of dangerous beliefs and doctrines with the assumption that they are biblical.

3) Sin

Whether committed knowingly or out of ignorance sin has the same consequences. The worst of the sins that can bring a wounded spirit include involvement in occult practices, sexual sins, unforgiveness of past hurts, and severe conflicts between a parent and a child.

Sexual sins have all kinds of bad fruits including bringing bitterness, anger, unforgiveness, rejection, humiliation or worthlessness for some when breaking up. "But a man who commits adultery lacks judgment; whoever does so destroys himself. Blows and disgrace are his lot, and his shame will never be wiped away," Proverbs 6:32-33.

Unforgiveness opens doors to a tormenting spirit. This is not a spooky spirit that enters and possesses a person. Rather it is an evil spirit that operates from an external position, an aspect of demonic influence, not demonic possession. An evil spirit gains entry into a person's life bringing heartache after heartache which brings much grief emotionally and mentally.

An individual faces a prison experience similar to the servant who refused to forgive his fellow servant (Matthew 18:26-34). Jesus ended the parable by saying "This is how my heavenly Father will treat each of you unless you forgive your brother from your heart," Matthew 18:35.

The prison sentence ends when he/she chooses to forgive. Please see the section on forgiveness in the social area of deliverance and healing.

4) Storms of life

Storms of life are unpleasant experiences that befall us out of no fault of our own. These include experiences of living under constant negative and critical words; experiences of betrayal (by a loved one; trusted person, or leader); death of a loved one; severe physical or emotional abuse experiences; living under a heavy control and disciplinary environment that brings fear; living under rejection; false accusations; terrible divorce experience (as the victim); traumatic experience(s), severe accident (e.g. surviving 911 terrorist experience, traumatic accident, casualty of war); having a physical or social disability; having a certain physical appearance society "persecutes;" severe racial, gender and ethnic discrimination or abuse; falling victim to false teachings; genuine trials of faith; and so on.

Depending on how we handle them storms of life can be our stepping stones to our promotion (like with Joseph) or they can be our downfall. They can be assets the Holy Spirit can use to our good or they can be assets Satan can use to block us from moving forward.

History has amazing examples of people who ended up in a palace of life instead of a prison of life through storms they went through. God can do awesome work with matters that ordinarily disadvantage us if we trust him to be more powerful than our limitations.

Effects of a Wounded Spirit (broken or crushed spirit)

Each of us has some level of scars in our spirits from whatever unpleasant past experiences. Two matters determine whether or not these past experiences have any negative effect on our present: 1) our reaction to them, and 2) the severity of the experiences. The degree of their effect varies from person to person and in different areas of our spiritual faculties (mind, emotion and will).

You may notice one or more effects below that describe you. No cause for fear. It's when one or more of these areas become barriers to leading a normal life that serious treatment is required. These barriers may manifest in the spiritual area, social, material or even physical (health) areas. The sub-topic after this on healing the wounded spirit covers on how to treat or heal a wounded spirit, whether severe or minor areas.

Mental Effects:
*Recurring bad dreams
*Recurring memories of a past hurt(s)
*Prone to memory losses or distorted memories, exaggerating the negatives
*Focused on faults of others and shifting blame
*Easily critical of others
*Difficulty in forgiving some people
*Either extremely overconfident even when heading the wrong way, or on the opposite end extremely pessimistic
*Either obsessed with cleanliness (clean freak) & hygiene, or on the opposite end extremely dirty (skunk (as an adult, not a teenager))

Emotional Effects:
*Either exceptionally withdrawn (extreme introversion), or on the opposite end exceptionally outgoing & people pleaser (extreme extroversion)
*Inferiority complex
*Exceptionally fearful, suspicious and distrustful
*Easily controlled by habits and compulsions like alcohol, drugs, food, television, etc
*Overwhelming feelings of guilt of some harm done (e.g. military personnel returning from war)
*Easily offended and angered - very sensitive
*Difficulty to give and receive love, praise or approval
*Either overprotective and possessive, or on the opposite end extremely permissive and indulgent

Effects in the will:
*Either excessive workaholism, or on the opposite end complete unconcern for work, career or obligations (sluggard, couch potato, leisureholic, lazybones)
*Either excessive perfectionism (picky, fussy), or on the opposite end loose morals and inability to care on doing what's right (chaotic)
*Either extremely cautious to life, or on the opposite end extremely impulsive and reckless, prone to jumping from fire to fire
*Either extremely domineering personality (control freak, planet, godzilla, bridezilla), or the opposite end extremely weak-willed and easily manipulated (doormat or welcome mat, wimp)

*Exceptionally self-centered
*Exceptionally defensive (even where wrong) & easily shifting blame on others
*Either very stubborn & insensitive to correction (bullheaded, brain-dead), or on the opposite end easily influenced (flip-flop, spineless), preferring peace over integrity
*Either extremely self-driven & unhealthily independent, or on the opposite end extremely others-driven & helplessly dependent on others

Other characteristics surface through the personality make-up of each person. There are two personality extremes: introversion or extroversion. These are terms and studies from the secular academic world of psychology. There is nothing wrong or sinful about the secular academic world in its non-infiltrated context. It's matters that contradict or undermine the bible that are no, no for us.

Each of us, regardless of having or not having wounds has some combination of introversion and extroversion. The degree of introversion or extroversion varies from person to person depending partly on hereditary factors and partly on upbringing factors. No trait is better than another. They complement each other. The extreme flaws or spiritual wound effects of each trait are both as destructive.

Introversion
Introversion is a tendency to be shy, inward drawn and interested in one's thoughts and feelings than in other people or external events in the world. People with a high degree of introversion are characterized as introverts. They are said to be shy, quiet, less sociable, sensitive, cautious, constantly in deep thoughts and minding their own soul-searching business.

Extroversion
Extroversion is the opposite of introversion. It is a tendency to be self-confident in public, outgoing, social, friendly, and interest in things outside oneself than interest in inner feelings or thoughts. People with a high degree of extroversion are characterized as extroverts. They are said to be uninhibited with other people, sociable, friendly, outgoing, impulsive and many times in a jovial mood to please others.

Although these terms from the secular academic world of psychology are quite simplistic in describing our make-up quantitative research has shown the nature of extreme negative flaws that characterize each of the traits. The extreme flaws are called the weakness tendencies of each trait. In our Christian context we can call them effects of spiritual wounds on each trait.

Spiritual wounds predisposed to extroverts
The extreme negative flaws that characterize extroverts are usually opposite to introverts. They are more outward than inward. They include anti-social behavior, inability to care on doing what's right, violence, aggression,

criminal behavior, prostitution, and so on. Some extroverts may have extreme tendencies that are predominant among and characteristic of introverts but this is an exception rather than the norm. Having such tendencies could be due to having a high combination of introversion traits.

At their worst level of spiritual wounds extroverts end up harming other people, being a problem to society, and in prison if law enforcement agents take action. Needless to say that human law enforcement is desperately lacking in enforcing its authority on people that harm others through direct or indirect means such as greed, exploitation, harmful illegal drugs, detrimental and immoral products, services, songs, films, etc.

If many of these sinful acts that harm others could successfully be prosecuted there would be more people punished for adversely harming others. Many super rich people would be among them.

As Christians we have God's spiritual law enforcement agents that are far thorough in taking action than human law enforcement agents (police, legal system, etc). God ensures that matters intended to work against us are either blocked by his angels or are ultimately made to work to our good. We're able to seek his intervention with our spiritual weapons of war that are far mightier than human weapons (like arguments, lawsuits, physical confrontation, war, and so on). With punishment and vengeance ultimately being in his hands and power he is able to ensure the guilty are punished or mercifully have their eyes opened.

Spiritual wounds predisposed to introverts

The extreme flaws that characterize introverts include nervous and mental diseases that include depression, schizophrenia, worry and anxiety disorders, excessive perfectionism, feelings of inadequacy, hopelessness, mental illnesses and so on. At their worst level introverts end up under psychological care, in metal hospitals or attempt suicide. Some introverts may have extreme tendencies that are predominant among and characteristic of extroverts but this is an exception rather than the norm. This could be due to having a high combination of extroversion traits.

Why are introverts more prone than introverts to have spiritual wounds of such nature? Lucinda Bassett, from Midwest Center for Stress and Anxiety says it is because introverts are very analytical. They are natural born thinkers who have a tendency to analyze and ponder on matters –spiritual, social, economical, scientific, etc.

This is a natural gift they have because they have the mental energy and commitment to go an extra mile in using their minds. However, when this energy of thinking and analyzing is turned inward it easily turns into negative energy. The introvert begins to overanalyze matters that everyone goes through or are not new under the sun, and which others do not easily allow them to bring their spirits down.

The analytical and introspective traits of introverts can develop into unhealthy tendencies of perfectionism and sensitiveness. Common imperfections and ups and downs of life can easily break the inner strength of some introverts and cause them to break down.

Severe experiences are even more so unbearable to such who want everything in life to work perfectly smooth. By learning to see the world in its fallen state and overcoming the compulsion for perfection introverts nursing a wounded spirit can be able to deal with life's obstacles in a positive way. Healing becomes automatic.

Instead of destructive or negative thinking and analysis a constructive or positive thinking approach to matters in life can lift up one's spirit into a whole new experience of life. It can open new levels of faith, hope, experiences and opportunities that would never have been realized during the time of being preoccupied with the past or any imperfections.

Many that are stuck in a cycle of destructive or negative thinking and analysis are actually very intelligent and talented people (though many don't know that). Universities and history itself has a long list of the smartest at some point suffering from mental disorders.

When self-inflicting introverts overcome their destructive approach, cease playing the low self esteem and negativity inner songs many can find themselves in the most fulfilling careers, positions, outreach work, marriages, you name it... Developing their attitudes and perceptions on life can help them express the many talents they already have (though many don't even know what they have). A cloud of witnesses in heaven are cheering for them to utilize their gifts and make a difference in this world.

It's often said that our attitude more than our aptitude determines our altitude in life. Our attitude in the spiritual sense is faith in action. "By faith the people passed through the Red Sea as on dry land; but when the Egyptians tried to do so, they were drowned," Hebrews 11:29. What would otherwise drown somebody can be a path to success for a person of faith (positive attitude).

It's also said that, "All the water in the world won't sink a ship - unless it gets inside it." How we react to matters in life, not the matters themselves, influences how we'll navigate our way forward. The unpleasant water is all around us. Our challenge is to insure it does not get inside our boats of life.

Other spiritual wounds predisposed to introverts
The psychology of introversion and extroversion leads us to include other matters that secular and Christian counselors deal with. These matters can be said to be more prone among introverts than extroverts. They include a sensing of someone or something watching the victim. Or it may be a feeling of a presence behind or around the victim.

Other extreme cases include seeing evil spirits or hearing voices. It may also include spiritual attacks through dreams such as having frequent nightmares or sexual encounters in dreams. Some victims of spiritual wounds are constantly suspicious or fearful of others plotting against them.

They may be suspicious of even the closest people that matter most to them or that are reaching out to help them. Others are able to smell foul smells of demonic beings that others can neither see nor smell.

Some experiences may manifest in the physical. A believer may lose things and have no clue how they disappeared. Or a sudden breakdown of car, computer or whatever. Explaining these experiences to someone unfamiliar with what's going on makes him/her think the believer has mental problems.

Other experiences may be in a social area. People easily pick a negative perception of the believer with no apparent reason. They just look down on him/her. He/she may find himself moving from one job to another, one location to another or worse still, one relationship to another.

Such is an extreme case and usually involves one who has opened doorways through sins such as sexual sins, sins of unforgiveness, bitterness, harmful false doctrines, and so on.

Seeing such experiences in the life of an unbeliever may not be surprising. However seeing such experiences in a Christian this is very unfortunate because they can be avoided by applying the right biblical principles. May the Lord effectively use all that is being shared in this book to bring freedom in all the areas under demonic attack.

There is a lot of negative spiritual energy around one dealing with severe wounds of the spirit. That is why the bible says, "a crushed spirit who can bear?" Proverbs 18:14.

Life can be hard to bear for one with a severely injured spirit as well as for people around him/her. All kinds of hard to bear experiences, like the ones covered in this sub-topic, can come from one spiritually wounded. But thank God there is hope - plenty of hope. "With man this is impossible, but not with God; all things are possible with God," Mark 10:27.

Healing the Wounded Spirit: the Christian Approach

Healing the wounded spirit is primarily the work of the Holy Spirit. Many secular counselors, psychiatrists or psychotherapists have something to offer but a lot has to be integrated with spiritual principles.

There is actually much research and information we can benefit from the secular world of psychology and related medical fields. On the other hand, secular academics have also benefited from the bible by learning most workable principles from the scripture (with little or no acknowledgment to the bible). God's prescription is always the ultimate prescription.

Without the integration with spiritual or Christian principles the secular prescription is largely limited in its effect. That is why many under secular treatment are under perpetual care that they fail to stand and deal with matters on their own.

Secular counselors, psychiatrists or psychotherapists are popularly known as shrinks in USA. Its sarcastic meaning descends from an old term "headshrinker." This means a shrink shrinks the brain of a person by disabling him/her from thinking for himself or herself. In extreme cases a person literally ends up under the constant care of a counselor year after year. The word "shrink" now refers to all counselors, secular or Christian.

The challenge for those seeking counsel is to find a counselor who does not shrink one's brain but empowers it. By any rate the best counselor is one who connects a person with his/her true Counselor, the Holy Spirit. "I will ask the Father, and he will give you another Counselor to be with you forever-- the Spirit of truth. The world cannot accept him, because it neither sees him nor knows him. But you know him, for he lives with you and will be in you. I will not leave you as orphans," John 14:16-18.

The Holy Spirit lives inside each inside each of us born again Christians. We are like cared for orphans and not like ones left to struggle on their own against forces more powerful than them. The Holy Spirit has a parental role over us. He is able to bring true healing when we enable him to work in the innermost parts of us. Certain mindsets that evolved throughout our upbringing and through various experiences are transformed into Christ-like nature.

The transformation of our minds directly affects the other areas in our spirits - emotion and will areas. Only the Holy Spirit knows how to piece together matters of our past and use them to work to our good not against us. Secular counseling cannot enable this.

This is also not to say all of us Christian counselors are better than secular counselors. There are some Christian counselors who use false teachings in their counseling or deliverance ministries. These false teachings end up doing as much damage, if not worse, on innocent believers seeking deliverance.

Of major concern are deliverance ministries that easily jump to bind and cast out demons from people who are under demonic influence, not demonic possession. They shrink the brains of innocent believers who seek deliverance by casting out demons that are not in a believer.

When the Christian returns home in the same state he/she assumes he could have some powerful demons inside him. Christian shrinks have done the harm by focusing on non-applicable matters. Once these innocent souls finally get to where there is biblical deliverance it can be quite a battle in convincing them that the problem is not demonic possession but demonic influence.

Other battles include moving them away from harmful false teachings innocently adopted through books, multimedia and ministries that preach false doctrine. Some are preoccupied with binding and loosing demons, pleading the blood of Jesus against evil spirits (which is a way of talking to them), speaking in so called spiritual warfare tongues, spiritual warfare or deliverance prayers against evil spirits, and so on.

Most of them are very intelligent Christians yet can still be misled when they seek deliverance out of desperation not biblical truth. The believers can end up with more demonic activity after embracing harmful false teachings.

That is why this book was inspired - to enable Christians to avoid deliverance ministries that invite more demonic activity and to equip the body of Christ with biblical principles of deliverance as well as spiritual warfare. These principles if applied provide the required counsel for biblical deliverance and healing in areas of interest.

No need of further counseling if one reads and applies the biblical principles in this book. Reading through more than once may help in grasping certain unclear areas. Plus there are more resources online at our websites: JesusW.com and SpiritualWarfareDeliverance.com (the two websites for Jesus Work Ministry are interlinked through easy navigation).

Avoid rushing to any nearest deliverance ministry that tries to cast out demons that are actually operating from outside, not inside. You'll avoid much heartache by following Christ-centered principles instead of demon-centered ones. Christ-centered principles may not have a lot of drama and sensation yet they work.

So where do we start in applying the Christ-centered principles that enable the Holy Spirit to bring deliverance and healing to the wounded spirit?

1) Drawing closer to God, effectively connecting with the Holy Spirit

A wounded spirit is a result of matters in the distant past even in areas unknown or long forgotten. It can also include recent afflictions one may be going through. To identify the root causes from thousands or even millions of experiences in life is not humanly possible. Only the Holy Spirit who's knowledge is infinite knows how to take care of such a puzzle.

That is why secular psychology and related fields of study are limited. Much has been unearthed through these noble fields. But they cannot replace a responsibility that is primarily spiritual. How else would you explain former prisoners, drug addicts, prostitutes, homosexuals, victims of abuse, emotional wretches, and son on, being more likely to change and receive deliverance through God's word than through all the secular counseling they could get?

Even Christian counseling ought to admit its limits in such a work of piecing together one's entire life and hoping to fix it. I grieve with anyone who ended up with more wounds after innocently visiting deliverance ministries that apply false doctrine on deliverance. There are heaven destined born again Christians today having a hard time living on earth partly due to spiritual wounds and partly due to having fallen into the wrong hands.

From these deliverance ministries a councilor (usually the pastor) would listen to a problem and before long begin to identify spirits attacking the victim. For instance it could be alleged that they are generational spirits, territorial spirits, spirits of lust, witch spirits, spirits of infirmity, familiar spirits, jezebel spirits, spirits of homosexuality, spirits of prostitution, and so on.

The entire life of a believer is said to be in the hands of one or more of these spirits. Once they are cast out freedom comes. The spirits are ordered to come out but deliverance does not come. Why not? The evil spirits were not even in the believer in the first place. Demonic influence from an external position was the cause, not demonic possession, the indwelling of demons. What may follow in a believer's life is usually application of false doctrine after false doctrine hoping to find freedom.

But there is a way out for every sincere believer. No need to blame any ministry embracing false doctrine for any further losses you may have faced - spiritually, socially, materially and so on. Categorize the experience as a storm of life in which God allowed it to occur without choosing to stop it.

If he allowed it in your sincere search he knows how to work the entire experience to your good. The ministries that embrace false doctrines on deliverance are mostly sincere but deceived saints. It is not deliberate misinterpretation of scripture if it's from deceived saints. Explaining why God allows such harmful deception in the body of Christ is another lengthy topic with its own limitations.

Our work as Christian counselors in deliverance ministry is to enable wounded believers, most of whom are intelligent people, to effectively connect with the Holy Spirit. God desires to walk with each of us on a personal, one to one level, not through another human being who assumes to be more spiritual. When this direct relationship is consolidated we're able to effectively deal with matters in our own lives.

In the case of a wounded spirit the Holy Spirit will be able to make the matters to work to our good instead of against us. He is also able to show us the key doorways that are allowing demonic influence (not demonic possession).

2) Prayerfully searching for doorways of entry
As we draw near to God and submit to his will we also prayerfully search for doorways that are allowing demonic influence. There is no need to wait for some strange discernment or a supernatural word from God while searching. God may speak in a still small voice in our hearts but this usually comes in the midst of the search. Staying still and hoping God will speak is as dangerous as transcendental meditation and yoga.

God gave us a mind to use and he usually speaks through it. It is not evil to think. The only difference with unbelievers is that we have "the mind of Christ" (1 Corinthians 2:16) controlled by the Spirit of God.

After praying to hear from God the next step is to apply your faith of believing that he has answered your prayers. You begin to think and think, read and read, on areas relating to your obstacle.

Key matters of the past that need to be effectively dealt with may have come through any of the four doorways: 1) deception, 2) ignorance, 3) sin, and 4) storms of life (when responded to in a wrong way).

3) Basic steps of faith to deliverance and healing

The doorways that have been found need to be placed on his mercy seat (through repentance). One can now move to applying the basic steps of faith to deliverance and healing:

1) prayer of repentance for walking outside God's will,

2) ceasing all known association and practice of matters that bring bondage through a) deception (false teachings), b) through ignorance (lack of knowledge), c) through sin, and d) through storms of life (when responded to in a wrong way),

3) being familiar with and applying biblical requirements in areas were deliverance and healing is sought (most biblical requirements in different areas are covered in this book), and

4) a simple prayer to ask God for continued guidance, equipping and grace in opening one's eyes to true biblical living.

Repentance on matters that came through storms of life is necessary when our response to them was in a sinful way. For example if one had an abusive upbringing and remains bitter about it, the bitterness and anger constitutes unforgiveness. Unforgiveness is a sin. Repentance for being bitter, angry or vengeful begins the healing process.

Prayer and fasting may be necessary on certain matters. We are dealing with spiritual strongholds that have consolidated their make-up in our lives. These are mindsets, emotions and defense mechanisms that have evolved throughout years of our upbringing and through various experiences. They become our identity and demonic influence has reinforced their hold on us.

Prayer and fasting is one of, if not, the greatest key to deliverance and healing. Please see the section on prayer and fasting as a major weapon to deliverance and healing.

Prayer and fasting enables the Holy Spirit to effectively work in the innermost parts of us. He is able to overcome certain mindsets, emotions and defense mechanisms that we find difficult to give up or unwilling to let go. He transforms our minds to value his ways than our ways.

The transformation of our minds directly affects the other areas in our spirits - emotion and will areas. However he also works on these areas individually until we each have "a spirit of power, of love and of self-discipline," 2 Timothy 1:7.

Power is an aspect of the Holy Spirit's ability to act, love is an emotional aspect of his nature and self-discipline is the will aspect of his nature. He throws away our nature which has no power to act over spiritual influences, he removes the dirt in our emotions while putting love in them and he removes our un-disciplined will which fluctuates according to circumstances and other external influences.

Above all the Holy Spirit enables us to grow in having "the mind of Christ," (1 Corinthians 2:16) so that we can effectively be under his influence, guidance and nature.

Once a human spirit begins to take on his nature the healing is in progress. Being under his nature is a lifelong work because the sinful nature in us always tries to return to its former throne. Demonic influence works through the sinful nature. That is how Adam and Eve fell. And that is why the bible cautions us to flee influences and situations that feed on the sinful nature.

People will notice the difference by the time the Holy Spirit reaches an advanced stage in working inside us. We will be producing not fruits from our negative past but the fruit of the Holy Spirit. "The fruit of the Spirit is love, joy, peace, patience, kindness, goodness, faithfulness, gentleness and self-control. Against such things there is no law. Those who belong to Christ Jesus have crucified the sinful nature with its passions and desires. Since we live by the Spirit, let us keep in step with the Spirit," Galatians 5: 22-25.

One who is bearing such fruit in abundance has a healthy spirit. He/she may not be perfect in every way or may not have all she desires yet she is an overcomer in the spirit realm. Demonic influence bounces off for as long as the Holy Spirit works in her life.

No demons cast out. Simply a truth encounter in God's word, abiding in Christ, prayerfulness and allowing the Holy Spirit to effectively work deep inside of us. Prayer and fasting actually does a lot of cleansing in us. It allows the Holy Spirit to search us and expose matters we easily took for granted.

Once healing progresses and a healthy spirit sets in we're able to effectively focus on the work of Christ. Instead of constantly being overwhelmed with our own problems we're able to see clearly problems of a lost world. Instead of bearing a wounded spirit from the devil's assault we begin to take on the marks of Christ. The marks of Christ come from enduring persecution and living a sacrificial life.

Living a sacrificial life is something that hardly preoccupies us when nursing a wounded spirit. It sounds nice and heroic but we feel it's for some people out there. A healthy spirit on the other hand, is burdened with love for its worldwide neighbors. It is abounding in the fruit of the Holy Spirit.

A healthy spirit can lay its interests down in preference for bigger problems around it. It is outward focused rather than consumed with itself or consumed with trying to fit in among the Joneses of this world.

Whatever it is able to give a healthy spirit willingly stretches out. It could be prayers, prayer and fasting sacrifices, finances, time or skills, it willingly stretches out. A healthy spirit adopts a biblical formula for reaping a blessed life without even realizing it.

Is getting to this level really possible? It is as the bible says it thousands of times in word and through hundreds of examples. Please apply the principles to deliverance and healing and you will be amazed over time as the Holy Spirit works in your life.

If you are burdened for someone please do not neglect the discipline of prayer and fasting. It is a powerful weapon against spiritual strongholds. It's not an easy cross to carry with all kinds of excuses we can have. But it's more than possible through God's enabling. "God is able to make all grace abound to you, so that in all times, having all that you need, you will abound in every good work," (2 Corinthians 9:8).

Healing the Wounded Spirit: the Secular Approach

In the secular professional world matters dealing with the wounded spirit are classified as anxiety disorders. The Anxiety Disorders Association of America (ADAA) groups anxiety disorders in the following categories: a) generalized anxiety disorders, b) panic disorders and agoraphobia, c) obsessive-compulsive disorders, d) posttraumatic stress disorders, e) social phobia (social anxiety), and f) specific phobia.

The study of anxiety disorders is a relatively new science that's still evolving. Caution and personal research is needed in seeking proper treatment to avoid ending up as a failed experimental guinea pig. Caution is particularly needed when one is prescribed medication. Medication has more controversy than psychotherapy as will be covered below.

There are two main types of treatment available for all anxiety disorders: a) medication, and b) psychotherapy. There are different medications and different psychotherapy treatments for different anxiety disorders. Some treatments have been known to work for another or combination of anxiety disorders while others have been known to have disastrous results. Unique differences of anxiety disorders among individuals have also added to the complexity of treatment for anxiety disorders.

A) Medication
Medication has from its onset had its controversies. It has had its fierce opponents like Lynn Henderson, who directs the Shyness Clinic in California, and Philip Zimbardo, a psychologist at Stanford University, who believe medication only tries to sweep issues under the carpet and not solve anything.

There are different kinds of medications that have been used to treat social anxiety disorders. The WebMD lists the following: "antidepressants, like Paxil; tranquilizers (benzodiazepines), such as Xanax, Librium, Valium, and Ativan; beta-blockers, often used to treat heart conditions, may also be used to minimize certain physical symptoms of anxiety, such as shaking and rapid heartbeat," (WebMD, Inc, webmd.com).

The main issue to note about medication is that it can help in the short run in adjusting. However, in the long-run it has the potential of being addictive to the point of not being able to function without it. That is why it has fierce opponents. People can get stuck on medication for years or for life, without dealing with the root causes.

Side effects of some medication include drowsiness, dizziness, headaches, nausea, and weight gain. Withdrawal symptoms have been experienced by some when they stop taking medication. Withdrawal symptoms have included severe depression and suicidal thoughts or attempts.

B) Psychotherapy

Psychotherapy has more advocates than for medication although the two can easily be used in combination by mental health professionals. Psychotherapy involves talking with a trained mental health professional, such as a psychiatrist, psychologist, social worker, or counselor to learn how to deal with problems like anxiety disorders.

Advocates for psychotherapy, like Thomas A. Richards, argue that psychotherapy has the best approach to solving anxiety disorders. A term was born in the 1980s to define the psychotherapy treatment method for anxiety disorders: cognitive-behavioral therapy (CBT).

The major aim of CBT is to reduce anxiety by eliminating beliefs, mental associations and behaviors that bring about the anxiety disorder. Cognitive-behavioral therapy, as its name suggests, has two parts: 1) the cognitive component, and 2) the behavioral component.

The National Institute of Mental Health (NIMH) says the cognitive component helps people change thinking patterns that keep them from overcoming their fears. For example, a person with a social anxiety disorder might be helped to overcome the belief that others are continually watching and harshly judging him or her.

The behavioral component of CBT seeks to change people's reactions to anxiety-provoking situations. A key element of this component is exposure, in which people confront the things they fear.

For example, a person with social anxiety may be encouraged to spend time in feared social situations without giving in to the temptation to flee. In some cases the individual will be asked to deliberately make what appears to be slight social blunders and observe other people's reactions; if they are not as harsh as expected, the person's social anxiety may begin to fade.

Some people who have successfully conquered their fears through cognitive-behavioral therapy (CBT) can experience a relapse after long periods of success. The NIMH says that, "Recurrences can be treated effectively, just like an initial episode. In fact, the skills you learned in dealing with the initial episode can be helpful in coping with a setback," (National Institute of Mental Health (NIMH).

CBT has its offspring among professionals who have modified the principles to the point of creating different approaches. A notable one is known as Solution-Oriented Brief Therapy (SBT) or Solution Focused Psychotherapy. Its approach is less past or problem-centered and more solution-centered, a process which is more effective, brief and more empowering.

Michele Weiner-Davis is a proponent of Solution-Oriented Brief Therapy (SBT), an approach that she uses to help people overcome their obstacles on their own rather than relying on so called "experts" for constant care. She believes professionals like her are meant to empower clients to solve their own obstacles rather than dump matters on counselors to solve them.

In her audio book, *Fire Your Shrink*, Weiner-Davis says, "The countless people who have triumphed over physical illness, poverty, abuse, loss, and emotional devastation, are true experts (in overcoming obstacles on their own). Let's learn from them, instead of obsessing over humanity's dark side then running to professionals (psychotherapists, counselors, etc) in the hope that they can cure what ails us.

"The idea that "experts" don't have all the answers may not win any popularity contest. A tremendous amount of security is derived in believing in "experts." But it's a false sense of security that in no way compares to the strength you get from knowing that you can depend on yourself.

"Since I'm one of those so called "experts" I realize that it may seem somewhat paradoxical for me to tell you to take expert advice off its pedestal (and see it for what it really is), but it's not paradoxical at all… My goal is to put the self back in self-help (to be your own expert and thereby help yourself overcome obstacles)," Weiner-Davis, *Fire Your Shrink* (parentheses added for clarification).

Weiner-Davis' book and audio book can be purchased online at her website, DivorceBusting.com. The website is more than about "divorce busting," that is why she has books such as *Fire Your Shrink.* Click on the top link "Divorce Busting Store," or on the left link "Audio CDs and Tapes." The book version of *Fire Your Shrink* has been renamed to *Change Your Life and Everyone in It.*

About the book and audio book, her website says, "The truth is, as Michele Weiner-Davis discovered when she set out to practice psychotherapy, you don't have to go on a psycho-archaeology expedition to solve your problems (like the CBT approach tends to emphasize with its problem centered approach).

"Exploring your childhood doesn't help you to escape the stranglehold of the past. Knowing why you behave destructively doesn't stop you from overeating or overreacting, curb depression or panic attacks, or build healthy, happy relationships. Even worse, continually thinking and talking about problems makes you feel hopeless.

"Determined to find a better way, Michele developed a radically different approach, based on the principles of Solution-oriented Brief Therapy (SBT). Suddenly she was witnessing spectacular triumphs. People who had been stuck for years turned their lives around within days. The transformations were real, immediate, and lasting.

"Drawing on more than a decade of experience with individuals, couples, and families, Michele explains:
- why looking to the past for understanding prolongs the problem
- how to find "the expert within" and break free of unproductive ways of thinking, feeling, and acting
- how to translate overwhelming problems into achievable goals
- how, despite what you've been told, you can change other people as well as yourself."

Other recommended secular professionals include, Lucinda Bassett, from Midwest Center for Stress and Anxiety. She has a self-help, drug free program called Attacking Anxiety & Depression. Her material is more expensive at around $450.00 compared to Weiner-Davis' $9.95 for her audio book. Her approach is similar to that of Weiner-Davis, focusing on empowering people than shrinking their brains.

Bassett actually does emphasize the importance of spiritually in dealing with matters in life though she falls short of stating what religion she believes is the answer. One hopes people will interpret it to be Christianity. Her website is at StressCenter.com.

Please check out our website at our spiritual warfare and deliverance section (SpiritualWarfareDeliverance.com) for any updates we may later have on Christian as well as secular approaches to healing the wounded spirit.

God's "Plan B" and Maintaining a Healthy Spirit

Maintaining a healthy spirit is a lifelong exercise and challenge. There are no stops. A believer can graduate from one level of spiritual health and healing to another only to fall down and suffer some spiritual wounds. God forbid that any of us ever experiences any other spiritual injuries.

Maintaining a healthy spirit comes through avoiding matters that can bring spiritual injury thus result in a wounded spirit. It comes through avoiding matters that Satan can use as legal entry into our lives. His legal entry comes through any of the spiritual doorways covered in this book. These are through 1) deception, 2) ignorance, 3) sin, and 4) storms of life.

Avoiding matters that give access to Satan does not come by shear personal determination. It's not by personal might, nor guts, nor power. The bible is clear on this. It comes through our intimate walk with God. This enables the Holy Spirit to effectively live in us, his temples, and overcome anything contrary to his nature.

Through the Holy Spirit we are enabled to know "all truth" (John 16:13) in required areas that Satan seeks to gain entry through 1) deception, 2) ignorance, 3) sin, and 4) storms of life.

He also enables us to look at sin the way it really is. We're able to see sin as a fake coating of honey containing nothing but poison that is harmful to us spiritually, socially, materially and physically. Temptation may come but his inner voice will enable us not to succumb to it.

As for storms of life the Holy Spirit uses them as assets to work to our good. Instead of being assets that Satan would like to use to block us from moving forward the Holy Spirit closes his access. God allows storms of life to happen but does not plot them against us. He only does not stop them.

If God allows them to come our way, as bad as they may be, he surely has plan B to ensure whatever happened eventually benefits us. God's "plan B" is anything good he can fulfill out of whatever negative matters we may experience in life. Instead of Satan bringing destruction upon us God frustrates Satan's plans and fulfills the unimaginable out of them.

Think of Joseph, the man who later told his bad brothers, "You intended to harm me, but God intended it for good," Genesis 50:20. It's nice to read the story but imagine yourself in his shoes. You get sold as a slave, stripped off all your human dignity.

All the lovely dreams of royalty vanished, your childhood robed, family bond robed, and anything else you would want to live for. You know there is a mighty God out there but what have you done to find yourself in this? Nothing.

Maybe you gain some hope that somehow this God will rescue you. So you keep going faithfully serving in your slavery. Then more strange events happen. You're accused of attempting to rape a wife of a high ranking governor. It's all over the media. You're further reduced from a slave to an animal that lives on instinctive drives rather than reason.

Could this God have forsaken you? Can anything get worse than this? I've worked jobs where a lot of cash is handled and the mere suspicion that I was pilfering made me want to quit. Being thought of as a thief was hurting enough to bring distress. What more an accusation Joseph got?

We seem to have a lot of easy answers on how Joseph coped with the severe storms that befell him. But the whole truth is that God kept him in the midst of it all.

Joseph did not have some high determination and guts to continue trusting in God. He was as frail as any of us. And he had no bible to read on the faithfulness of God. Put in his shoes many of us would rather be dead. Yet God in his power is able to sustain us if we go through the worst of experiences.

When we get out we even wonder how we came out alive, sane and still Christians. It's unfortunate when some depart from the faith or end up in sin or compromise that brings more bondage. This is another side of the story, but glory be to God for those of us who came out alive and Christian.

May he use us to save others that can be vulnerable to Satan's schemes during storms. No one deserves to face destruction, especially after becoming a Christian. May God use us to stand in the gap and allow him to frustrate Satan's attempts while fulfilling his plan B.

Through God all things are possible, bearable, and can be overcome. Unlike Joseph we have the bible to encourage us. With God's word richly living in us the Holy Spirit is able to effectively use it when storms come. He enables us to effectively respond to storms in a way that blocks Satan from using them to work against us.

During my worst trial or is it worst experience of reaping from igno-rance, I concluded the best option was dying. Not through suicide but asking God to take my life. I cried almost daily seeking to be in heaven than in this weird world. Seeing that death never came I kept praying and fasting for God to do something about it if I was to be of any use here on earth. He did - eventu-ally, after six torturous months.

Between the trial (or reaping to ignorance in my case) and the break-through Satan had no room of using the experience to bring destruction. God took over and kept working out plan B on matters he never orchestrated. He probably tells his angels, "Satan can try whatever he wants but I can still use any situation for good."

God used it to reveal the false teachings on spiritual warfare and deliv-erance, inspired this book, brought the call into deliverance ministry, and many other matters that cannot be quantified. For anyone in a storm please forget not the discipline of prayer and fasting. Fasting is a powerful weapon in the realm of the spirit. It enables God to fight for us and work on "plan B."

Storms of life do not spell doom for us for as long as our response is in a way that blocks Satan from using them against us. Whether from past or current experiences God can still use them to work to our good. He did it for Joseph, for Jesus, the early disciples and many saints of God throughout history. Why not for us? Yes he still does today. He's the same God who changeth not.

Past or present storms of life are unpleasant experiences that befall us out of no fault of our own.

They include experiences of living under constant negative and critical words; experiences of betrayal (by a loved one; trusted person, or leader); death of a loved one; severe physical or emotional abuse experiences; living under a heavy control and disciplinary environment that brings fear; living under rejection; false accusations; terrible divorce experience (as the victim); traumatic experience(s), severe accident (e.g. surviving 911 terrorist experience, traumatic accident, casualty of war); having a physical or social disability; having a certain physical appearance society "persecutes;" severe racial, gender and ethnic discrimination or abuse; falling victim to false teachings; genuine trials of faith; and so on.

A victim of whatever storm of life ought to focus on God's power, sovereignty and love in fulfilling "plan B." For instance, one can say to himself/herself, "Satan may have created this mess but God who is more powerful knows how to use it to bring out the best for his glory." Not saying it out of arrogance but out of humility of being God's child. He is the God who fights our battles. God will make a way, where there seems to be no way... Most of us know the song.

Another may say to himself/herself, "It was not a mistake to be born in family Y or living with guardian(s) Y. Neither was it a mistake to be born or living in location Z.

"I am not a mistake, regardless of how, where or when I was born, my appearance, gender, race, tongue, having certain strengths, having certain weaknesses, abilities, disabilities and so on. God "fearfully and wonderfully," (Psalms 139:14) put all these ingredients together for a particular purpose.

"I may not understand everything but bit by bit I'll be seeing his purposes unfold in my life. I may not like everything about this whole set up but he knows how to work every piece to work to my good. He's more powerful than forces that may try to set limits against me due to matters I only found myself into. My role is to focus on him, obey his word and allow him to fulfill his ultimate plan over this entire set-up I found myself in."

For any of us our resolve ought to be that whatever our limitations they cannot hinder God from fulfilling his ultimate plans for our lives. He's the one in charge, not our circumstances.

Our circumstances whether from past or present experiences can roar like Goliath if they want to. But the final choice is on each one of us. Whose report will you believe -the report of circumstances or the report of the Lord in his written word? One is proclaiming doom while the other proclaiming hope. One is proclaiming a curse while the other is proclaiming a blessing.

"See, I am setting before you today a blessing and a curse-- the blessing if you obey the commands of the Lord your God that I am giving you today; the curse if you disobey the commands of the Lord your God and turn from the way that I command you today by following other gods, which you have not known," Deuteronomy 11:26-28.

The Lord is still saying the same words to each of us today. We either obey his word or obey our circumstances. Satan will try to be crafty enough to influence us to make choices based on circumstances so that our lives are hindered -spiritually, socially, materially, physically and so on. He did that to Adam and Eve.

He's still busy doing this in the lives of many people, Christians and non-Christians. Scripture says we're to be vigilant and alert of his tactics. "Be self-controlled and alert. Your enemy the devil prowls around like a roaring lion looking for someone to devour," 1 Peter 5:8.

During severe storms (God forbid) it's good to confide in someone that can continue drawing you closer to God. Avoid discussing your obstacles with people that Satan can use to fulfill his scheme of destruction. They are destiny killers, blocking God from working out "plan B." Some could even be Christians -sincere but deceived.

You can cry all your lungs out before God but not before fellow power-less souls. Same may even be happy you're in a fix so don't waste your time. You can share your burdens with a Christian confidant who has proved to be really interested in helping.

He/she does not have to entirely agree with your approach to the problem but is still able to pray with you. If you have none you can seek counsel from our ministry at JesusW.com and SpiritualWarfareDeliverance.com (the two websites for Jesus Work Ministry are interlinked through easy navigation).

Fast as often as you can though with understanding on principles of fasting. Please see the section on prayer and fasting as a major spiritual weapon to deliverance and healing. Great if your Christian confidant is also able to fast with you. Fasting is essential during crisis moments.

This is seen in the Israelite history. They fasted during crisis moments and more often than not God quickly came to their rescue. So fasting does facilitate the deliverance and healing process. Also continue a serious search for any doorways of Satan's legal entry in your life.

Deliverance from Hearing Voices, Seeing Demons, etc

This is one area of a wounded spirit. Some believe they're demon pos-sessed because they sometimes sense, see, hear, smell or even feel evil spirit beings. So demons have to be cast out.

Though this book deliberately makes repetitions on key point to stress their importance it may not be worth a detailed repetition here that a Christian cannot be demon possessed. Please read Chapter 6 on this topic. The bible is clear here no matter what scriptures some may try to twist to say otherwise.

Being God's children our spirits are sealed as God's own temples. They cannot be defiled by any evil spirits. However, our spirits being sealed does automatically translate to our bodies and human senses (hearing, sight, smell, touch) being sealed. Anything that is temporal, that we'll leave behind, is not a big issue to God – compared to our spiritual identity that we'll take with us.

If God extremely cared about our outward issues believers would all turn out to have supermodel looks, be super rich, super healthy, have super minds and he'd never allow us to face any problem. This will be so in heaven. Not so in this life. Down here God has chosen to be more concerned with one major area – our spiritual identity.

That is why God allows trials of faith into our lives. They're not pleasant but they really strengthen our walk with him. He also allows persecution which to him is a blessing to us. What? We're even to rejoice over it because great is our reward in heaven. No kidding. "Blessed are you when people insult you, persecute you and falsely say all kinds of evil against you because of me. Rejoice and be glad, because great is your reward in heaven, for in the same way they persecuted the prophets who were before you," Matthew 5:11-12.

Thus God may allow unpleasant matters to come our way while also guarding matters that can compromise our spiritual identity. In addition our lives may also have open doors in certain areas. These areas give access to demons to cause trouble.

So demons can have access to what may not be the ultimate of God's concern - his concern is our spiritual identity. Plus their access can only be from an external position, an aspect of demonic influence. Even where a believer actually feels strange things moving in the body it does not imply they are inside. The body is not the spirit part of us. It's just a vessel our human spirits use to relate with the physical world.

If demons get any access to the body it's still from any external position since the real part of us, the spirit, which demons would love to possess is not accessible to them.

Remember Paul who received a thorn in the flesh from Satan that brought much pain and discomfort in his life. Was he demon possessed? "There was given me a thorn in my flesh, a messenger of Satan, to torment me," 2 Corinthians 12:7.

And the demonic torment in his body that he experienced was not an entry of demons into his body. Just as they cannot enter our spiritual faculties they cannot enter our physical bodies. They can however have such access to our bodies from an external point that it may seem like they're inside. Remember these are spirits that have no physical boundaries.

What some believers and ministries easily classify as demonic possession is actually demonic influence. Seeing, smelling, sensing, or hearing demon spirits implies one previously tapped or got access into the spirit world through whatever doorway: 1) deception, 2) ignorance, 3) sin, or 4) storms of life.

An individual is now able to sense, see, smell, or hear spirit beings that we're not to ordinarily perceive. People involved in the occult and witchcraft are more prone to this. Some sincere believers previously involved in false teachings on spiritual warfare that bombard evil spirits are also prone. So are some who once experienced severe emotional or physical abuse.

This does not imply an individual is possessed by these beings - at least not after receiving Jesus as Lord and Savior. Rather it is that his/her eyes are now open to seeing the supernatural. Demons (fallen angels), like God's angels are all around us. We just don't see them. We are not supposed to. God gave us the earth to take care of not the heavens or the spirit world to be preoccupied with.

In rare cases God can allow any one of us to see activities in the spirit world. For example God allowed Elisha's servant to see the vast angels protecting them when he was afraid of enemy forces (2 Kings 6:16-17). It would be a wonderful experience seeing God's angels, not demons.

When my mother was departing she was full of joy with angels singing around her. The experience was confusing to my siblings but she was having a great time receiving a welcome party to heaven.

An individual who can see and hear demonic spirits does not mean the demons have gained more power over him/her. They are as powerless as the ones not seen. They can scream and say "we're watching you," but that does not mean they have any power over you.

If someone comes to your house and screams at you with threats and demanding you to get out does not make him/her powerful. Besides there are police officers right around you and you have access to all government's legal authority.

The same is the case in the spirit realm. You have God's angels right around you and you have access to God's throne to block them should they try to get to you. You may not see God's angels but they are around us 24/7. As long as God has broken the legal hold of demons over you they have no power over you. Let them scream and talk but ignore them as if they don't exist.

Deliverance and healing

How does one receive deliverance from hearing and seeing demons or evil spirits? The same way as all the other areas requiring deliverance. In God's eyes the cure is the same for all afflictions. However we have made it seem like some afflictions need special deliverance because of their severity. Believers being told they need special deliverance end up moving from one "deliverance ministry" to another, sometimes coming out with worse afflictions than before.

Firstly, a believer needs to be open to searching for doorways in his/her life that may have given access to experiencing and seeing in the spirit world. It could have been through any one or combination of 1) deception, 2) ignorance, 3) sin, or 4) storms of life (when responded to in a wrong way).

1) Deception, and 2) Ignorance
These two usually go hand in hand

Some could be beliefs embraced by certain churches that are not biblical. These include erroneous teachings on spiritual warfare, spiritual warfare prayers, deliverance prayers, binding and loosing demons, most of modern day speaking in tongues, the Rosary and praying to Mary (instead of to God, our heavenly Father), pleading the blood or sprinkling the blood of Jesus (instead of taking holy communion like Jesus instructed us), transcendental meditation, yoga, horoscopes and so on.

(In case you need detailed info on modern versions of speaking in tongues, etc, please visit GotQuestions.org. It's a Christian website that answers questions from a biblical perspective. They do not dispute all modern day versions but caution on going into non-biblical practices (some of us learnt of it the hard way). You can type in your query in the search bar. Please make use of such resources, including resources at our website and public or church library resources for questions unanswered in this book. Do email us a question to consider answering in the next edition or adding to the website. But the volume of email received makes it unbearable to reply to every person that writes).

Most of these can open doors to seeing and hearing demonic forces. The beliefs and practices tap into the wrong spirit world, making Christians able to see or experience unpleasant demonic activities.

What is required is only repentance for the non-biblical practices, occasional fasting for some, and the truth being applied. Deliverance follows while healing may not be overnight. Please read sub-topics that distinguish between deliverance and healing.

3) Sin
The most common sins associated with such experiences include bitterness, anger, unforgiveness, vengeance, and so on, over past wrongs one innocently experienced as a victim. Culprits or offenders against innocent people are also prone though they may also experience other non-spiritual torment.

Deliverance and healing here needs to be combined with aspects of social healing. Please see the next section of Chapter 9 (Part 5) which focuses on deliverance and healing in social areas.

4) Storms of life
Storms of life are unpleasant experiences that befall us out of no fault of our own. These include experiences of living under constant negative and critical words; experiences of betrayal (by a loved one; trusted person, or leader); death of a loved one; severe physical or emotional abuse experiences; living under a heavy control and disciplinary environment that brings fear; living under rejection; false accusations; terrible divorce experience (as the victim); traumatic experience(s), severe accident (e.g. surviving 911 terrorist experience, traumatic accident, casualty of war); having a physical or social disability; having a certain physical appearance society "persecutes;" severe racial, gender and ethnic discrimination or abuse; falling victim to false teachings; genuine trials of faith; and so on.

Victims of trauma are among common cases of people that experience spiritual torment to the extent of seeing, hearing, and experiencing demonic activities. But there is a solution through Christ no matter what incidences opened one's spiritual faculties to be able to see, hear and experience the evil side of the spirit world.

Closing the legal doorways

After finding matters that were root causes of demonic visions and voices a believer needs to deal with these areas to close the legal doorways. No demons need to be cast out of a born again Christian. The problem is with external influence (an aspect of demonic influence), not with internal influence (an aspect of demonic possession).

A believer's prayer and appeal to God is to seek God to close his/her spiritual eyes and faculties from seeing, hearing and sensing these spirit beings. He'll need to continue seeking the Lord's deliverance and healing from not being able to see, hear and sense these spirit beings.

When the Lord brings this victory it means that his faculties have been restored to the level we are ordinarily made of - not being able to see, hear nor sense evil spirits.

This will not mean their demonic influence (not possession) attempts have ended. It will only mean their power to inflict underserved spiritual torment from their external influence has ended. They can no longer be seen, heard or sensed so they can make all the noise they wish but a person is shielded from seeing into the spirit realm. If we all could ordinarily see into the spirit realm it wouldn't be a pleasant experience constantly watching ugly beings.

It'd be nice to sometimes see God's angels conquering the demons though. Our faith would be energized, knowing that those who're with us are more than those against us. But that'll be walking by sight (what we see) instead of faith (trusting God and his word). Maybe that's why God doesn't allow it.

Please read Chapter 6. Exception for Direct Confrontation where the distinction between demonic possession and demonic influence is made. Chapter 2: Our Territory and Nature of Our Christian Authority explains what binding and loosing according to the Bible is, not according to some "deliverance ministries."

All this is emphasized so that you don't have to run to ministries that bring more bondage instead of deliverance, by being preoccupied with casting out demons that have already been evicted by the Holy Spirit. Being Christ-centered instead of demon-centered is the key to deliverance and healing

Standing in faith and obedience to God throughout healing process

No need to speak to spirit beings. In fact please do not speak to them. Some believers I have counseled have said speaking to them makes them leave for a while. But they still come back.

There is no need to keep going in circles. The demons end up playing hide and seek. They claim to be inside a believer (an aspect of demonic possession), when they are actually operating from outside (an aspect of demonic influence). Playing their game keeps them working through the doorways.

There is no scriptural example where someone was speaking to spirit beings except those demon possessed. You or your born again loved one cannot be demon possessed. A born again believer cannot be Holy Spirit possessed and demon possessed at the same time. Your experiences are a result of demonic influence and not demonic possession.

Speaking to evil spirits in thin air is not scriptural. Yes Jesus spoke to the devil in the wilderness but look at its context. Did the prophets do it? No. Did the disciples do it? No. Did the apostles do it? No. Neither should we.

Speaking to evil spirits only invites their presence. It is calling them forth or summoning them into a sphere that your spirit and senses are able to recognize and interact with them. It is tapping into the spirit world, the wrong spirit world. Once your spirit and senses are able to recognize and interact with them the experiences are nothing but ugly.

Some experiences may seem like one is demon possessed yet it is mere demonic influence. Some so called deliverance ministries rush to categorize some experiences as demonic possession that are actually from demonic influence. They cast out evil spirits that are not even in a person. Because this is not what's required a person who has non-existent demons cast out ends up never experiencing any deliverance. He/she feels more confused wondering why the demons have not gone.

This is because the demons were never inside. The individual may begin feeling more discouraged and defeated. He may assume there could be something wrong with him for having demons not being able to be cast out. What is actually wrong are the deliverance ministries that label nearly every problem as an aspect of demonic possession. It is the deliverance ministry, not a believer in the wrong.

Sometimes the intensity of demonic influence increases after going to these supposed deliverance ministries. Their intensity increases not from an internal influence (an aspect of demonic possession), but from an external influence (an aspect of demonic influence). The demons taunt the individual that they will never get out. He/she is their home. Yet those are only lies to continue focusing on their none existent internal presence. As long as one focuses on the wrong causes there will never be a solution. God forbid.

Sometimes out of desperation a believer may try all kinds of remedies to get rid of their harassment. Some begin to bind and cast them out, to plead the blood of Jesus against them, to plead the blood of Jesus upon themselves, rebuking the demons, seeking deliverance ministers to cast demons out, getting into spiritual warfare prayers or deliverance prayers that directly confront the demons, and so on.

Unfortunately most of these assumed remedies are the very avenues that demons are invited into a realm where one's spirit and senses are able to experience them. So believers or deliverance ministries who practice them only invite more demonic activity.

Under no circumstance are we to speak to demons in cases of demonic influence. We're to speak to God only in the spirit world. Ignore the evil spirits and get into a prayer session, speaking to God who will eventually close your eyes from seeing evil spirits in the spirit world. Prayer combined with fasting also helps.

Until God completely closes your access into the spirit world your focus should be on him not the evil spirits being seen or heard. In his time God will bring the required covering to your spiritual eyes and senses. You'll be like the rest of us who are covered from seeing and hearing these evil beings.

Continue doing your part of seeking God's intervention and walking an upright life. If you're interceding for someone facing spiritual attacks your challenge is ensuring you're a clean vessel for the Lord to use.

Our obedient lives are weapons of righteousness that enable our prayers not to be hindered. This is indirect spiritual warfare. "Submit to God and be at peace with him… *You will pray to him, and he will hear you*… He will deliver even the one who is not innocent, who will be *delivered through the cleanness of your hands*," Job 22: 21,27,30.

Praise and worship music is another weapon against spiritual attacks. Through his continued disobedience the Lord allowed a tormenting spirit to come upon Saul. "Now the Spirit of the Lord had departed from Saul, and an evil spirit from the Lord tormented him," 1 Samuel 16:14.

One of his servants knew a remedy to this. "See, an evil spirit from God is tormenting you. Let our lord command his servants here to search for someone who can play the harp. He will play when the evil spirit from God comes upon you, and you will feel better," 1 Samuel 16:15-16. Another servant recommended David who was at this time hardly known.

The music from David proved to be good medicine for Saul. "Whenever the spirit from God came upon Saul, David would take his harp and play. Then relief would come to Saul; he would feel better, and *the evil spirit would leave him*," 1 Samuel 16:23.

The evil spirit could not stand music from an anointed person like David who earlier on had been anointed by prophet Samuel. Saul however did not know at this time that God had chosen David to replace him.

Praise and worship music can therefore be one of the prescriptions in facilitating healing from spiritual attacks. You can sleep with your radio tuned in to a Christian station if it helps. Praise and worship music however does not replace all the other matters that God requires us to follow through. These include walking in obedience and closing any identified legal entries that give access to demons.

Deliverance and Healing from Spiritual attacks through Dreams

Some may experience frequent bad or nightmare dreams. Others may experience sexual encounters with demons in dreams. They come as fine looking humans of male or female gender. Most of their sexual acts are violent or repulsing. You know once you wake up that it was a dream from hell. But fear not. You have not sinned in God's eyes.

Neither should you feel any condemnation. Your consistent fearlessness will eventually drive out experiences of these dreams. The deliverance principles shared in the above sub-topic apply in this area as well.

Deliverance and Healing from the Occult, Witchcraft or Satanism

While I have zero personal experience in such areas deliverance and healing principles are the same for all problems whether resulting from false doctrines in the body of Christ, from false religions, from past abuse, from sin, or from involvement in the occult, and so on. At least this is the case when applying biblical principles, not psychiatry, medicine or other non-Christian approaches. What matters most is the area where deliverance is required - spiritual, social, material or physical.

Some deliverance ministries have complicated and polluted biblical deliverance principles with rituals, constant "spiritual medications" such binding and loosing demons, and so on. These have only brought more demonic attacks on individuals.

Please read the key sections of this chapter on deliverance and healing, particularly Part 1, Part 2, Part 3 and this Part 4 section. These four parts cover on key biblical principles on deliverance and healing that are also helpful to anyone seeking deliverance from the occult, witchcraft or Satanism.

Some involvement in the occult may have been minor yet resulted in strange experiences and demonic attacks. *If people that where deeply entrenched in occultism can be delivered and healed how much more a one time or casual encounter?* What brought their deliverance and healing is nothing but their willingness to follow through the biblical principles God has given us. And he is no respecter of persons in showing his grace and love to those willing to receive it according to his Word.

Please stick with God's plan for your salvation and see what he'll do in your life. Avoid deliverance ministries that try to bind and loose demons in their attempts of casting out demons. It is true that extreme involvement in the occult can result in demonic possession. Yet it's also true that deliverance from demonic possession comes through accepting Jesus Christ as personal Lord and

Savior. When Christ is invited one's spirit (inner self) is reborn into a new nature that is under the ownership and possession of a new Spirit, the Holy Spirit.

The deliverance from demon possession is instant. Healing from past possession is what can prove to be challenging for some. Because some individuals' faculties remain open to seeing, hearing, and experiencing the activities of these spirit beings that we ordinarily are not designed to see their tormenting attempts can persist way after deliverance.

If the new believer, who is now God's child, is not wise he/she may believe the spirits still own or possess him. The fact is that they do not own or possess him. They no longer live inside him. Their attempts and fights to return may seem like demonic possession yet it is an aspect of demonic influence (not possession), from an external position.

They are now operating from the outside, from an external position. This is an aspect of demonic influence, which everyone is liable to. The only difference is that the individual's faculties remain open to seeing, hearing, and experiencing the activities. His prayer and appeal to God is to seek God to close his spiritual eyes and faculties from seeing, hearing and sensing these spirit beings.

He'll need to continue seeking the Lord's deliverance and healing from not being able to see, hear and sense these spirit beings. When the Lord brings this victory it means that his faculties have been restored to the level we are ordinarily made of - not being able to see, hear nor sense evil spirits.

This will not mean their demonic influence (not possession) attempts have ended. It will only mean their power to inflict underserved spiritual torment from their external influence has ended. They can no longer be seen, heard or sensed so they can make all the noise they wish but the individual is shielded from seeing into the spirit realm. If we all could ordinarily see into the spirit realm it wouldn't be a pleasant experience.

Please read Chapter 6. Exception for Direct Confrontation where the distinction between demonic possession and demonic influence is made. Chapter 2: Our Territory and Nature of Our Christian Authority explains what binding and loosing according to the Bible is, not according to some "deliverance ministries."

All this is emphasized so that you don't have to run to ministries that bring more bondage instead of deliverance, by being preoccupied with casting out demons that have already been evicted by the Holy Spirit.

You may also find Jeff Harshbarger's book, *From Darkness to Light* helpful. Harshbarger is a former Satanist now in Christ and is the director of Refuge Ministries International (website: RefugeMinistries.cc (Not .com)). By the way, there were no demons cast out of Harshbarger when he was delivered from Satanism. Being Christ-centered instead of demon-centered is the key to deliverance and healing.

9.5 Christian Deliverance and Healing, Part 5: Social Areas

CHAPTER 9. PART 5: SOCIAL HEALTH AREAS - SUB-TOPICS:
- Deliverance from Unforgiveness Curses
- Deliverance from Generational Curses
- Deliverance from other Curses
- Deliverance from Family Curses
- Familiar Spirits

Deliverance from Unforgiveness Curses

We call them unforgiveness curses merely because of the problems that result from unforgiveness related areas. Could there be someone that hurt you in whatever way that you are failing to forgive?

Forgiveness does not mean becoming best friends with the person even though this would be quite a testimony. It implies letting go of all his/her wrongs and wishing him God's mercy rather than wrath. God may punish him/her but you have no role to play on the negative side.

Your role is to ask God to open the person's eyes to truly see his/her faults so that he/she can repent and obtain forgiveness from God. The person may not need to meet with you or you going to express your forgiveness. It's the place he/she occupies in your heart that matters. He/she needs to move out of the area that holds bitterness, anger, unforgiveness, hate, vengeance, and so on, into the area that overlooks all the past wrongs.

You also search for something that shows that although evil came your way God ultimately brought good out of it. This enables you to say like Joseph, "You intended to harm me, but God intended it for good," Genesis 50:20.

If nothing good can yet be associated with the harm please trust God to bring good out of it. It's difficult to figure out how he will but this is where God does things in such an awesome way beyond our understanding.

Tears may flow at a mere reflection of the harm but trust him to ultimately bring good out of it. Then move on to doing your part by forgiving. There is a prayer in the Chapter on Christian Persecution –A Deliverance Exception, on areas we can pray for over those who bring harm against us.

By not forgiving one may face a prison experience similar to the servant who refused to forgive his fellow servant (Matthew 18:26-34). Jesus ended the parable by saying "This is how my heavenly Father will treat each of you unless you forgive your brother from your heart," Matthew 18:35.

God does the sentence, not Satan. The prison experience may be spiritual, social, material, physical or whatever combination. It certainly brings unanswered prayer since the one not forgiving is still serving hard labor. The prison sentence ends when he/she chooses to forgive. Forgiveness can be referred to as "informed self interest." It is doing something for someone in exchange for a favor. In this case the favor comes from God when forgiveness is applied.

Deliverance from Generational Curses

What are generational curses? Generational curses are not a result of familiar spirits. Familiar spirits are discussed at the end of this chapter. How this association with familiar spirits came up among some "deliverance ministries" is a bit strange because in regard to generational curses it is God who said he'd visit each generation under his curse (Exodus 20:5).

He said this in the second commandment which forbids idolatry. He did not say he would assign evil spirits from Satan to do the work. The idea of evil spirits bringing generational curses is therefore way off the scriptures.

If it is God who actually brings generational curses then we can breathe with a big sigh of relief that the whole generational curse topic has no validity. First because it assumes generational curses come from evil spirits and not God. Secondly, because it assumes Christians can suffer from generational curses.

Since it is God only who can bring generational curses are we to assume he assigns generational curses on Christians as well? No Christian can face generational curses for any reason. We are free from the curse of the law, through Christ having been made a curse for us.

"Christ redeemed us from the curse of the law by becoming a curse for us, for it is written: 'Cursed is everyone who is hung on a tree.' He redeemed us in order that the blessing given to Abraham might come to the Gentiles through Christ Jesus, so that by faith we might receive the promise of the Spirit," Galatians 3:13-14.

Non-believers may face generational curses because Christ has not yet freed them from the curse of the law. However, even if they may face generational curses the source of such curses is God, not Satan nor any demon spirits from his kingdom.

Conducting generational prayers to break generational curses is therefore a waste of time. The only solution is to pray for their salvation so that they may come under the covering of Christ.

Salvation enables all their sins to be covered by the blood of Jesus, including any sins of parents that the law may hold them accountable for. "To him who loves us and has freed us from our sins by his blood, and has made us to be a kingdom and priests to serve his God and Father--to him be glory and power for ever and ever! Amen," Revelation 1:5-6.

God's salvation is therefore what enables him to automatically break generational curses. He is the curse breaker, not some "deliverance ministry" preacher or "deliverance ministry" church. Deliverance ministry churches are supposed to lead people to Christ to do the deliverance work, not themselves.

Certain traits and matters among believers may seem like generational curses but this is not scriptural. Scripture even cautions us against those who follow endless genealogies. Such only teach false doctrines that try to resurrect the law we were freed from, at least in this capacity. "Command certain men not to teach false doctrines any longer nor to devote themselves to myths and endless genealogies," 1 Timothy 1:3-4.

Our defense against traits, experiences and matters that may seem like generational curses is to bring them before God. We "remind" him that through Christ any family curse, parental curse or ancestral curse has been broken. We remind him that any curse against us is undeserving because of Christ having been made a curse on our behalf. We ask for our rightful bread which is his blessing not his curse. We also endeavor to live lives that are worthy of our calling.

Deliverance from other Curses

"Like a fluttering sparrow or a darting swallow, an undeserved curse does not come to rest," Proverbs 26:2. An undeserved curse no matter where it's from cannot rest or settle on an innocent person. It would be a violation of God's spiritual laws if it did.

So there is no need for a believer to worry about coming under a generational curse by being born in a certain family, coming under a territorial curse by living in a certain neighborhood or region, coming under a soul tie curse from previously repented sexual sins, and so on.

As for people who may curse us by speaking evil against us the scripture is more than clear here. "They may curse, but you will bless; when they attack they will be put to shame, but your servant will rejoice. My accusers will be clothed with disgrace and wrapped in shame as in a cloak," Psalms 109:28-29.

It may not work out exactly the way we envision over our opponents. However we are not to be concerned that their words will have any effect on us. God will ensure no undeserving curse reaches us.

"Like a fluttering sparrow or a darting swallow, an undeserved curse does not come to rest," Proverbs 26:2. There are no exceptions. Even curses from witches, voodoo curses, curses from people in the occult have no legal power over a Christian.

In one biblical example, Balak, a son of a Moabite king tried to seek protection for his kingdom by means of sorcery or witchcraft. The Israelites, under Moses, were taking over one territory after another. The Moabites knew they were next and had heard the miraculous conquests of the Israelites. Not a good story about wiping out other ethnic groups in our New Testament Christian era where God loves all people and wants all to be saved.

Balak knew sorcery from his own Moabite people would have no effect against the Israelites. So he sought for an Israelite who would put a curse on his own people, that is, would seek the Israelite God in cursing the Israelites. Balaam, an Israelite prophet was given a huge amount of money called a "fee for divination," (Numbers 22: 7). It could have been millions of dollars worth in our day.

It appears that Balaam somehow wanted the fortunes. He knew the Israelites were God's people and could not be cursed. But he kept looking for a way for God to bend the rules. The Lord showed him in miraculous ways, including having his donkey speak to him, that his cursing attempts would not prosper.

In the final stages of the cursing attempts Balaam told Balak, "God is not a man, that he should lie, nor a son of man, that he should change his mind. Does he speak and then not act? Does he promise and not fulfill? I have received a command to bless; *he has blessed, and I cannot change it*." Numbers 23:19-20.

The same is true over Christians, spiritual Israelites through Christ. Balaam confessed about his fellow Israelites, "God brought them out of Egypt; they have the strength of a wild ox. There is no sorcery against Jacob, no divination against Israel. It will now be said of Jacob and of Israel, `See what God has done!' Numbers 23:22-23.

In applying the above passage to Christians we can say, "God brought them out of their Egypt, a bondage to sin that goes back to Adam. They are now saved through Christ who purchased them through his blood. They are now under God's blessing, not the curse of the law nor any other curse.

"There is no sorcery, no divination, not occult curse, no involuntary curse, no territorial curse, no generational curse, no satanic curse, no demonic curse, no witch curse, no voodoo curse, nor any other curse against those whose sins are under the blood of Jesus and are children of God."

We do not have any business to speak to demons or evil spirits about our freedom in Christ. It speaks for itself and whatever any evil spirits or human agents attempt against us will not prosper.

We faithfully go about minding our own business and walk with God, without being preoccupied with what demons in the spirit realm are up to. God has assigned angels to our defense who outnumber demons. "Are not all angels ministering spirits sent to serve those who will inherit salvation?" Hebrews 1:14.

We are also not to be preoccupied with what human agents of demons, such as those in the occult, are up to. In fact human agents are scared of Christians that know their position in Christ. Ask any former high level witch, wizard or occult member.

Like with Job and the Israelites there is a hedge of protection around us that neither Satan, his demons, nor human agents can penetrate into our lives. Unless God, in his sovereign will lifts this hedge, there is no way any evil powers can penetrate our lives.

Deliverance from Family Curses

What are family curses? By family curses here we mean curses that come through serious family conflicts. The topic has nothing to do with generational curses. By serious family conflicts we mean conflicts that result in unpleasant words being uttered against a family member and both or one of them holding bitterness against another.

Serious family conflicts without any reconciliation result in distressing experiences among those not willing to settle scores. The trauma that results may be spiritual, social, physical, material or any combination. This may seem like a contradiction after confirming that undeserved curses are powerless. However the area of family politics seems to be a biblical exception.

There is something about family issues, especially between parents and children. Family politics can make or break the course of the lives of children. "Children, obey your parents in the Lord, for this is right. 'Honor your father and mother'--which is the first commandment with a promise—'that it may go well with you and that you may enjoy long life on the earth,'" Ephesians 6:1-3.

Notice that the commandment has a promise—"that it may go well with you and that you may enjoy long life on the earth." The promise is hindered or goes unfulfilled when serious conflicts come in between the parent(s) and a child.

The passage that follows talks about parents' input to their children. "Fathers, do not exasperate your children; instead, bring them up in the training and instruction of the Lord," Ephesians 6:4.

From here we realize that it's a two way street. If parents treat their children well the children are likely to treat them with honor. There is no single formula of ensuring a two way healthy relationship but it can take so much work, prayer, occasional mistakes, differences, breaking and making up. In the final outcome making up must win to ensure that it "may go well with you and that you may enjoy long life on the earth."

Parents have immense biblical authority to influence the destiny of their children for better or for worse. Their words are not mere words. They carry with them the power to bless or to curse -socially, spiritually, materially or physically. Children don't have this privilege over their parents. Their words are mere words. Their privilege lies in continuing the family lineage

In case a parent uttered cursing words against you or someone you love and channels of reconciliation are still closed please continue praying for God to open them up. It may require sessions of prayer and fasting for God to break the spiritual strongholds over emotions, memories and thoughts that are blocking the way. Like any relationship there is no single formula to reaching a break-through. Praying and entrusting it to God will enable him to work in their hearts and minds.

He may also create matters and events that can facilitate healing and reconciliation. There is no requirement to bind and loose demons in any way. Some resort to binding and loosing spirits they categorize as spirits of division, spirits of unforgiveness, spirits of rebellion, spirits of disrespect, spirits of divorce and so on. It ends up being a ritual of inviting more demonic attacks.

The bottom line is that you or anyone you're burdened for would like to close any doors that may provide legal access for problems that come through parent-child conflicts. But you need to follow prescriptions that are in line with scripture, regardless of the urgency. No short-cuts to deliverance, unless endorsed by the bible. Commit more days of prayer and fasting if possible. Fasting brings amazing breakthroughs. Walk in love, mercy, charity, read more on biblical deliverance on family matters, etc.

Any one in courtship with someone who has scores to settle with parents is better off waiting and praying for the conflict to be settled before getting into a marriage. Without the conflict settled you could have a rough road ahead. Consolidating such areas constitute materials for a strong foundations against life's storms.

Another area that can bring family related curses is when one side of parents refuse to approve a marriage partner of their child. For example some multiracial relationships end up in major problems and eventual separation not because of supposed cultural differences. Many of us have more than one racial descent, however long ago, so at least no one has room to assume there's any bias against interracial relationships.

Many of the major problems in multiracial relationships come from one or both sides of the marriage not approving the relationship. These lead to words said directly or in the absence of the children that curse the relationship. Tensions grow from the parent(s) disapproving with a determination to see the relationship fail.

Some of the tension may even be unknown to the children. Certain spiritual forces at one point or another create havoc in the couple. For such reasons I wish God never gave parents such influence that can bless or curse their children. But he is God. We will some day know why he has made this set-up, giving our parents some god-like powers.

In a non-racial or ethnic example a minister and his fiancée went ahead and got married when the parents to his wife strongly disapproved. This is a man after God's heart, serving in front-line ministry. But even this could not help save his marriage when the parents continued their disapproval. To some extent he and his wife did not see it as a major area of concern and probably devoted less prayer to it. Their heavy association with false teachings on spiritual warfare compounded the problem.

For anyone already in a marriage with some form of family tension identify your area of prayer and let God fight your battles. Many couples have prevailed whether from a disapproved marriage or one partner having personal conflict with a parent. God has now joined you together. Let no man or woman pull you apart because of some spiritual influence God gave them which they're misusing to curse instead of bless. But devote much prayer to it (and occasional fasting) so that reconciliation, healing and approval wins the day.

The following principles define the nature of family politics and how it needs to remain a work of team effort rather than one of personal interests.

1) It's all about the team, not one team player or one special group trying to win a game on their own,

2) It's God who chooses our team members. How we deal with them depends on each one of us and determines our individual and overall success. The team God picks he also equips it for as long as it remains dependent on him.

3) Parents remain team captains over their children regardless of the children's age and status. If they refuse to participate in or approve a particular game God also opts out. Sure defeat follows if the children stubbornly try to pursue matters objected by parents.

The only way is to peacefully or skillfully resolve the areas of conflict until their approval is secured. Most times all they need is to receive some respect and consideration. After that they're usually willing to tolerate conflicting agendas,

4) Parents may be completely wrong on particular matters concerning their team members. This does not nullify their biblical authority nor justify dishonoring them. All who tried to resolve matters this way failed miserably in one area of their lives or another.

Some are very famous or powerful yet live in pain and a tormenting hell they can easily avoid. The only way to resolve the mistakes of parents is to skillfully and respectfully show the wrongs until they consent to the errors,

5) The obligation to honor and support our parents doesn't depend on their level of contribution to our lives. Most times it's through no fault of their own. Even when it was is no justification. Denial of their due biblical honor and reward only result in curses in a child's life, in one area or another,

6) There's not enough room for competition in a team. When competition comes in team unity and cooperation go out,

7) Team players may make mistakes but none deserves to be expelled or disqualified. Skillful disciplinary action may be required. Expulsion is not, since it exposes the member to thoughts of rejection, inferiority and worthlessness. This can result into many long-term problems for the individual,

8) The make up of the team is always unequal. Some members may be extremely helpful to the team, doing most of the good work. It's more of a privilege than a burden to be a key player.

Others may be average performers -socially, spiritually, materially or physically. Others may be "free riders" not willing to put in much and caring less. Some may even be liabilities, draining resources from the team -socially, spiritually or materially.

Other liabilities include those who assume it's about themselves, their needs and desires that matter most not those of everybody else in the team. It's understandable for the early 20s and below but can be a nightmare for those older. Skillfully dealing with such a wired set-up can be a challenge particularly for those doing a lot of the work.

However there's no other alternative since the blessings only come through remaining united. Helping the most irrelevant or problematic member may also turn out to be the most rewarding sacrifice for the team,

9) Nearly each team member has one area or another that can be a topic of ridicule and condemnation from others. Learning to prayerfully and skillfully deal with these areas keeps the team united. Some may have the negative areas due to willful sin thus "deserving" it.

Others may be going through a trial of faith or a moment of crushing. Some may not be as intelligent, as strong or privileged and thus more prone to problems -socially, spiritually, materially or physically. For others God may for a special purpose allow a blinding deception from hell to stubbornly pursue ventures others know are foolish and destructive.

Skillfully and prayerfully dealing with such problems overcomes them faster than constant conflict which serves to increase division,

10) Parents have immense biblical authority to influence the destiny of their children for better or for worse. Their words are not mere words. They carry with them the power to bless or to curse -socially, spiritually, materially or physically. "The tongue has the power of life and death, and those who love it will eat its fruit," Pr 18:21.

Children don't have this privilege and influence over their parents. Their words are mere words. Their privilege lies in continuing the family lineage. It doesn't do parents any good in the long run to see their children living miserable lives. The children will also be hindered from effectively fulfilling their obligations of being sources of strength to the parents as they age. Avoiding the negatives comes through divine wisdom, prayers, skillful diplomacy and words of blessing that break any cycle of curses any child may experience.

Familiar Spirits

What are familiar spirits? There is confusion as to what familiar spirits are, as defined in the Bible. Some assume familiar spirits are evil spirits that are familiar with a person's ancestral past. They use their familiarity to bring the same curses and problems that a person's parents or ancestors encountered. In other words familiar spirits are carriers of generational curses, passing the same afflictions from one generation to another.

However the bible's version is far from this. *Bamford's Bible Diction-ary*, says the term familiar spirits applies to the practice of communicating with the spirits of the dead.

As *Easton's Bible Dictionary* says, the practice involved sorcerers, me-diums or necromancers, who professed to call up the dead to answer questions. These individuals were said to have a "familiar spirit," of another dead person.

In actual fact, the different voice that came out a person claiming to call the dead was not that of a dead person but that of a demon spirit. Any apparition was also the work of demons. A demon spirit could fake the voice or image of a dead person.

That is why God strictly forbade this heathen practice among the Israel-ites (Leviticus 19:31). The consequences God said would result in defilement and excommunication from the community (Leviticus 20:6, Deuteronomy 18:10-13). The one acting as a vessel or medium for a familiar spirit to talk through was to be stoned to death (Leviticus 20:27). That was the heavy hand of the law in the Old Testament (Old Covenant).

Saul, the first king of Israel tried it (1 Samuel 28v3-25). He went to a sorcerer to call up dead prophet Samuel for some urgent advice. Sure enough Samuel appeared, though it was a demon spirit.

This finalized Saul's fate. He was cut off from Israel as the Philistines came against Israel with many casualties, including Saul and his sons. He actually requested to be struck dead after being severely wounded. He and his sons' bodies were later burned by their enemies (1 Samuel 31). Not a good ending for a person with such royalty and anointing as king.

The term "familiar spirits" therefore has to be applied only in its biblical context for it to make any scriptural sense. In case anyone was involved in the practice of seeking the dead there is hope in the New Covenant. You or anyone involved in any other occult practices will not be cut off from God's blessing if you have repented of the practice.

The previous part of this Chapter (Part 4) covers on required principles for biblical deliverance and healing from occult practices. Please particularly read the sub-topics on repentance and ceasing the non-biblical practices.

9.6 Christian Deliverance and Healing, Part 6: Financial Areas

CHAPTER 9. PART 6: FINANCIAL HEALTH AREAS - SUBTOPICS

This entire area on financial and material rewards is adapted from my incomplete book still on the shelves with a proposed title: *Seed Time & Harvest Time - and God's Mercy*. Every part of it is related to deliverance from financial bondage, breaking the curse of poverty, biblical financial victory, steps to financial freedom and so on.

Christianity is burdensome when one does not understand the ways of God. It is difficult to accept or obey what we cannot understand. One of the most practical examples is the monetary side of our required obedience. This is in the area of monetary contributions, offerings and charitable giving.

Financial lack is still among the worst areas of affliction among believers, though for non-believers as well. Some are in unresolvable debts. Others are lacking basic resources in their lives and Christian living. And so on.

As believers God has given us biblical principles that relate to our material well-being. We can at least overcome areas within our sphere of responsibility. Applying God's principles may not bring all we desire but it can eliminate avoidable and needless distress. I'm therefore not endorsing in this section the prosperity health and wealth "gospel" circulating among some of our spiritual siblings in the body of Christ.

Same Principles, Different Limits

A text in Malachi that talks about tithes and offerings is a key reference to how God works through our financial obedience or disobedience. *It is important to note that tithing, that is, giving ten percent of our income, is not required in the New Testament (New Covenant) era we're in.* We are freed, through Christ, from religious rituals of the Mosaic Law.

If tithing is still a requirement then we need to resurrect the whole Old Testament law. And all of us who go to church on Sunday would have no place in heaven until we returned to Seventh Day worship.

Violation of the Seventh Day worship law is more eternally serious than violating requirements on tithes and offerings. Seventh Day worship is among the ten commandments while tithing is tucked among the numerous minor laws that are basically religious rituals and social policing laws.

So let no one deceive you that giving ten percent of our income is still our required minimum limit. Neither let them deceive you that a traditional church is the only accepted avenue for giving in the body of Christ.

However, the principles under tithing and offering requirements still apply in our day. So the text in Malachi still speaks to us today. The financial requirements in the New Testament era actually demand more than the old ten percent (tithe) minimum limit. We're required to deny ourselves and to offer ourselves as living sacrifices. Making ourselves as offerings to God is giving everything we have for his interests.

The early church in the book of Acts is a good example though not necessarily to be applied the same way they did. They sold their belongings and gave the funds to the apostles as stewards for all believers. Please don't try this even if you hear a voice claiming to be from God. Continue you good deeds with bible based financial principles that are not based on emotions or strange voices.

And let no ministry manipulate you by claiming to bring special rewards from heaven when you give to them. The bible talks about believers' motives for giving while saying nothing on which ministry is more acceptable than another on financial matters.

We're requested to be rich in good deeds, which is a way of storing up our treasure (wealth) in heaven. Our security is meant to be in what we're saving up in heaven through good deeds rather than in how much our savings or earthly investments are worth (Matthew 6:19-21).

It's a complete opposite paradigm or standard from the secular approach. How much is required to be stored up in heaven is therefore as much as we can possibly manage. No percentage limits.

"Command those who are rich in this present world not to be arrogant nor to put their hope in wealth, which is so uncertain, but to put their hope in

God, who richly provides us with everything for our enjoyment. Command them to do good, to be rich in good deeds, and to be generous and willing to share. In this way they will lay up treasure for themselves as a firm foundation for the coming age, so that they may take hold of the life that is truly life," 1 Timothy 6:17-19.

Obedience is the Key

Like in the old covenant era God brings whatever results based on our financial obedience or disobedience. He said to those who desired financial deliverance and freedom:

"Bring the whole tithe into the storehouse, that there may be food in my house. Test me in this and see if I will not throw open the floodgates of heaven and pour out so much blessing that you will not have room enough for it. I will prevent pests from devouring your crops and the vines in your fields will not cast their fruits, says the Lord Almighty," (Malachi 3:10-11).

So this is God's way of providing material necessities. It is through giving. A tithe (ten percent) of ones income was the minimum in the Old Testament.

Something is a gift when the giver requires nothing in return. It maybe financial, material, service of one's talents and time, counsel and so on. It's something that will contribute to the well-being of someone or group at the expense of the giver's input.

Through the gifts, God says he is moved to "throw open the floodgates of heaven" to bless the giver. It may not be instant or come in a way the giver may assume. However God works everything out in his way and timing to bless the giver.

Not only does he open doors for his blessings he also prevents the enemy from undoing our blessings. You probably know people who received much only to loose it all in mysterious ways, to suffer crippling health problems or other misfortune. God works to prevent such experiences for as long as we continue obeying his word.

On the highest level we're requested to "Seek first his kingdom and his righteousness and all these things will be given to you as well," (Matthew 6:33).

It means putting his ways of righteous living, evangelism interests and charitable interests ahead of our personal earthly interests. They need to matter to us more than our interests and needs. All the things we need for our earthly living are given to us as we pursue his interests.

God's Ways or Ours?

God has given his ways to open the floodgates of heaven. But some may decide to look for their own ways they consider more convenient. All sorts of "justifiable" excuses may come up. The most common are, "I don't have enough to give anyone," "I've so many critical obligations that giving would not be practical," "I've not yet started earning my own income."

Thus we devise other ways to receive from God. We hold long prayers, sometimes accompanied with fasting. Some who misunderstand spiritual warfare resort to binding and rebuking demons from holding their material blessings.

At the end of the day nothing moves. We may even begin to question ourselves: "May be God wants us to remain in lack?" After all, the bible strongly warns against the love of money. So living day to day on subsistence provisions by the grace of God could be his will for our lives.

All this is not true. We are only applying the wrong principles for the wrong purposes. We still end up walking in financial disobedience and harvesting fruits of financial disobedience.

Our Lord waits for us to apply what he has prescribed for us. Until we respond according to his word he continues to wait. Resorting to sinful ways and other worldly ways may work but only to bring in other worse problems in the long-run. On another note, a believer may have other issues outside giving that may be contributing to financial woes. All these are hindrances to what God has promised through his word.

Still Under Manna or in Canaan?

God fed the Israelites manna during their 40 years in the wilderness. Manna was enough for the day and no more for the next. Any attempt to lay aside some for a succeeding day failed, except the day immediately preceding the Sabbath. Attempts of preservation only led to the manner to rot.

After 40 years the disobedient generation of military age had all gone except Joshua and Caleb who had obeyed God. Then God asked Joshua to circumcise the sons of the disobedient generation. After he obeyed this and observed the Passover God opened the door for them to eat their own produce in Canaan. The manna stopped (Joshua 5) and the Israelites were no longer bound to daily rations.

Their reproach, which was a sign of bondage, was rolled away when the new generation matured and it fulfilled its obedience through Joshua. "Today I have rolled away the reproach of Egypt from you," Joshua 5:9.

Their reproach was not rolled away when they crossed the sea with Moses. It was after more than 40 years when they qualified to inherit their promised blessing. All along they were still in some form of bondage like in Egypt. It was a material bondage. No wonder they complained so much that some even asked to return to Egypt where they had no freedom.

This could be the case for some believers in their material lives. Spiritually they are no longer in bondage. Materially things have not changed or have worsened. Some even consider returning to sinful ways of gaining material means. They consider sacrificing their spiritual freedom for material gain. They have prayed and begged God for years but little if anything has changed.

Yet God is saying some are in a financial wilderness of their own making because of disobedience to his financial principles. Prayer and begging is not a requirement in this area of our Christian lives. According to his word there is a better way out than resorting to sinful or spiritually compromising ways. His ways may take longer than the sinful ways but are more than worthwhile in the long run.

So some may be living in a financial wilderness of their own making because of disobedience. There are only two wildernesses in life – one is God-made while the other is man-made. Jesus entered a God-made wilderness when he was led to be tempted by the devil. His wilderness was a general trial of faith and not a financial one.

Our God-made financial wilderness is mostly during the years of our upbringing. We receive manna we never worked for. The manna is just enough to get by and scarce enough to continue looking forward to our own means.

During this period, God wants us among other things to learn obedience and submission to higher authority. It is also training ground for our submission to God and his ways. During God's ordained wilderness our parents and guardians not only have heaven's commission to care for us, they also have the means to exercise their authority.

No wilderness is exciting. As we grow older we desire more to be free from the financial wilderness of being on the receiving end. For some the mere thought of others sacrificing their lives for them is tormenting. They look forward to freeing their parents or guardians from their burden of looking after them.

For others the manna itself becomes increasingly unbearable. And so on. A God-made financial wilderness is at least one we're not to regret. We found ourselves under particular parents or guardians of certain means and other characteristics. It was God's own design. It's a self-made one that is a problem.

Financial Curse (Wilderness) -A Father's Discipline

The wilderness that we can somehow live to regret for having gone through is the self-made one. It comes as a result of disobedience to God. Here an individual has the power of choice but misuses it by ignoring God's principles.

In the God-made wilderness there is nothing we can do except endure it. In the self-made one there is everything we can do to get out of it. It's presence is a sign that there is something God requires of us that we're not fulfilling.

When the Israelites disobeyed God they paid the penalty by being caged into a wilderness for forty years. They received manna just to keep them alive while paying for their sin. The same happens to us when we disobey his principles. He leaves us to survive on manna that is just enough to get by and scarce enough to continue looking forward to being free from such mere survival.

It may seem like God is a strict disciplinarian waiting to punish every disobedience. However scripture and history show that his hand of mercy is more prevalent than his hand of justice. His greatest act of mercy was having his Son, Jesus, die for our sins. We would be paying for every sin if it wasn't for Christ. For most of us who have not been perfect this would be serious bondage, worse than slavery.

But to say God is no disciplinarian would be a big lie. Try getting into certain sins, especially the sexual sins and you'll be sorry for it. Repentance is the ultimate rescue but may not stop all the sinful harvest. He will also eventually work it to your good but the process of getting to obtain that good can be painful. God does discipline us, out of love, not out of his wrath when we stray. "The Lord disciplines those he loves, and he punishes everyone he accepts as a son," Hebrews 12:6.

So God disciplines us when we disobey his biblical financial principles. His discipline is what enables us to return to his ways when we stray. He allows a financial curse or wilderness to develop in our lives. To him disobedience to his biblical financial principles is robbery. We robe God of what belongs to him. He said, "Will a man rob God? Yet you rob me…in tithes and offerings. You are under a curse – the whole nation of you because you are robbing me" (Malachi 8-9).

A whole nation or household can be under a curse because of one of the heads of a household is walking in disobedience. The curse of not giving is living in scarcity and continual harassment from the devourer (devil) either through a financial misfortune, losses, theft, money going to cover for sickness, and other unnecessary burdens. And because God is merciful he gives manna to the disobedient so that they survive by the day. Until obedience is fulfilled the manna continues.

Breaking the Curse of Poverty Through Obedience

The curse is only changed into a blessing when one starts giving. Ten percent was the Old Covenant minimum but it can be a safe level to start on. There is no other substitute. Our monetary and material means that are given as gifts are the only worthy seeds for a material harvest.

We can also freely give our time and talents that have financial value to Christian causes. This can be a way of making up for low financial contributions in the manna years of scarcity.

Merely praying or fasting will do almost nothing. *Prayer and fasting only water the seeds. Without the seeds no amount of water will bring anything from the ground. No seed falling to the ground no harvest.*

Usually prayer and fasting are not necessary to material harvests. This is because material seeds work on God's principle: "A man reaps whatever he sows." (Galatians 6: 7).

If material harvests came from prayer then only Christians would have the material means. The rest would be on manna until they got born again. Evangelism would be so easy, if at all it would be needed. Unbelievers would seek salvation once they got tired of the manna.

God has set aside prayer (and occasional fasting) for more important seeds -evangelism. He wants us to concentrate on watering (praying and fasting) over seeds of salvation and liberty among lost souls. We can pray over our evangelism efforts or those of other ministries to produce their intended harvest of souls.

In the financial or material area God personally opens the windows of heaven to bless us. This happens as we apply the principles of seed time and harvest time. We do not need to pray or ask him to open the windows of heaven.

Here he wants to be tested and not be prayed to. Can you imagine God asking his creatures to challenge, test or tempt him? He said, "*Test me* in this and see if I will not through open the floodgates of heaven and pour out so much blessings that you will not have room enough for it" (Malachi 3:10).

There is so much in heaven that God had to build floodgates - figuratively speaking. Floodgates are for stopping floods. God's kingdom is flooded with blessings waiting to be poured out on obedient souls in the biblical financial principles.

Wanna go for a one on one with God, the Almighty, All Powerful and so on? He says "test me," "try me," or in our street language "go on, dare me!!." In paraphrasing he is saying "let's see who is going to win in the giving game between you and I. Let's see if what you give to me will be more than what I give back in return to you." It's easy to know who the winner will be.

God's victory of giving more than the giver may not come in the short-run. Any short-sighted person can have a difficult time understanding how God works. Many times the desired means also do not come the way an individual expects.

For instance, he may open doors for your children into schools and professional positions that you could only dream of. This way your children become your most exciting part of your senior life. Seeing the faithfulness of God fulfilled in their lives gives you more reasons for living. Such a blessing may take 30 or more years to materialize. Yet you kept sowing throughout those decades. God is faithful – in his time and way.

How God Opens the Floodgates of Heaven

The floodgates of blessings God pours out are in the form of avenues that he opens for us to receive from him and be under his protection. One avenue is through divine ideas. For instance, God told Isaac to plant crops in drought season and he "reaped a hundred fold" (Genesis 27:12).

God can drop ideas into the heart of an individual on how to run or start a particular business, where to look for employment, or if it's a promotion, how she should conduct herself for promotion.

Another avenue is God commanding favor in the hearts of other people towards an individual and her particular calling. "Let love and faithfulness never leave you…then you will win favor and a good name in the sight of God and man," (Proverbs 3:3-4). This favor or grace is the anointing of God upon an individual and his/her particular calling.

The individual may not be as educated as her associates, or as good looking, as old or young, as talented, or whatever is desired, yet the anointing upon her will make her to be exceptional in one way or another. The individual can be a farmer, lawyer, nurse, retailer, an evangelist, consultant, teacher, and so on. People will be attracted to her and be more willing to receive from or transact with whatever she offers than with others.

The academic world may be the most meritorious system in the world. One gets a certificate, degree or grade depending on their ability in a selected field. Merit or ability not favor or chance is the ultimate determinant. The professional world operates in a somewhat chaotic way. Merit (ability) and favor coexist with one being more prominent than the other in different fields and places.

Making it in such a chaotic world may need more than merit for some. For others ability may be all that will be required. God opens doors for mastering the ability and where necessary grants favor in securing a position, business, property, interest or whatever.

God even lays burdens in the hearts of some people to give in monetary or material form to the individual. Our Lord Jesus and his disciples lived under this favor. Jesus made Judas Escariot, a perpetual thief, his treasure to show how unconcerned he was for material provisions. No matter how much Judas embezzled supplies never ran out.

How God Prevents Satan from Destroying the Blessings

"I will prevent pests from devouring your crops, and the vines in your fields will not cast their fruit," (Malachi 3:11).

Pests are problems and misfortune that arise in areas of interest in our lives. The comparison scripture uses is related to farming. A farmer labors sowing seed, tenders it while eagerly expecting a great harvest as the final outcome. However pests come and ruin all his labor. He worked hard but this time it was all in vain. He worked to feed the pests, not himself or his/her family.

In our lives Satan and his agents are the pests. They work to destroy everything we endeavor in that is godly and scriptural. Destruction is their only ministry. Their ministry succeeds where we do not have God's protection. So if our financial areas have no covering our labor may be in vain.

God prevents Satan's access when we start to apply the biblical financial principles. We do not need to pray to him to rebuke the devourer. He does it on his own. Our obedience breaks the curse of poverty for as long as we remain in obedience. We do not need to be even concerned how Satan is working in his ministry of trying to frustrate our lives. Our concern should be on how we're obeying God in fulfilling our required input.

When our obedience is fulfilled to God's principles he works to rebuke or prevent the devourer affecting our lives. Knowing God's principles in every area of our lives is therefore our only refuge.

The enemy feeds on our ignorance. When we know the truth in a given area Satan can devise any plan of destruction but God's angels will prevent him from fulfilling it. No need of binding and loosing evil spirits of this and that.

Non-believers survive by the mercy of God. The devourer has easy access into their lives. The financial area is where more people are trapped in the curse of poverty than are out of it.

This includes believers. Satan may be the thief that comes to steal the blessing but he is not the problem. The problem is believers themselves. We give him access to spoil the harvest if we do not live by biblical financial principles. Living outside biblical principles gives pests as much access to us as they have to unbelievers in their finances.

For instance one may save a good amount of money only to loose it through a misfortune. An illness or accident may come along and eat some of it. He/she may invest into something only to see it collapse. One way or another money seems to be coming in and quickly going out through another door.

Another situation may be borrowing for matters one shouldn't have. The individual could still survive without them. But the tempter shows up with wonderful ideas on how one's life will be better off if they borrowed to obtain certain desires. The funds will after all be repaid at a low interest. Before long the individual is having trouble paying the interest, leave alone the loaned amount. It is like being caught up in a prison of working to pay someone else. This someone is part of the pests that have entered to eat whatever one labors in.

This is how curses operate. They keep people from making any progress in areas of interest. People try hard only to fall back, or ending up worse off. A worse off situation arises where an individual gets into increasing debts. Another can be through other problems coming up to eat every form of piece of mind one desires to have in life.

We see this in many so called celebrities. Many live tormenting lives confronting one serious problem after another. They have money and earthly fame but they have no peace. Having peace only comes from the Prince of Peace (Isaiah 9:6).

Most of us saved have this peace. We did not buy it. It was freely given upon receiving Jesus as our Lord and Savior. We have the most expensive blessing that no wealth, power, beauty, fame or worldly pleasure can buy. Any believer that does not have it ought to search what is grieving the Holy Spirit from bringing his peace and comfort.

Sometimes trials may overwhelm but only some times. Most times the Lord enables us to bear our trials of faith, knowing he is the one in control, not our circumstances, nor other people, nor Satan.

During my worst trial or is it worst experience of reaping from ignorance I concluded the best option was dying. Not suicide but asking God to take my life. After all he did that to Elijah who was as human as any of us. Having no children or spouse to leave behind during the experience made it safe to say such "self-centered" prayers.

Like with Elijah it was time to go to a better place. "I have had enough, Lord," he (Elijah) said. "Take my life; I am no better than my ancestors," 1 King 19:3-4. Then God revealed the cause of the problem - bombarding hell in the name of spiritual warfare prayers and deliverance prayers. Applying all that was required and correcting interpretation on spiritual warfare ended all the torment.

In the midst of the torment I had all the peace as to whom I served, where I was going after dying and knowing who was in control over my case. A colleague who was an unbeliever was puzzled to think of someone not being afraid to die. Fellow believers understood the salvation principle though they of course disagreed on making such prayers.

Well, God tossed out all such prayers then later revealed the cause. This book, other books and the ministry work would not have materialized had he answered the prayers. I would have been in heaven but would have also received a smaller crown. And many would have been deprived of what he purposed to fulfill from the experiences.

The Bottom Line

The whole truth about financial rewards is that any giver prospers. "A generous man will prosper; he who refreshes others will himself be refreshed," (Proverbs 11:25). It does not matter whether one gives to the work of God or to the work of men. Neither does his religion or spiritual state matter. The law of seed time and harvest time applies to all of us. One harvests whatever he sows.

A mango seed will always harvest mangoes no matter the soil it is planted in. It cannot change to oranges. Same with material or financial seeds. That is why many people in the occult are very wealthy. They are not wealthy because they are in occultism. It is because they know and aggressively apply the law of seed time and harvest time. But they have their major problems that amount to severe bondage.

Some of what individuals and companies call as charitable giving to non-profits, sports clubs, schools, hospitals and communities are activities of increasing their wealth so that they can increase their mischief. Their seed is of the flesh and the material harvest is of the flesh. Whatever the sacrifice it has no reward in heaven.

Some individuals and companies may even give for extreme occult reasons. You may have heard rumors of some companies contributing some of their profits to satanic churches. Most rumors are hoaxes made by up their competitors. But it shows such activity is there. Some companies reap large profits by sowing some of their finances to demons.

Same Harvest, Different Taste of Harvested Material Fruits

The only difference between Christian and all other forms of giving is that one sows to the Spirit (of God) and the other to the flesh (sinful nature). Monetary and material gifts by a Christian with genuine motives to other believers or needy people in society are material seeds sown to the Spirit. The recipients may include one's local church, an evangelistic ministry, and a Christian charity.

On the other hand, monetary and material gifts by a non-Christian, even with right motives, sown to needy people in society are seeds sown to the flesh. One cannot buy his/her way to heaven by good works. Good works that have value in heaven are from us who already are counted as God's children. The good hearted non-believer will be blessed materially and have quite a respectable life on earth but that's about it.

You may have met or heard of good-hearted non-Christians doing all kinds of charity work. Many lead quite admirable lives that many self-righteous Christians may have much to learn from. I have met many in various areas including in charity ministry. I pray for their salvation which is a free gift from God. "It (salvation) is the gift of God not by works, so that no one can boast," Ephesians 2:8-9.

While salvation and a plot in heaven is a free gift through Christ the crown is not. Christians that may think works are not important have not read the bible. They have not read how much believers had to sacrifice for the gospel and godly work. On judgment day Jesus' judgment will be based on what we have done not just for being saved by grace. "My reward is with me, and I will give to every one according to what he has done," (Revelations 22:12).

It gets more complicated where scripture adds that not all our good works will be accepted. Like those of unbelievers some of our works may be rejected. They will have no value in heaven. They will bring material rewards here on earth. But they will not be credited in heaven.

Here is a warning from scripture regarding our good works. Note that the one whose entire good works are rejected will narrowly escape the fire (hell) and will also suffer loss.

It does not elaborate what kind of loss but the mathematics in the scripture points to seeds of the flesh = fruits of the flesh, that is, problems spiritually, socially, physically, etc.

"If any man builds on this (salvation) foundation using gold, silver, costly stones, wood, hay or straw, his work will be shown for what it is, because the Day will bring it to light. It will be revealed with fire, and the fire will test the quality of each man's work. If what he has built survives, he will receive his reward. If it is burned up, he will suffer loss; *he himself will be saved, but only as one escaping through the flames*," 1 Corinthians 3:12-15

With such a warning we can now proceed to the principle of reaping whatever we sow. Since the scriptures can never be broken each seed will reap it's own nature.

"The one who sows to please his sinful nature (flesh), from that nature will reap destruction; the one who sows to please the Spirit; from the Spirit will reap eternal life," (Galatians 6:8). One group of seeds harvest fruits that bring destruction on the individual. The other group brings health and life to the individual.

They are all monetary seeds but they harvest different types of monetary fruits. For instance, lemon and orange seeds are both citrus seeds. When planted they both produce citrus fruits. However, the taste of the fruits differ. One group is bitter while the other group is sweet.

The same is the case with monetary and material seeds. Flesh and spirit monetary seeds have one thing in common: they are both monetary seeds. They therefore both produce monetary fruits. However, the taste of the fruits differ.

One group is bitter, the other group is sweet. One group of monetary wealth brings sorrow, trouble and death. The other group brings trouble free rewards.

"When God gives any man wealth and possessions, and enables him to enjoy them, to accept his lot and to be happy in his work - this is a gift of God. He seldom reflects on the days of his life (with regrets), because God keeps him occupied with gladness of heart," (Ecclesiastes 5: 19-20).

"The blessing of the Lord brings wealth, and he adds *no trouble* to it," (Proverbs 10:22). His blessings add no trouble because they are fruits one reaps from sowing to the Spirit.

Scripture says the fruit of sowing to the Spirit (of God) is "love, joy, peace, patience, kindness, goodness, faithfulness, gentleness and self-control," (Galatians 5: 22-23).

On the other hand, the fruits of sowing to the sinful nature (the flesh) include, "Sexual immorality; impurity and debauchery; idolatry and witchcraft; hatred, discord, jealousy, fits of rage, selfish ambition, dissentions, factions and envy; drunkenness, orgies, and the like. I warn you, as I did before, that those who live like this will not inherit the kingdom of God," (Galatians 5: 19-21).

"The Lord's curse is on the house of the wicked, but he blesses the home of the righteous" (Proverbs 3:33).

The measure of material rewards is therefore not on the scale of quantity but on quality. To what extent are they either curses or blessings on the lives of those that have them? To what extent are they facilitating their walk with God. To what extent are they blocking it? David prayed to God, "Turn my heart towards your statutes and not towards selfish gain. Turn my eyes away from worthless things," (Psalm 119:36-37)

If what is sown to God's work has selfish gain motives in it then it is likely to reap a flesh harvest. Orange trees when not tendered properly while growing can turn into lemon trees. Lemons are basically bitter oranges and not the other way round.

The same change can happen to monetary seeds sown to the Spirit, that is, God's work (evangelism and Christian charity) when not tendered properly or if they are sown with selfish gain motives. They produce bitter monetary fruits in the sower's life.

Christianity is a call to total self-denial. Whatever comes into one's hand must go back to extending God's interests not ours. For instance, if an individual is called into business ministry, the more profits God blesses him with, the more he must sow towards God's interests. He should not stick with the old testament ten percent rule and shift the rest on personal gains of acquiring a fleet of cars and other unnecessary personal additions. His selflessness must be expressed in his zeal in God's interests and lack of interest in himself.

About self denial our Lord said "If anyone would come after me, he must deny himself and take up his cross and follow me. For whoever wants to save his life will lose it, but whoever loses his life for me will find it," (Matthew

16:24-25). The measure of our obedience is determined by how much we deny our interests and lose our lives by burying them in the work of Christ in whatever calling God puts us in. "Where your treasure (interest) is, there your heart will be also," (Matthew 6:21).

Where to sow

Much of what has been shared may have clarified this. It may be worthwhile to summarize it. Wherever you sow as long as it's in Christian related causes matters less than your motives for sowing. You will receive financial rewards for whatever financial sacrifice you make. God remembers them all and will reward you in due season.

Your concern should be whether or not your financial sacrifices will have a heavenly reward. You may be desperate now to care less on what you'll later receive but I advise you to minimize your desperation. The more in a hurry you are the more God may test your faith and try to align your motives to suit his.

He can therefore delay your purposed reward or transfer it to your children altogether. He may instantly reward but you will be a rare exception. Many of us have had to walk by faith and learnt to give for the sake of the gospel for years and years and years. God has blessed us in many ways that toil and sweat cannot manage. However it has all been in his way and measure, not ours.

Another counsel is on ministries claiming to be fertile ground. I believed this until the Lord revealed these matters. The only fertile ground is you the individual believer not an entire ministry.

If it was a ministry then our heavenly rewards will be based on which ministries we gave to regardless of our motives. Even non-Christians would be rewarded for helping Billy Graham, Joyce Meyer, T.D. Jakes in their evangelism work or supporting Betty and James Robison in their charity ministry that ministers to physical needs of the poor.

The scripture says the soil (good or bad) is the believer. The parable about the good and bad soil is in Mark 4:13-20. The parable is more about how we apply God's word in our lives than about finances. Regarding finances we will reap wherever we sow even with wrong motives or in wrong areas.

Our concern needs to be on our motives and areas that the bible supports - Christian causes. Where to sow is therefore in areas that can be considered as Christian causes or responsibilities of the body of Christ. They need to be part of God's household mentioned in Malachi. God's house is the body of Christ that is beyond a single ministry, denomination or structure.

A traditional church easily fits the description because of our conservative views. However the early church structure is far from what we have today. It was wherever people met and wherever believers did God's work. They even denounced temple buildings that the Israelites considered being sacred houses of God. Stephen got stoned to death for such remarks (Acts 7:48-50).

Paul, the one who supervised his stoning went on after his conversion to establish Stephen's divine inspired version of non-traditional temples. The early Protestants like John Wesley followed this up in their non-traditional ministries.

There is no ten percent rule of paying tithe like in the old testament. Neither is there a rule on sowing to a single ministry or to multiple ones. However it is good not to walk away from your local church. They survive and grow based on your support and you probably have been blessed by their teachings.

Attending a local church Sunday after Sunday and never helping out in their financial needs is spiritual robbery. Maybe you feel that they don't deserve your help. Then you're better off moving elsewhere you'd be willing to contribute at least on a level you feel grateful for their role in your life.

The other problem is when manipulation and deceit is used to obtain financial support. For instance when some claim sowing to their ministry will bring a financial breakthrough or break yokes in certain areas.

It is not wrong to say God will bless you. He will bless you because of your obedience to his word on giving, not obedience to someone's word on where to give, when or how much. It is wrong when God's blessing is linked to giving to a certain ministry, certain ministry programs and giving certain amounts.

If the blessing comes quickly enough you may end up assuming it came because you obeyed someone's word. He/she ends up getting the credit and not God's unbreakable word on giving that was actually fulfilled as you gave.

You're better off staying away from manipulative ministries. They may hinder some of your blessings because they make people focus on the assumed power of their ministry and not the real power of God's word when obeyed. Fellowship with a ministry that does not create such hindrances. There are enough hindrances to deal with already.

So certain amounts can be set aside for local and other ministries that have been a blessing to you in one way or another. Bless them materially for the spiritual empowerment they have sown in your life. "If we have sown spiritual seed among you, is it too much if we reap a material harvest from you?" 1 Corinthians 9:11.

The material support is anticipated to come from those being assisted spiritually. "In the same way, the Lord has commanded that those who preach the gospel should receive their living from the gospel," 1 Corinthians 9:14.

If our work has blessed you and you'd like to support our ministry please visit our support pages at JesusW.com and SpiritualWarfareDeliverance.com (the two websites for Jesus Work Ministry are interlinked through easy navigation).

Certain amounts can go to ministries you love to support in their work and care less of hearing or benefiting from them - spiritually, socially and so on. These can include Christian charities helping materially disadvantaged people. Certain amounts can go to your own personal ministry like helping your parents (or former guardians), needy members of your extended family, personal evangelism and so on.

Helping your own immediate family (spouse and children) is like helping yourself so it will not count as a sacrificial seed. But your immediate family still counts as part of your personal ministry.

Here is the best part on where to sow financial seeds. Sowing with the right motives and in Christian causes is what brings sweet fruits as opposed to bitter fruits. The gifts sown are also counted as a reward in heaven's bank account.

The sweet fruits and heavenly storing is what we all desire from our good deeds. We want to support the body of Christ in evangelism and charitable work for the worthy sake of the work even if no earthly reward came. However we also want heaven to honor our sacrifices on Judgment day rather than trash them in the fire. "If I give all I possess to the poor and surrender my body to the flames, but have not love, I gain nothing," 1 Corinthians 13:1.

If we cared less how heaven will value our good deeds then we could give with wrong motives and/or to non-Christian causes. The eventual outcome would still be a financial harvest, but one with bitter fruits and with no heavenly account. No sincere Christian would want this to his/her name.

Besides, bitter financial fruits are as distressing and many times worse than having no fruits at all. "Better a little (wealth) with the fear of the Lord than great wealth with turmoil," Proverbs 15:16. "He who increases his wealth by exorbitant interest amasses it for another, who will be kind to the poor," Proverbs 28:8.

How to Start

Having a giving lifestyle may be easy for some while difficult for others. Some who grew up with generous parents or guardians may have easily caught on this discipline. For those that may have problems you have God as your helper. Ask him to give you a heart and mind that is selfless and a heart that will help you in obtaining material blessings based on his principles.

A generous heart is God's spiritual gift of being empowered to apply the biblical financial principles. "But remember the Lord your God, for it is he who gives you the ability to produce wealth, and so confirms his covenant," Deuteronomy 8:18.

This ability or anointing to produce wealth (material resources) is not some magical or mysterious power that turns everything we touch into gold. It is being empowered with a generous heart that easily gives and gives without being preoccupied with its own needs or what it's getting in return.

A generous heart is blessed in the long run while one that keeps withholding receives no reward. "One man gives freely, yet gains even more; another withholds unduly, but comes to poverty," Proverbs 11:24. The spiritual laws of seed time and harvest time work in favor of the generous giver in the long run. It is important to pray for God's ability to have a generous heart if one lacks one. It is a spiritual gift known as the gift of giving or of helps (1 Corinthians 12:28).

Scripture encourages us to desire all spiritual gifts in whatever measure God, the giver, is able to give us (1 Corinthians 14:1). Better asking for too much and receive some than asking for a little and receive a minimum that God desired to give. Gifts are for helping us in doing good works. They have little or no relationship with showing how spiritual one is.

This book was written through one or more of these gifts working through me. It does not necessarily mean I am more spiritual than those who may not have the ability to share God's truths in this way. The same goes with the gift of giving. It will not mean it's a spiritual promotion once God gives it to you after asking for it.

Spiritual promotion comes through submitting to God in such an intimate way that his Spirit is effectively enabled to produce his fruit through us. The nature of his fruit that is produced in our lives is diverse.

Scripture says, "The fruit of the Spirit is love, joy, peace, patience, kindness, goodness, faithfulness, gentleness and self-control. Against such things there is no law. Those who belong to Christ Jesus have crucified the sinful nature with its passions and desires. Since we live by the Spirit, let us keep in step with the Spirit," Galatians 5: 22-25.

Having the fruit of the spirit is therefore far more important than having the gifts of the Spirit:

"Now I will show you the most excellent way. If I speak in the tongues of men and of angels, but have not love, I am only a resounding gong or a clanging cymbal. If I have the gift of prophecy and can fathom all mysteries and all knowledge, and if I have a faith that can move mountains, but have not love, I am nothing. If I give all I possess to the poor and surrender my body to the flames, but have not love, I gain nothing," 1 Corinthians 12:31-13:1-3.

Without love, a fruit of the Spirit, all our gifts have no value in heaven, no matter what we accomplish thorough them. Having the fruit of the Spirit flow through us is what makes our gifts of the Spirit acceptable to God.

So please be mindful as the Lord gives you many gifts, including the gift to possess much material resources that it has little, if anything, to do with a spiritual promotion. It does not indicate that you're closer to God even if people easily judge one's closeness to God by how much he/she is doing in the body of

Christ. "Man looks at the outward appearance, but the Lord looks at the heart," 1 Samuel 16:7.

We'll be amazed in heaven the little reward some will receive after we have labeled them as great men and women of God because of what they outwardly accomplished. God looks at how much was driven by love and his other fruits as opposed to how much was driven by ambition, material gain, fame, power and so on.

Some have gone on to manipulate innocent believers that they have a special anointing on them that if you sow to their ministry God will break whatever yokes in your life. Sowing to their ministry, not following the biblical ways of God has been made the focus. They are more focused on their ambition to grow their ministries than to connect people to God and his spiritual ways in the bible.

So please be mindful that spiritual gifts have nothing to do with a spiritual promotion. Do not look down on people that may not have certain gifts as if they are less spiritual than you. They are as close to God, if not closer, if their lives are overflowing with the fruit of the Holy Spirit -love, joy, peace, patience, kindness, goodness, faithfulness, gentleness and self-control. "To love your neighbor as yourself is more important than all burnt offerings and sacrifices," Mark 12:33.

After asking for the gift of giving you begin looking at whatever you have to give. If you have enough food to eat and a basic form of shelter the rest is a luxury. If your luxury is hindering you from giving you can work on minimizing all that you can live without.

Relocating to a cheaper residence maybe necessary if you are paying too much rent. Remember that God does not need your giving. It is you that needs his giving. To receive his giving he requires you to give first. It is therefore wiser to get rid of stuff that hinder you from giving. With all the hindrances around you God will continue waiting until you do your part.

As said earlier praying for God's material blessing will achieve little, if at all anything. Praying for God to help you in making priorities is a worthy prayer. Beyond that you're asking him to disobey spiritual laws he has set up for our own benefit. If he could provide material resources just through prayer there would be no poverty among Christians.

There are many Christians worldwide who pray fervently and overflow in the fruit of the Holy Spirit but still suffer avoidable financial afflictions. Why? "Unless a kernel of wheat falls to the ground and dies, it remains only a single seed. But if it dies, it produces many seeds," John 12:24.

A particular seed must therefore fall to the ground first before any harvest comes. On material harvests the particular seed required is a material seed, not prayer. Prayers are seeds for evangelism and for seeking God's ability to obey and fulfill his spiritual laws. They are not for asking God to make some short-cuts.

Where funds are scarce material items can be given or sold with the funds going to Christian evangelistic or charity causes. Items you can live without may be idle seed that could be sown for your future harvest. There is much around us that can be worthwhile seed. It's worth looking around.

If all you have is yourself, that is, no source of income there is still something to give – yourself. You can volunteer in Christian evangelistic or charity causes. Wherever your time or skills are needed can be a starting point.

Your labor won't be in vain. In due season God will begin to open strange doors that will enable you to give even financially. Or he may take care of your material needs in such a way that other people will be drawn to helping you materially. Some may even be good-hearted unbelievers. You can pray for their salvation.

Another counsel concerns borrowing. Some may assume borrowing in order to sow financial seed may be acceptable. God discourages borrowing, likening it to inviting servitude or bondage. "The rich rule over the poor, and the borrower is servant to the lender," Proverbs 22:7.

So borrowing in the Christian sense has its limited areas - on really, really critical matters like student loans in a career that one knows he/she is willing to excel in (or at least afford to repay the loan) after graduating.

If any ministry asks you to borrow for certain programs while promising God's blessing please leave that ministry faster than you got involved with it. They have put their ministry agenda beyond your welfare spiritually, materially, socially and so on. Avoid such ministries like a plague.

God, not their ministry is the one who will release your blessing. It will be based on what he has promised in his word not based on what a ministry has said. And his word certainly has nothing to do with borrowing in order to receive a blessing.

9.7 Christian Deliverance and Healing, Part 7: Physical Areas

CHAPTER 9. PART 7: PHYSICAL HEALTH - SUB-TOPICS:

- **Natural Physical Health**
- **Food as Medicine and other Natural Cures for Natural Health**
- **Supernatural Physical Health**

There are plenty of scriptures on physical health deliverance and healing. More direct scriptures focus on physical health deliverance and healing than on social and material deliverance and healing.

For example, fewer scriptures discuss directly on deliverance and healing from a marriage crisis or a financial crisis. Most of what we have in these areas is drawn from digging deep into the context and meaning of particular passages.

This should be great news for those seeking deliverance and healing in physical health areas. The bible affirms that being in good health is important. Desiring to be healthy physically is not wrong. It makes it harder to effectively do God's work in the harvest field if one's body is not in a healthy state. Jesus called physical healing "the children's bread," Matthew 15:26.

It is a gift from God intended for his children in their everyday lives. However, this needs to be seen in its context to avoid making it a "health and wealth gospel."

Natural Physical Health
a) What to eat and drink

What to include in your diet. Lot's of home-cooked greens and some garlic (natural or processed garlic). Some greens like fruits may be expensive for some. There are collard greens, lettuce, spinach and cabbage which are quite cheap. They are of great nutritional value as well as being helpful to the digestive system with their rich fiber levels.

In his book, *The China Study*, T. Colin Campbell, Professor Emeritus of Nutritional Biochemistry at Cornell University says, "So, what is my prescription for good health? In short, it is about the multiple health benefits of consuming plant-based foods, and the largely unappreciated health dangers of consuming animal-based foods, including all types of meat, dairy and eggs, " (*The China Study*, p. 21).

Greens are actually cheap in most third world countries where they can be grown on vast extra land. In Kenya lettuce is called "sukuma wiki." In

Swahili it literally means extend the week. It implies the greens help you afford to stay alive for another week.

The vegetables are seen like manna the Israelites had in the wilderness – just enough to live by the day. Understanding the health benefits of sukuma wiki and its cheap green relatives could lead to giving it a better name. Sukuma wiki is great with any non-pork meats in moderation to keep you healthy for decades ahead.

Meats other than pork are good if you can afford them but not in excess. Eliminating meats altogether is not wise. Two extremes, one of excess and another of abstinence are equally unhealthy. Unless occasional eggs are taken to supplement the needed for protein.

There are natural or organic foods in stores though many can be a bit more pricey than ordinary foods, many of which are not grown naturally. For most living in developing countries organic foods are abundant particularly in rural areas. The dilemma on food quality is mainly in the Western world.

Drinking more water instead of soda or other refined drinks is also more beneficial. God didn't make a mistake for making water, as tasteless as it is - when one is not thirsty. Water is king or queen, over all other human made drinks.

Plain boiled tap water is ok unless highly contaminated with impurities other than germs. The benefits of spring water over tap water are usually said to be minimal. However the debate on how much better spring water is over tap water can be controversial. Joseph Mercola says tap water should be avoided if possible because it contains chlorine and may contain fluoride in levels that in the long term can harm the body.

b) What not to eat

In the area of physical health God will enable you to know and avoid matters harmful to your body. In general please avoid eating pork. Pork mixes maybe, but pure pork is another story. Pork is not cheap meat. It is cheap poison meat.

No wonder the Jews were forbidden from eating it. There are lots of medical principles in the bible that the medical field keeps drawing from. I am therefore cautioning on eating pork for health reasons not religious reasons.

In the new covenant we can eat whatever food we like and still be under no condemnation. However, "everything is permissible but not everything is beneficial," 1 Corinthians 10:23. Jews do not eat pork to this day. Wise guys.

Drinking too much milk or milk products may also be unhealthy. Moderation is always the key. The quality of milk has diminished because of the way cattle are reared in developed nations like USA. The cattle are fed high growth hormones and other chemicals that are not good to our human bodies. They make the animals grow faster, bigger or produce more milk, thus yielding more profit with lower costs than through the natural process.

Dr. Joseph Mercola, an osteopathic physician (medical doctor) and natural health professional, says at Mercola.com, that some cases of breast cancer, prostate cancer, thyroid cancer, colon cancer, and so on are directly linked to genetically engineered substances like the Recombinant Bovine Growth Hormone (rBGH) that is given to some cows to increase their milk production.

The use of rBGH on cows is banned in Europe and Canada because of its proven effects on humans. The non technical term for food that has harmful extraneous substances in it is "contamination." Food can be contaminated for deliberate reasons because certain chemicals and substances given to it increase its yield, or its taste, its shelf life or for whatever motive.

It's helpful to stay informed rather than being ignorant and then start paying later for our negligence. For our children it's even more important to watch out for them.

However, it's not a call to be a health freak but a call to be aware of what's going on and take worthwhile measures where necessary. The level of greed among some in the business world is so shocking that profit maximization is their sole motive without any consideration for what's in the best interest of consumers. In the food industry the biggest problem has been adding substances that increase profits even when they are deemed harmful to consumers.

This is partly why there are increasing cases of obesity and other "modern" ailments. It is not because people have started eating more or exercising less. This has a factor but not compared to what is being put into our food supply to increase production and reduce costs. The times when people could afford to eat a lot have been around in developed nations for centuries. Why the sudden explosion of obesity in the last twenty or so years?

If you hear the amount of food being claimed as the main factor to obesity consider it as a "pass on the blame," game that the food industry loves to advocate for. They want to sweep their share of responsibility underneath the carpet.

The same chemicals and hormones that make the cattle and other animals gain weight and grow quickly end up doing the same to us when consumed in excess.

If you love milk for calcium in sustaining strong bones there are many other alternatives to take instead of drinking too much of it. Calcium supplements in moderation can be taken. One can also spend time in the sun which is a far better natural supplement. The only thing to avoid is overexposure. There is enough literature out there about the pros and cons of being in the sun.

C) Rest and Inner Renewal

According to a 2004 Harris Poll in the US, of 1,017 adults surveyed 35 percent listed reading as their favorite pastime. Reading has been the top

response ever since the surveys began to be conducted in 1995. The following were the favorite pastime activities ranked in order of preference:
1. Reading: 35 percent
2. TV watching: 21 percent
3. Spending time with family and kids: 20 percent
4. Going to the movies: 10 percent
5. Fishing: 8 percent
6. Computer activities: 7 percent
7. Gardening, renting movies, walking, exercise (aerobics and weights), and listening to music: 6 percent
8. Entertaining, hunting, playing team sports, and shopping: 5 percent
9. Traveling, sleeping, socializing with friends/neighbors, sewing/crocheting, golf, going to church, and church-related activities: 4 percent

Sleep ranks at a low 4 percent among those surveyed in the US population. Spending time sleeping whenever an appropriate time arises enables the body to recuperate. This is only for workaholics who naturally perceive sleep as a waste of time – a waste of time from winning as many gold medals as possible. Even sleeping or idling in the sun (when it shows up in some of our places) can be so refreshing.

The body does not call relaxing anything done with some level of physical activity or mental exertion. We may call it relaxing because it's different from the routine. The body does not. Eventually the body's definition of relaxing wins. It's better to give it needed rest that pays the dues in later years of life.

The senior years may seem far away for some of us but they come like a thief without realizing it. Who wants to spend his/her senior years moving from one hospital to another or being under a truckload of medication? And not to forget the thoughts of being a burden to loved ones. It's better thinking of how you'll still be able to serve the Lord in your senior years.

Physical activity and exercise is vital but so is sleep. How much sleep is enough? At least 7 to 8 hours a day for most with some extra catch up sleep on weekends or whenever possible. The rule is if you feel tired, unable to concentrate you may need an extra hour, or two.

How you feel throughout the day says a lot about how sufficiently your body is getting sleep. There could be other factors, like stress, worldly cares and concerns, and some biological matters involved but sleep has its major role among them.

Exercise is important too, particularly for those who have careers that have little or no physical activity. Some think yoga is a relaxing exercise but it is a practice of a non-biblical religion.

Here is a full definition of yoga: "Hindu discipline - any of a group of related Hindu disciplines that promote the unity of the individual with a supreme being through a system of postures and rituals," from the *Microsoft Encarta Dictionary, 2003*. You be the judge.

Excessive exercise is worth avoiding too. Ask professional athletes who suffer from joint and other ailments in their later years. As in many matters moderation is critical in exercise. More is not always better. Even brisk walking or jogging each week can be sufficient without any need for intensive exercise programs.

For now this is all that can be said on maximizing our physical health the natural way - doing our expected part in managing our physical health. There is a lot of literature out there on natural health you may have already come across.

It may also be worthwhile to visit Dr. Joseph Mercola's website at Mercola.com. It's the most visited natural health website in the world according to Alexa.com rankings. Mercola's free newsletter is also said to be the most popular natural health newsletter. You can subscribe for it at the website, Mercola.com.

Food as Medicine and other Natural Cures for Natural Health

While eating and drinking what's good for the body acts as a defense against avoidable illnesses it is also a natural cure against some diseases. Simple dietary measures can be natural cures against common illnesses.

Nearly 2,500 years ago, Hippocrates, who is regarded as founder of modern medicine, said, "Leave your drugs in the chemist's pot if you can heal the patient with food." But today dashing for medicine is the norm even over the slightest problem.

Good food increases or maintains our immune system which is a natural defense mechanism against illnesses. It's often said that if the body were a nation, the immune system would be its army against foreign invasion. The foreign invaders are the millions of pathogens that threaten our bodies daily. Pathogens are disease-causing agents that include bacteria, fungi, parasites, protozoa, and viruses.

That is why diseases that overcome the immune system or cause it to malfunction win their battle in attacking the body. Dr. Lorraine Day, a physician (medical doctor) and advocate for natural alternative therapies for diseases, says "The best and only way to avoid all infectious diseases is to have your body in a maximum healthy state with a properly functioning immune system. If the body's immune system is working properly, it is virtually impossible to contract any infectious disease!" (Lorraine Day, GoodNewsAboutGod.com).

Does medicine boost the immune system? Dr. Linda Page says, "Drugs aren't the answer for immune enhancement. The immune system is not responsive to drugs for healing. Even doctors admit that most drugs really just stabilize the body, or arrest a harmful organism, to allow the immune system to gather its forces and take over.

"Each one of us has a unique immune response system. It would be almost impossible to form a drug for each person. Antibiotics used to fight infections actually depress the immune system when used (in the) long-term. Long courses of tetracycline and erythromycin are some of the most common and some of the worst for immune health.

"But natural nutritive forces, like healing foods and herbal medicines can and do support the immune system. They enhance its activity, strengthen it, and provide an environment through cleansing and detoxification for it to work at its best.

"I believe the only way to stay healthy during high risk times is to prepare your body for the defenses it's going to need. Even if you've improved your diet, take another look at it because a super nutritious diet is imperative when you're under attack," (Linda Page, HealthyHealing.com).

This does not mean it's not healthy or beneficial to use conventional medicine. It can be unhealthy when medicine is used on a prolonged basis or overused. Page says, "Three unwanted things often happen with prolonged drug use: 1) our bodies can build up a tolerance to the drug so that it requires more of it to get the same effect. 2) The drug slowly overwhelms immune response so the body becomes dependent upon it, using it as a crutch instead of doing its own work.

"3) The drug misleads our defense system to the point that it doesn't know what to assault, and attacks everything in confusion. This type of over-reaction often happens during an allergy attack, where the immune system may respond to substances that are not really harmful.

"Most of the time, if we use drugs wisely to stimulate rather than over kill, if we "get out of the way" by keeping our bodies clean and well nourished, the immune system will spend its energies rebuilding instead of fighting, and strengthen us instead of constantly gathering resources to conduct a "rear guard" defense. The very nature of immune strength means that it must be built from the inside out," (Linda Page, HealthyHealing.com).

Other natural medical approaches apart from good nutrition as a means for increasing or maintaining our immune system are practices popularly known as alternative medicine or natural cures. These include herbs, exercise, vitamins & minerals, pure water, sleep, rest, fasting, sunlight, and stress reduction products & programs (such as music, bible study, vacationing, watching cartoons (for some), comedies (for others), etc).

Some not included on the above list are associated with Eastern religions and thus are non-Christian religious practices. These include yoga, acupuncture and transcendental meditation.

In case you need detailed info on why they may not be Christian please visit GotQuestions.org. It's a Christian website that answers questions from a biblical perspective. You can type in your query in the search bar. It's a helpful website covering even on matters central to this book: biblical spiritual warfare, territorial spirits, can Christians be demon possessed, tongues, praying to Mary, etc.

Some of us from Africa, South America and the Caribbean may assume herbs are not Christian. It depends which herbs one is talking about. In some parts of these regions, particularly in rural areas, there are herbal doctors known as witch doctors. As the name implies, witch doctors include witchcraft practices that embrace non-biblical interactions with the spirit realm. They prescribe clean herbs but they also practice non-Christian spiritual beliefs.

In Congo (DRC), parts of Cuba, Malawi, South Africa, Zambia, and Zimbabwe a witch doctor is largely known as nganga, Mganga in Swahili, sangoma in Zulu, and boko in Haitian Creole.

It's important to note that most of these regions are very Christianized. A few choose to integrate their Christian beliefs with traditional practices. In South Africa, some sangomas have progressed and ended black magic associations. These prescribe herbs without any association to occult practices.

For such their herbal prescriptions have no occult connection. The question comes over those that include non-biblical practices in their profession. It taints their clean side. One may not be able to distinguish what's been associated with the evil spirit realm and what's not. Unless he/she is well informed.

Any search for herbs ought to be from those that do not have beads, images, animals' bones, weird outfit and all the superstitious items common among witch doctors. They ought to be professional herbalists not spiritualists or witch doctors.

Developing countries have a longer way to go in separating the two professions - herbalists versus spiritualists (witch doctors). They're ahead in natural, non-genetically altered foods that are essential for our immune system.

Herbs that are worth using are those produced by those who do not associate their products with the evil spirit realm. By the way, some of modern medicine does consist of herbs. They are just herbs that have successfully been patented. Those in business know why patents have brought modern medicine to where it is today - big business with profit maximization sometimes at consumers' expense.

Some may ask where these clean herbs can be found. A good book to read is *The Christian's Guide to Natural Products & Remedies: 1100 Herbs, Vitamins, Supplements and More!* by Frank Minirth et al. Many other books and resources on herbs out there could be helpful sources - including library and Internet resources.

Another point to note is that some advocates for alternative medicine or natural cures have been harassed indirectly or directly. Some have been labeled as quacks. This is an old reference to an untrained person who pretends to be a physician (medical doctor) and dispenses medical advice and treatment. Because they do not use modern medical treatment as their primary approach they automatically are labeled as quacks.

For instance, Dr. Lorraine Day, who is actually a trained and licensed physician (medical doctor (MD)) has received her fair share of accusations of practicing quackery after abandoning emphasis on modern medical treatment. The main reason for such assaults is preservation of big business in maintaining its hand on the billions it makes from its health products. Natural cures, if they gained prominence would take over their dominance. They're to be conquered from being a business threat. The secular business world is predatory and can be ruthless.

Thinking that the pharmaceutical industry (manufacturers of modern medicine) is lovingly and tearfully looking out for your utmost interests is basically running from reality or just a love for ignorance. They are among the business giants working on the creation of the New World Order. Need I say more?

Individuals in alternative medicine like Lorraine Day (DrDay.com), Linda Page (HealthyHealing.com), and Joseph Mercola (Mercola.com) have been compelled to publish disclaimers to avoid being bullied into oblivion through lawsuits.

Here is a disclaimer example from Joseph Mercola, "The entire contents of this website are based upon the opinions of Dr. Mercola, unless otherwise noted. Individual articles are based upon the opinions of the respective author, who retains copyright as marked. The information on this website is not intended to replace a one-on-one relationship with a qualified health care professional and is not intended as medical advice. It is intended as a sharing of knowledge and information from the research and experience of Dr. Mercola and his community. Dr. Mercola encourages you to make your own health care decisions based upon your research and in partnership with a qualified health care professional," (Joseph Mercola, Mercola.com)

The good news is that professionals practicing alternative medicine or natural cures have fought back and won a few battles - in USA where the medical field is strongly regulated. Many alternative medicine practitioners are actually licensed medical doctors (MDs) that have chosen to treat diseases outside modern medical procedures we call Western Medicine or Hippocratic Medicine.

Many alternative medical fields have been recognized as legitimate health fields in their own area of specialization of alternative health. For instance naturopathic medicine is recognized and practitioners must have a Doctor of Naturopathic Medicine (abbreviated as N.D. or less commonly N.M.D.) from an accredited university in USA or Canada.

They're also required to pass licensing board examinations from an individual state or province Naturopathic Board of Medical Examiners. Linda Page, a Naturopathic physician, of HealthyHealing.com is an Adjunct Professor at Clayton College of Natural Health. She is the author of *Healthy Healing - A Guide To Self-Healing For Everyone*, used as a textbook for health and nutrition courses by some universities like UCLA (University of California, Los Angeles).

So the key is to seek legitimate alternative health professionals from a field that is as diverse as the Christian faith. Naturopathic medicine with its emphasis on nutritional and herbal procedures rather than acupuncture, yoga and transcendental meditation has a pass mark for us Christians. Websites like DrDay.com, Mercola.com, and HealthyHealing.com may be worthy resource sites.

Some Christians may have problems with naturopathic practitioners that embrace Eastern religious practices like yoga and transcendental meditation. How about the modern medical physicians who embrace yoga or whatever non-Christian belief and still come to lay their hands on your body? Does that contaminate you?

If you were to ask some how they maintain their health they may quickly tell you "secrets" they discovered in yoga or some other non-Christian beliefs. Many in the Western world know what I'm talking about - that our physicians are not necessarily Christian.

The drug manufacturers as well are not Christian institutions. Some have been linked to research on biochemical warfare, the New Age human weapons of warfare. Buying medicine from companies with such ties is like funding their research on evil agendas. Does this make you evil or contaminate you if you buy clean medicine made by these companies?

Why then are we quick to "stone" people who practice alternative medicine? Some have gone out to allege that they're demon possessed. Bird brain size thinking. Do you know there are many New Age and occult secret society members in the health care world of modern medicine? Does it lead to impartation of demons by buying medication from a manufacturer with many top level occult members or receiving services from a physician who happens to be an occult member?

The key therefore is you not being involved in the practice of the non-Christian beliefs. If a physician practicing modern medicine shares his/her non-Christian health "secrets" you're free to differ with his/her approach. If an alternative medicine physician such as a naturopathic physician recommends a non-Christian approach you're free to state your beliefs and seek only what's in line with your faith. This is the key, not what they believe in or what they do in their private lives.

Or maybe modern medical practices are seen as safer? They're expected to be safer since quantitative analysis is their foundation before being marketed. But once profit maximization became the primary goal among many giants in the pharmaceutical industry quantitative analysis took the back seat. Quantitative data is now prone to bias and manipulation.

For example, among psychiatric drugs a news article in USA Today said study results of drugs depend on who is paying for the studies. Studies funded by the company that makes the actual drug being studied produced favorable results about the drug 78% of the time. Independent studies produced favorable results about the drug 48% of the time. Studies funded by a competitor to the company that makes the drug being studied produced favorable results about the drug 28% of the time (USA Today, May 25, 2006, p. A1).

Why such a wide discrepancy? Aren't such studies quantitative analyses and thus free from bias? You don't have to be a researcher to answer such easy questions. Could such discrepancies be part of the explanation why some drugs get good test results only to end up being so harmful and later to be removed from the market? What about the independent safety monitoring agencies?

Now on our physicians: Are our physicians who practice modern medicine far more reliable than physicians in alternative medicine?

One may say the answer is both yes and no. It is yes when diagnosing or recognizing health problems. The knowledge and tools that have been developed over centuries in the modern medical field are largely better in diagnosing or recognizing health problems. They are better at finding what the problem is in one's body. That could explain why many alternative medical physicians use many of the tools in the modern medical field.

However, when it comes to treating or curing the health problems the answer is no. A BusinessWeek article based on Dr. David Eddy's findings says, "Even today, with a high-tech health-care system that costs the nation (USA) $2 trillion a year, there is still little or no evidence that many widely used treatments and procedures actually work better than various cheaper alternatives," (BusinessWeek, May 29, 2006, Medical Guesswork, p. 73).

Eddy, a heart surgeon turned mathematician and healthcare economist says, "Go to one doctor, and get one answer. Go to another and get a different one."

This is partly because physicians may be inclined to treat health problems in relation to their area of medical specialization. This is more pronounced among serious illnesses. "Go to a surgeon, and he'll probably recommend surgery. Go to a radiologist, and the chances are high of getting radiation instead," (ibid., p. 76).

On this matter, Dr. David E. Wennberg, says "Doctors often assume that they know what a patient wants, leading them to recommend the treatment they know best," (ibid., p. 76).

The good news is that physicians largely have a heart, unlike many giants in the pharmaceutical industry who have no heart. The only problem is not being honest or blunt with patients about their limitations. As Dr. Paul Wallace puts it, the challenge is, "really about transparency – being clear about what we know and don't know," (ibid., p. 78).

In America, The Foundation for Informed Medical Decision (online at fimdm.org) was formed (in Boston) to foster transparency with patients. It produces booklets, videos, and other material to educate patients about health-care and their various options in the system. The Foundation's formula is: Medical Evidence + Patient Perspective = Informed Medical Decisions.

Its mission: "To assure that people understand their choices and have the information they need to make sound decisions affecting their health and well being. The Foundation organizes and frames medical evidence in an unbiased manner to help people evaluate their options, particularly in instances where differences in individual preferences and perspectives are likely to affect personal choice," (The Foundation for Informed Medical Decision, fimdm.org)

So when going to health specialists it's wiser doing personal research rather than assuming they are gods. This includes physicians in both modern and alternative medicine, and psychiatrists. They're not gods – in the higher sense. Their profession is just as fallible and imperfect as any of our own professions.

The health care field is liable to err, liable to bias, or any other influence as any of our professions. Some of their errors can result in major consequences on your life or over your loved ones – physically, materially, socially, etc.

So it's wise to arm yourself with necessary info over the numerous options you may have. It's worth buying books, software and read internet or library resources in these fields.

Much more could have been shared including the placebo effect were a patient miraculously heals herself after being administered fake medication or treatment. This includes fake surgery and fake psychotherapy. The scientific explanation (though still a mystery) is that the mind can affect the body's biochemistry. Thus it's all in the mind or a mind over matter phenomenon, whereby the body is subject to the mind. In the Christian sense it's all according to one's faith. "According to your faith will it be done to you," Matthew 9:29.

In summary, all this has been shared to expand your understanding and empower you on physical health care. This section of the Christian Deliverance and Healing chapter on physical health attempts to provide helpful info with a balance on medical practices that are workable and applicable to Christianity.

Modern medical procedures have not been shared extensively because the information is right at our doorsteps. There are even plenty of "personal MD software" one can buy. I have one myself, a "Home Medical Advisor," and it's been helpful.

Health care institutions (hospitals, primary care units, clinics, etc.), the media and the academia "worship" modern medicine to the extent of preaching it as our ultimate answer to good health. This chapter serves to balance this view with reality.

As an informed Christian, with the mind of Christ (active not sleeping), you're at liberty to make your own health care decisions based on whatever you believe is workable for you.

Supernatural Physical Health

Supernatural physical health, faith healing or divine healing is physical health that is enhanced by our walk with God. It is not a license to neglect taking care of ourselves naturally. Rather it makes up for what we're unable to acquire naturally. The Lord is also able to graciously rescue us from health problems that we may have brought on ourselves through carelessness.

We all need the supernatural physical health to supplement our limitedness - some more than others and at different stages in our lives. It is perfectly fitting to seek God's supernatural deliverance and healing from health problems through his supernatural intervention.

While using modern medicine is great sometimes it may not be affordable or it may bring other complications. Plus modern medicine usually comes with its side effects, leave alone the fact that our genetic code widely varies between individuals such that for some certain medicines may just be more poison to their bodies. Thus our best medicine is seeking God's miraculous or supernatural deliverance and healing in major areas. For major illnesses modern or alternative medical procedures can be followed on a secondary level or in combination with seeking God's supernatural intervention.

There are plenty of scriptures that relate to our supernatural physical health or God's supernatural provisions for our spirit, soul and body. Among them are:

"They drove out many demons and *anointed many sick people with oil and healed them*," Mark 6:13

"Is any one of you sick? He should call the elders of the church to pray over him and anoint him with oil in the name of the Lord," James 5:14

"Blessed is he who has regard for the weak; the Lord delivers him in times of trouble…The Lord will sustain him on his sickbed and *restore him from his bed of illness*," Psalms 41:1-3

"May God himself, the God of peace, sanctify you through and through. May your whole spirit, soul and body be kept blameless at the coming of our Lord Jesus Christ. The one who calls you is faithful and he will do it," 1 Thessalonians 5:23-24

"For everyone who asks receives, and he who seeks finds, and to him who knocks it will be opened." Matthew 7:8

"If you spend yourselves in behalf of the hungry and satisfy the needs of the oppressed, then your light will rise in the darkness, and your night will become like the noonday. The Lord will guide you always; he will *satisfy your needs* in a sun-scorched land and will strengthen your frame;" Isaiah 58:10-11

"First let the children eat all they want," he told her, "for it is not right to take the *children's bread* and toss it to their dogs." Mark 7:27

9.8 Christian Deliverance and Healing, Part 8: Overcoming Setbacks

CHAPTER 9. PART 8: OVERCOMING SETBACKS - SUB-TOPICS:

- The Reality of Falls and Lapses ("Setbacks," "Relapses")
- Rising Again After a Fall or Lapse
- Guarding Against any Fall or Lapse
- What Falling Down is Not

The Reality of Falls and Lapses ("Setbacks," "Relapses")

A dictionary definition of a fall, lapse, or setback means slipping from a higher or better condition to a lower one after apparent improvement. It is some level of deterioration after realizing an important improvement, recovery or healing. The level of deterioration may not necessarily be a complete return to a former lower condition, but does constitute a regression.

"Though a righteous man falls seven times, he rises again, but the wicked are brought down by calamity," Proverbs 24:16.

This topic is usually avoided by ministers or is looked at in a judgmental way: "As a dog returns to its vomit, so a fool repeats his folly," Proverbs 26:11. One scripture is talking about a righteous person (Proverbs 24:16 above) while the other is talking about a fool (Proverbs 26:11 later). These are two different categories of people.

Proverbs 24:16 says a righteous person can fall and it's not the end of the world as long as he/she rises again. Falling from a realized higher or better condition is nothing any of us desire or anticipate, be it spiritually, socially, materially, or physically. It is a nightmare to think about.

However, the bible says all hope is not lost when the unexpected somehow befalls us. Although the wicked are brought down by calamity (undesirable matters) the righteous are able to rise again when they experience them. We have God who graciously gives us strength to get up and recover.

Falling in any area of concern is therefore not a victory against us by Satan and his demonic influence schemes. It is not to be considered as his moment to gloat or rejoice over us. "Do not gloat over me, my enemy! Though I have fallen, I will rise. Though I sit in darkness, the Lord will be my light," Micah 7:8.

Noah, Abraham, Isaac, Jacob (Israel), Moses, Miriam, Elijah and other prophets, Peter and other disciples, Paul and other apostles, great ministers of church history, were by no means perfect. Who are we to assume we're exceptions?

Rising Again After a Fall or Lapse

Remember how Paul wrestled with matters that brought him down? "I do not understand what I do. For what I want to do I do not do, but what I hate I do... Now if I do what I do not want to do, it is no longer I who do it, but it is sin living in me that does it... What a wretched man I am! Who will rescue me from this body of death?" Romans 7: 15, 20, 24.

This is the person who ascended to the third heaven, received revelations God said were just for his consumption, and a person that God used to write a third of the New Testament! Yet he was still no superman. "What a wretched man I am! Who will rescue me from this body of death?" Romans 7:24.

Did Paul lose hope? Not according the verses that follow up: "Thanks be to God--through Jesus Christ our Lord... Therefore, there is now no condemnation for those who are in Christ Jesus," Romans 7:25; 8:1. Paul fought back by appropriating God's grace available through Christ's work on the cross.

Thus anyone that may experience a fall in any area he/she received deliverance and healing has plenty of hope - through Jesus Christ our Lord. There is no condemnation for the fall as long as one gets up again. Jesus paid the price for our freedom on the cross. God's grace that is granted to us on the grounds of Christ's work on the cross is available to enable us to get up gain.

The solution after falling down therefore is to rise up again. God's grace is already at work to enable us. How does one get up? By applying the same biblical principles that earlier brought deliverance and healing. A summarized version of what's needed to get up is as follows:

1) prayer of repentance for walking outside God's will,
2) ceasing all known association and practice of matters that bring bondage through a) deception (false teachings), b) through ignorance (lack of knowledge), c) through sin, and d) through storms of life (when responded to in a wrong way),
3) being familiar with and applying biblical requirements in areas were deliverance and healing is sought (most biblical requirements in different areas are covered in this book), and
4) a simple prayer to ask God for continued guidance, equipping and grace in opening one's eyes to true biblical living.

Falling does not mean the biblical principles failed or God failed in sustaining his part. It only implies that maintaining our health whether spiritually, socially, materially, or physically, is a constant battle throughout our lives. Once healed does not mean never to face the same challenge again. For as long as we're in this world we'll continue wrestling against Satan's schemes of demonic influence (not possession) and our fallen nature.

Guarding Against any Fall or Lapse

This is the part we all desire - to never fall down, particularly in major areas. Every fall has its levels of loss and regret, even if we end rising up. The more important the area the bigger the loss and regret.

The "secret" to guarding against any fall is to strive in managing our lives in such a way that we "Make every effort to enter through the narrow door, because many, I tell you, will try to enter and will not be able to," Luke 13:24. This isn't an easy journey yet is possible with God who provides the grace for it.

The bible says, "Grace and peace be yours in abundance through the knowledge of God and of Jesus our Lord. His divine power has given us everything we need for life and godliness ... Through these he has given us his very great and precious promises, so that through them you may participate in the divine nature and escape the corruption in the world caused by evil desires," 2 Peter 1:2-4.

The Christian life is a challenging call to perseverance and righteous living. Scripture doesn't say it's easy. That's why few make it or desire it. However the bible does say it's possible – through God. It'd be a dishonor to God to make up excuses or to lower the standards because of difficulties of meeting required standards. God is faithful in doing his part of sustaining us as long as we remain faithful in fulfilling our required input.

Sometimes we weaken in our faithfulness level yet his level of faithfulness is always the same. "If we endure, we will also reign with him. If we disown him, he will also disown us; if we are faithless, he will remain faithful, for he cannot disown himself," 2 Timothy 2:12-13

The bible's prescription for doing our part in guarding against any fall is: "Make every effort to add to your faith goodness; and to goodness, knowledge; and to knowledge, self-control; and to self-control, perseverance; and to perseverance, godliness; and to godliness, brotherly kindness; and to brotherly kindness, love. For if you possess these qualities in increasing measure, they will keep you from being ineffective and unproductive in your knowledge of our Lord Jesus Christ," 2 Peter 1:5-7.

Based on the above and other scripture we can simplify the bible's formula to a more practical level:

1) Watching vulnerable areas, guarding areas of weakness,
2) Employing biblical disciplines such as fasting when overwhelmed by challenges,
3) Cultivating intimacy with the Lord – deeper abiding with Christ,
4) Responding to life's storms the right way.

1) Watching Vulnerable Areas, Guarding Areas of Weakness

We become vulnerable if we let down our guard against Satan's schemes. For as long as we're in this world we'll continue wrestling against Satan's schemes of demonic influence (not possession) and our fallen nature.

We become vulnerable particularly during seasons of ease when we assume we've arrived and gone beyond falling. "If you think you are standing firm, be careful that you don't fall!" 1 Corinthians 10:12. There is no arriving in this life time. It is a journey of maturing from one stage to another and defending territory that has already been gained.

Areas we're most vulnerable to are areas we're weakest at. Each of us has different areas we're strongest at and different areas we're weakest at. Each of us knows best where these are (or at least should know better). Factors that influence our makeup of strengths and weaknesses include:

a) our inborn makeup (biological, personality and other nature factors),

b) our upbringing factors (educational level, area of training and skills, family upbringing, cultural upbringing and other nurture environmental factors), and

c) our spiritual rebirth factors (spiritual gifts given to us after being born again. These gifts operate in us regardless of our natural abilities, education, background, sex, age, personalities, and so on).

Areas of strength are not a challenge for us. Even Satan can labor all day to bring us down without any success. It's another story when it comes to our weaknesses.

For example, I've the grace in managing finances. Being entrusted with a billion dollars would not be a hell of a challenge for me. It's not an area of weakness. For others this could be their biggest area of weakness. Just a few pennies can cause them to fall.

On the other hand, I have my own biggest areas of weakness where it'd take a tiny dose to fall. Those in my inner circle are aware and help in being as backups in guarding against any fall. It's therefore the areas of weakness that I'm most vulnerable to. And it's wise to guard against these areas on a constant basis than areas of strength. Areas of strength also need guarding but not as much. "If you think you are standing firm, be careful that you don't fall!" 1 Corinthians 10:12.

Guarding against these areas of weakness includes staying away were possible or fleeing from instances and matters that expose one to danger of falling. It also includes applying the other biblical principles mentioned here, such as cultivating intimacy with the Lord – deeper abiding with Christ.

2) Employing Biblical Disciplines such as Fasting when Overwhelmed by Challenges

Does this need repetition here? Maybe not. Other chapters and sections in this book have more detailed info. See chapter 9.3 Christian Deliverance and Healing, Part 3: Prayer and Fasting.

3) Cultivating Intimacy with the Lord – Deeper Abiding with Christ

"Submit yourselves, then, to God. Resist the devil, and he will flee from you. Come near to God and he will come near to you," James 4:7-8.

The strength to lead righteous and empowered lives comes from God. Submitting or drawing near to him gives us more strength to victoriously confront matters that attempt to bring us down. "I am the vine, you are the branches. He who abides in me, and I in him, bears much fruit; for without me you can do nothing. ... By this my Father is glorified, that you bear much fruit," John 15:5,8 (NKJV).

4) Responding to Life's Storms the Right Way

This also may not need repletion here. All the parts of chapter 9 have so much info on this area.

What Falling Down is Not

This section is important before being misunderstood - it's worth addressing what falling down is not.

"Though a righteous man falls seven times, he rises again, but the wicked are brought down by calamity," Proverbs 24:16.

Firstly, falling down is not an aspect of inviting demonic possession. It concerns the righteous, God's children, who're possessed by the Holy Spirit. They are thus free from any danger of demonic possession.

Some have used a scripture on potential return of demonic possession and associated it with matters of falling down. "When an evil spirit comes out of a man, it goes through arid places seeking rest and does not find it. Then it says, 'I will return to the house I left.' When it returns it finds the house *unoccupied* (i.e. empty, without the Holy Spirit in it), swept clean and put in order. Then it goes and takes with it seven other spirits more wicked than itself, and they go and live there. And the final condition of that man is worse than the first. That is how it will be with this *wicked* (sinful) generation," Matthew 12: 43-45 (emphasis added).

Three things qualify for return of demons into a person: a) the individual was *previously* possessed by whatever demons that owned him; 2) he is *wicked* and has totally turned his back on the Lord and his ways; 3) after being delivered and then owned by the Holy Spirit he later becomes an *unoccupied* vessel, that is without having the Holy Spirit since he's totally walked out on God.

Thus while falling down has aspects of demonic influence it's got nothing to do with demonic possession. The righteous that fall down however many times and are able to rise up and continue being God's children. If God requires us to forgive others at least seventy-seven times a day (Matthew 18:22) how much more is able to forgive us?

The price for falling down among fellow humans may be huge if it's in a major area. Humans have quite a hard time taking a wrongdoer back completely –depending on the sin. However with God when a wrongdoer chooses to rise up he takes them back completely and wipes every bad record off his "black book."

Secondly, falling down is not falling from grace. While being once saved does not necessarily imply always saved, falling down cannot be equated to loosing one's salvation. The righteous that fall down have an open door to return to their Father's house. Their salvation is still intact through the door called "grace."

It is true however that one can depart from the faith. This takes a lot of serious wrong choices knowingly and after ignoring repeated convictions by the Holy Spirit. How else can we explain those who were once Christians and now want nothing to do with it? "The Spirit clearly says that in later times some will abandon the faith and follow deceiving spirits and things taught by demons," 1 Timothy 4:1. Needless to say that there is still hope to return for such individuals.

Departing from the faith should not be a concern to any of us doing our best to live by our required biblical standards. As long as we commit any negative matters we're facing into his hands the Lord will ensure we're ultimately victorious over them.

"No temptation has seized you except what is common to man. And God is faithful; he will not let you be tempted beyond what you can bear. But when you are tempted, he will also provide a way out so that you can stand up under it," 1 Corinthians 10:13.

10. Christian Persecution: A Deliverance Exception

One area where there is no freedom is Christian persecution. Others include trials of our faith that God allows us to experience. Enduring Christian persecution is where genuine marks of Christ come from. It's the true furnace that the Lord uses to refine us. The Lord may free us from one form of persecution but only to allow another to take over at some point. How we respond to it depends on each of us and our walk with God.

The scriptures are more than clear about persecution in more passages than many other topics. We would only be deceiving ourselves if we think we'll receive medals of approval from both God and the fallen world. "*Everyone* (not some or a few) who wants to live a godly life in Christ Jesus will be persecuted, while evil men and impostors will go from bad to worse, deceiving and being deceived," 2 Timothy3:12-13.

Nature of Christian Persecution

Baker's Evangelical Dictionary of Biblical Theology says the meaning of persecution includes "pursuing or pressing on, to oppress, harass (Deut 30:7; Job 19:22; Acts 8:1), and also to bring to judgment or punishment (Jer 29:18; Lam 3:43; Matt 5:11-12; Luke 11:49)."

On the nature of persecution it says, "Both the Old Testament and New Testament give examples of *physical, social, mental, and spiritual persecution*. Physical persecution includes taking another's life (Gen 4, Cain murdering Abel) or maiming the body (Exodus 22, 23). Social persecution (sometimes called discrimination) consists of making individuals or a group outcasts. An example of extreme mental and spiritual persecution is seen when Peter and John were threatened not to preach the gospel (Acts 5:28,40)."

In its reference to Christians persecution is therefore suffering inflicted on us by other people because of our beliefs. It comes directly from people not spirit beings. Satan who is said to be prince of this fallen world (John 16:11) influences people to persecute us, though only to the extent God allows. It can even go the extent of our lives being taken, as was the case with many prophets in the Old Testament and the early church apostles.

Persecution is highest in regions were Christianity is most hated. In many parts of Asia including the Middle East and North Africa Christians have been facing severe attacks from people including governments. To this day some are imprisoned and killed for their refusal to compromise their beliefs.

Persecution.org is a good website if you wish to familiarize yourself (or support believers under severe persecution) on persecution among believers worldwide. It belongs to the International Christian Concern (ICC) a ministry serving the highly persecuted believers in such regions.

In the Western world, a new era of oppression against Christians is growing. The freedom of worship and expression has been decreasing as people have attacked Christianity to be offensive against modern day lifestyles. "When the foundations are being destroyed, what can the righteous do?" Psalm 11:3. They want to destroy the foundational principles of Christianity under the veil of "religious tolerance."

These include some pro-abortion groups, gay rights groups, some extreme left-wing groups (e.g. some New Age crusaders) and extreme right-wing groups (e.g. Neo-Nazis).

For instance, in November 2003 a Chief Justice, Roy Moore, was dismissed for his refusal to remove the Ten Commandments monument from the Alabama state courthouse in USA. Moore was sued by the American Civil Liberties Union (ACLU), the Southern Poverty Law Center, and Americans United for Separation of Church and State.

They argued that references to God on a monument was a threat to the establishment of the official Alabama state religion, atheism. Similar arguments have led to the removal of bibles in public schools, abolition of prayer in public schools and so on.

To God persecution has its blessings. "Blessed are you when people insult you, persecute you and falsely say all kinds of evil against you because of me. Rejoice and be glad, because great is your reward in heaven, for in the same way they persecuted the prophets who were before you," Matthew 5:11-12.

Persecution does not include the strange experiences we face individually, in a family, among friends or in the church that come from being involved in the erroneous spiritual warfare and deliverance teachings. This tells us that there is something wrong with teachings that invite the enemy to come and "steal and kill and destroy," John 10:10.

If we cannot learn from the scriptures we are at least enabled to learn from the experiences it brings. The experiences are mere acts of destruction that come upon us because we have gone outside our area of authority. It is wrong for instance, to attribute severe illnesses, accidents, tormenting experiences, strange church problems or worse still the death of a loved one as persecution from the devil. Persecution comes from people not unpleasant circumstances and experiences.

Fruits of Persecution on us and Consequences on Persecutors

Persecution exposes how much treasure we have invested on earth in our egos or personal interests and how much is in heaven. If we have invested more in loving ourselves and in being loved by others than being loved by God we will be bothered when that investment is threatened.

Anything that appears to endanger or threaten that area of self will induce fear, anxiety, anger or hurt. Why? Because, "Where your treasure is, there your heart will be also," (Luke 12:34, Matthew 6:21).

Our Lord Jesus invested all his treasures in heaven and his heart naturally followed where his treasure was. He was not therefore moved when his character was threatened among people. Neither was he looking for any approval from them.

Even the Pharisees who hated him acknowledge it. They said, "Teacher, we know you are a man of integrity. You are not swayed by men because you pay no attention to who they are; but you teach the way of God in accordance with the truth," (Mark 12:14).

Jesus did not worry about what others thought of him. All he cared for was his heavenly agenda that concerned fulfilling God's will and obeying his voice even if it brought opposition.

As Jesus' followers we are called to be like him. Our Lord endured the cross by denying himself at all costs against himself for the sake of others. The persecution he endured shows us how little he cared about his ego needs.

For us his followers persecution is meant to remove the self in us and replace it with his selfless nature. He rebuked Peter for trying to restrain him from going through what God ordained – the cross. He said to him, "Get behind Satan! You are a stumbling block to me; you do not have in mind the things of God, but the things of men," (Matthew 16:23).

Then he turned to the rest of his the disciples saying: "If anyone would come after me, he must deny himself and take up his cross and follow me."

As we mature spiritually we come to accept that a lot of God's leading involves self-denial. He leads us in areas that can kill the self. The self-centered and self-led part of us is a stumbling block to his leading and lordship over us.

With natural strength, defeat is inevitable in situations were our self-interests are threatened. But as we keep drawing strength from God - in prayer and his word we're able to deny ourselves and put the interests of others ahead of us.

We're able to accept that our opposition is not people or circumstances but Satan. And God only allows certain acts of the enemy's attacks for the purpose of refining our motives, interests and commitment in carrying the cross of self-denial.

Needless to say that some that persecute us receive instant judgment from God. Much to our amazement that the Lord can be so angry against some that trouble his children. Especially his children in front-line ministry (pastors, deacons, elders, intercessors, music artists and so on). "I will bless those who bless you, and whoever curses you I will curse; and all peoples on earth will be blessed through you," Genesis 12:3.

Notice on the cursing role that it is God that does it not us. We are only permitted to bless while leaving the cursing and vengeance for him to take care of. Our role is to pray for those cursing and persecuting us. God may choose to use the cursing (unpleasant) experiences he brings upon them to draw them to himself. Others may receive instant Mercy without going through unpleasant experiences.

Persecuting Jesus

Those who persecute us indirectly persecute Jesus. When Jesus appeared to Paul on the road to Damascus he asked Paul why he was persecuting him. He said, "'Saul, Saul, why do you persecute me?' 'Who are you, Lord?' Saul asked. 'I am Jesus, whom you are persecuting,' he replied," Acts 9:4-5. Fortunately enough, Paul received salvation, not judgment from Christ.

However Paul suffered the most among all the apostles in proclaiming the gospel. "This man is my chosen instrument to carry my name before the Gentiles and their kings and before the people of Israel. I will show him how much he must suffer for my name," Acts 9:15-16.

Many found salvation through his sufferings. His salvation opened doors to the greatest outreach among the early apostles.

Others persecuting us therefore find salvation, thus receiving God's mercy. We can only pray they all receive God's mercy instead of his wrath. It's Satan fighting against us as he works through their fallen nature. That's why the Bible says, "our struggle is not against flesh and blood, but against the rulers, against the authorities, against the powers of this dark world and against the spiritual forces of evil in the heavenly realms," Ephesians 6:12.

Scripture also says we're to walk in forgiveness. We forgive our persecutors and count their acts as being done out of not knowing what they're doing. Forgiveness obtains blessings for us and for those who wrong us. After Job prayed for his friends who kept judging him God restored twice all that he previously lost (Job 42:10).

When Stephen forgave those stoning him Paul received God's mercy that later brought his salvation. Meanwhile Stephen received a hero's welcome in heaven.

Scripture says, "Do not repay evil with evil or insult with insult, but with blessing, because to this you were called so that you may inherit a blessing," 1 Peter 3:9. Forgiveness enables us to inherit the blessing God has for us in every area we're being challenged to forgive. One of the great blessings is being forgiven by him.

"Forgive us our debts, as we also have forgiven our debtors. And lead us not into temptation, but deliver us from the evil one," Matthew 6:12-13 (NIV, ASV, NKJV, BBE).

Praying for persecutors is a way of forgiving their debts and trespasses against us. These may include some family members, relatives, friends, workmates, other acquaintances, strangers, those who persecuted or currently persecute you and even people that seem not to deserve forgiveness like thieves, criminals and so on.

Praying for Persecutors

You may wish to include the following prayer in praying for those persecuting you or persecuting others you're interceding for.

Our heavenly Father, I present to you, in the name of Jesus, the people who are persecuting me. Lord the condition these individuals have yoked themselves in through the schemes of Satan is something I cannot ignore. The yoke is in many dimensions:

1) their salvation is at stake,

2) they stand to reap in multiples the negative seeds they are nursing in their hearts,

3) Their behavior separates them from your hearing as 1 Peter 3:12 says, "the face of the Lord is against those who do evil,"

4) their problems that they desire you to solve will therefore continue as Isaiah 57:21 says, "There is no peace for the wicked," irrespective of the size of wickedness,

5) they risk not being forgiven by you as our Lord Jesus said in Matthew 6:15: "If you do not forgive men their sins, your Father will not forgive your sins,"

6) they risk procuring a curse from you as your word says in Proverbs 3:33 "The Lord's curse is on the house of the wicked, but he blesses the home of the righteous,"

7) They are away from your refuge and therefore can easily be opposed by Satan to whatever degree their sins give him the legal grounds to interfere with their lives,

8) Their sins will harm their children in one way or another as Isaiah 14:20-21 and Leviticus 26:39 say,

All this is working to the advantage of the devil whose ministry is to destroy people's lives. It profits you nothing for them to remain in such a hopeless state. Your word says in 2 Peter 3:9 that you do not want "anyone to perish, but everyone to come to repentance." Neither does it profit me anything to see them sawing seeds of bondage against themselves unknowingly. This leads me to my second petition.

Therefore my second petition, in the name of Jesus, is that you answer my petition to pardon their sin and therefore free them from paying their sins in the multiple ways mentioned above and any other ways. I forgive them for their sinful attitude towards me and I hold nothing in my heart against them. The Lord Jesus said to us his disciples: "if you forgive anyone his sins, they are forgiven," John 20:23.

Thank you that the enemy has been robbed of what he had wanted to destroy on my side and the side of those persecuting me. (*If prayed among two or more*): Thank you that you have considered my petition as binding just as Jesus said in Matthew 16:19 "whatever you bind on earth will be bound in heaven." Thank you that the enemy cannot unbind it since you who is mightier than him have bound it in heaven.)

Thirdly, I ask in the name of Jesus, that you cause these individuals to repent. Lord of the great harvest, open their mental and spiritual eyes so that they see their sins. Satan who is the god of this age has blinded their minds from knowing your truth.

Your word says "The god of this age has blinded the minds of unbelievers so that they cannot see the light of the gospel of the glory of Christ, who is the image of God," 2 Corinthians 4:4.

Verse 6 says it is you who healed the blindness of the minds and hearts of those of us who now can see: "For God, who said let light shine out of darkness, made his light shine on our hearts to give us the light of the knowledge of the glory of God in the face of Christ."

Heavenly Father, I ask you to let your Holy Spirit to heal the hearts of these individuals. May your Spirit open their eyes and shine his light in their hearts to give them the light of the knowledge of your ways. Some of these individuals are believers who already have the seal of your Holy Spirit in them.

However, they're grieving your Spirit by their sinful behavior and thereby hindering or limiting what you've purposed to fulfill in through them. Please allow your Spirit to convict both the believers and the unbelievers of their sins so that they can live lives worthy of your callings. In Jesus' name I pray, Amen.

Appendix 1: Weapons of Spiritual Warfare

Appendix 1: Weapons of our Spiritual Warfare

The following are among the major weapons of spiritual warfare. As the scriptures say these weapons of spiritual warfare look simple but are powerful in overcoming the enemy.

Please note the focus of the 20 "weapons" listed. All, except one, focus on God and us doing our part. There is only one exceptional "weapon" that directly targets the devil - weapon #4 -Exercising authority over unclean spirits. This involves casting out evil spirits dwelling in people (see chapter on Exception for Direct Confrontation).

The rest of the 19 weapons of spiritual warfare focus on God and us doing our part. They are by no means exhaustive. Other "weapons of spiritual warfare" can be found in the scriptures and be added to them. However they all focus on God or us doing our part.

This is not to say we fight God. It implies that God takes care of any obstacles in our lives as we abide in him. Our weapons of spiritual warfare are therefore "weapons of righteousness" (2 Corinthians 6:7) that the Lord uses to confront the enemy and set captives free. This may come as a surprise since we expect weapons of warfare to be used directly against enemy forces and territory. The case is a bit complex in the realm of the spirit because there is one group of forces in the natural realm and another in the spiritual.

In the natural realm there is us, God's servants on one side and on the other there are people knowingly or unknowingly being used by the devil, our main enemy. In the spiritual realm there is God almighty and his entire government of angels in their various roles and ranks. On the other spiritual realm side is the devil and his entire alliance of fallen angels in their various roles and ranks.

Explaining how and why the war rages may be another lengthy topic with its own limitations. The only important matter to note is that we have the entire heavenly government on our side including our Lord Jesus who stands as our intercessor (Romans 8:34) and our advocate in heaven's highest court (1 John 2:1, Job 16: 19-20). Our main concern here is the part we, as God's servants, play in this war. The scripture has laid this out quite clearly.

Most of what we see from the scripture is that the battle is his and our concern is to focus on him rather than on Satan. In fact, Satan's influence over the outcome of any battle is so insignificant that he's the one to be pitied for having started any battle – if only we do our part.

That is why the scripture says we're more than conquerors in any battle we may encounter. "In all these things we are more than conquerors through him who loved us. For I am convinced that neither death nor life, neither angels nor demons, neither the present nor the future, nor any powers, neither height nor depth, nor anything else in all creation, will be able to separate us from the love of God that is in Christ Jesus our Lord," Rom 8:37-39.

Thus the distortion that Satan is the focus in any battle ought to be totally demolished. This has been explained extensively in this book.

Weapons of Spiritual Warfare

1. **Prayer – (among weapons of spiritual warfare against all forms of evil, including sin, real failure, walking outside God's will)**

"Simon, Simon, Satan has asked to sift you as wheat. But *I have prayed for you*, Simon, that your faith may not fail. And when you have turned back, strengthen your brothers," Luke 22:31-32

"I (Paul) urge that supplications, prayers, intercessions, and thanksgiving be made for all men, for kings and all who are in high positions, that we may lead a quite and peaceable life, godly and respectful in every way. This is good and acceptable in the sight of God our Saviour, who *desires all* men be *saved* and come to the knowledge and truth," 1 Timothy 2:1-4

"I have posted watchmen on your walls, O Jerusalem; they will never be silent day or night. You who call on the Lord, give yourselves no rest, and give him no rest till he establishes Jerusalem and makes her the praise of the earth." Isaiah 62:6-7

"The prayer of a righteous man has great power in its effects," James 5:16 (our righteousness is in Christ Jesus: "Christ Jesus, who has become for us wisdom from God--that is, our righteousness, holiness and redemption," 1 Cor 1:30

"When I shut up the heavens so that there is no rain, or command locusts to devour the land or send a plague among my people, if my people, who are called by my name, will humble themselves and *pray* and seek my face and turn from their wicked ways, then will I hear from heaven and will forgive their sin and will heal their land. Now my eyes will be open and my ears attentive to the prayers offered in this place," 2 Chronicles 7:13-15

*"Submit to God and be at peace with him... *You will pray to him, and he will hear you*... He will deliver even the one who is not innocent, who will be *delivered through the cleanness of your hands*," Job 22: 21,27,30.

"A time is coming and has now come when the true worshipers will worship the Father in spirit and truth, for they are the kind of worshipers the Father seeks. God is spirit, and his worshipers must worship in spirit and in truth," John 4:23-24

"The Spirit helps us in our weakness. We do not know what we ought to pray for, but the Spirit himself intercedes for us with groans that words cannot express. And he who searches our hearts knows the mind of the Spirit, because the Spirit intercedes for the saints in *accordance with God's will*," Romans 8:26-27

*"If you remain in me and my words remain in you, ask whatever you wish, and it will be given you. This is to my Father's glory, that you bear much fruit, showing yourselves to be my disciples," John 15:7-8

*"The Lord is far from the wicked, but He hears the prayer of the righteous," Proverbs 15:29

*"When men are brought low and you say, `Lift them up!' then he will save the downcast. He will deliver *even one who is not innocent*, who will be delivered through the cleanness of your hands," Job 22:29-30.

2.   The Word of God -the sword of the Spirit and the belt of truth– (among weapons of spiritual warfare for evangelism and self defense weapon against ignorance, deception, false doctrines, spiritual poverty, sin, and against walking outside God's will)

3.   Fasting -(among weapons of spiritual warfare against heavy oppression that prayer alone may not overcome)
"*When* (not, if or in case) you fast, put oil on your head and wash your face, so that it will not be obvious to men that you are fasting, but only to your Father, who is unseen; and your Father, who sees what is done in secret, will reward you," Matthew 6:17-18
"His disciples asked him privately, "Why could we not cast it (the demon) out" And he said to them, "This kind cannot be driven out by anything but prayer and fasting," Mark 9:28-29, Matthew 17: 21, (KJV, ISV)
"Is not this the kind of fasting I have chosen: to loose the chains of injustice and untie the cords of the yoke, to set the oppressed free and break every yoke? Is it not to share your food with the hungry and to provide the poor wanderer with shelter-- when you see the naked, to clothe him, and not to turn away from your own flesh and blood? Then your light will break forth like the dawn, and your healing will quickly appear; then your righteousness will go before you, and the glory of the Lord will be your rear guard. Then you will call, and the Lord will answer; you will cry for help, and he will say: Here am I," Isaiah 58:6-9

4.   Casting out unclean spirits living in people (not in thin air) (Matthew 10:1, Mark 6:7,13, 16:17-18, Luke 9:1-2). Notice that this is the only area we have any direct confrontation with evil spirits. It's the only area we have believers' authority over evil spiritual forces. Any other role that works as spiritual warfare involves our focus on God and doing our part of walking in obedience.
*"The reason the Son of God appeared was to destroy the devil's work,"1Jn3:8
*"As the Father has sent me, I am sending you," John 20:21
*"How God anointed Jesus of Nazareth with the Holy Spirit and power, and how he went around doing good and healing all who were under the power of the devil, because God was with him," Acts 10:38
*"Anyone who has faith in me will do what I have been doing. He will do even greater things than these, because I am going to the Father," John 14:12
*"From the days of John the Baptist until now, the kingdom of heaven has been forcefully advancing, and forceful men lay hold of it," Matthew 11:12
*"I have given you authority to trample on snakes and scorpions and to overcome all the power of the enemy; nothing will harm you," Lk 10:19
*"Do not be afraid or discouraged because of this vast army. For the battle is not yours, but God's," 2 Chron 20:15
"The seventy-two returned with joy and said, "Lord, even the demons submit to us in your name," Luke 10:17

5.   Walking in obedience and consecration -the breastplate of righteousness- (among our weapons of spiritual warfare against sin)

*"Does the Lord delight in burnt offerings and sacrifices as much as in obeying the voice of the Lord? To obey is better than sacrifice, and to heed is better than the fat of rams," 1 Samuel 15:22.

*"Seek first his kingdom and his righteousness, and all these things will be given to you as well," Matthew 6:33-34

*"This is the one I esteem: he who is humble and contrite in spirit, and trembles at my word," Isaiah 66:2

*"You do not delight in sacrifice, or I would bring it; you do not take pleasure in burnt offerings. The sacrifices of God are a broken spirit; a broken and contrite heart, O God, you will not despise," Psalm 51:16-17

"When I shut up the heavens so that there is no rain, or command locusts to devour the land or send a plague among my people, if my people, who are called by my name, will humble themselves and pray and seek my face and turn from their wicked ways, then will I hear from heaven and will forgive their sin and will heal their land. Now my eyes will be open and my ears attentive to the prayers offered in this place," 2 Chronicles 7:13-15

*"If my people would but *listen to me*, if Israel would follow my ways, *how quickly would I subdue their enemies and turn my hand against their foes*," Psalm 81:13-14

*"Submit to God and be at peace with him… You will pray to him, and he will hear you… He will deliver even the one who is not innocent, who will be delivered through the cleanness of your hands," Job 22: 21,27,30.

6.   Walking in love, repentance and forgiveness -the shoes of the gospel of peace- (among our weapons of warfare against curses, sickness and hatred)

In Love: "By this all men will know that you are my disciples, if you love one another," Jn 13:35

*"If I have a faith that can move mountains, but have not love, I am nothing. If I give all I possess to the poor and surrender my body to the flames, but have not love, I gain nothing. 1 Co 13:2-3

*"This is how we know what love is: Jesus Christ laid down his life for us. And we ought to lay down our lives for our brothers," 1 Jn 3:16

"Let no debt remain outstanding, except the continuing debt to love one another, for he who loves his fellowman has fulfilled the law," Romans 13:8

*"Unless your righteousness surpasses that of the Pharisees and teachers of the law, you will certainly not enter the kingdom of heaven" (Matthew, 5:20

*In Repentance and Mercy (to God and to one another):
*"Because of the Lord's great love we are not consumed, for his compassions never fail. They are new every morning; great is your faithfulness …" Lament. 3: 22-23

*"Let us then approach the throne of grace with confidence, so that we may receive mercy and find grace to help us in our time of need," Hebrews 4:16

*"Blessed are the merciful, for they will be shown mercy," Matt. 5:7

*"Forgive us our debts, as we also have forgiven our debtors," Mat 6:12

*"Be merciful, just as your Father is merciful. Do not judge, and you will not be judged. Do not condemn, and you will not be condemned. Forgive, and you will be forgiven. Give, and it will be given to you...For with the measure you use, it will be measured to you," Luke 6:36-38.

<u>Healing through Repentance</u>

*"Therefore confess your sins to each other and pray for each other so that you may be healed," James 5:16

*"Bless the Lord, O my soul, and forget not all his benefits, who forgives all your iniquity, who heals all your diseases," Psalms 103:1-3

7.   **Walking in fellowship- (among our weapons of spiritual warfare against spiritual unfruitfulness, spiritual weakness,, spiritual poverty, sin, deception)**

8.   **Walking in agreement- (among our weapons of spiritual warfare against division, conflict, unanswered prayers, etc.)**

*<u>In Word:</u> "He who guards his mouth and his tongue keeps himself from calamity," Pr 21:23

*"The tongue has the power of life and death, and those who love it will eat its fruit," Pr 18:21

*"To man belong the plans of the heart, but from the Lord comes the reply of the tongue," Pr 16:1

*<u>In Deed:</u> "Again, I tell you that if two of you on earth agree about anything you ask for, it will be done for you by my Father in heaven. For where two or three come together in my name, there am I with them," Mat 18:19-20.

*"Two are better than one, because they have a good return for their work. If one falls down, his friend can help him up. But pity the man who falls and has no one to help him up!" Eccl 4:9-10

*Agreement with the Lord makes three cords: "Though one may be overpowered, two can defend themselves. A cord of three strands is not quickly broken," Eccl 4:11

*"Every matter must be established by the testimony of two or three witnesses," Deut 19:15, Mat 18:16, 2 Corinthians 13:1

9.   **Walking in humility- (among our weapons of spiritual warfare against pride, egoism, arrogance, disrespect)**

*"The meek (humble) will inherit the land and enjoy great peace," Ps 37:11

*"Blessed are the meek, for they will inherit the earth," Mat 5:5

*"Ask of me, and I will make the nations your inheritance, the ends of the earth your possession," Psalm 2:8

*"And you will be called priests of the Lord...You will feed on the wealth of nations," Isaiah 61:6 (Nations' wealth is our inheritance for our priestly duties)

*"A sinner's wealth is stored up for the righteous," Pr 13:22 (the righteous use it for the gospel)

*"Humility and the fear of the Lord bring wealth and honor and life," Pr 22:4

*"Humble yourselves before the Lord, and he shall exalt you," James 4:10

*"God opposes the proud but gives grace to the humble," Jas 4:6, 1 Pet 5:5

*"A man's life is not his own; it is not for man to direct his steps," Jer 10:23.

*"This is the one I esteem: he who is humble and contrite in spirit, and trembles at my word," Isa 66:2

*"The sacrifices of God are a broken spirit; a broken and contrite heart, O God, you will not despise," Ps 51:17

*"Everything comes from you, and we have given you only what comes from your hand," 1 Chron 29:14

10.   Walking in submission- (among our weapons of spiritual warfare against self-ambition, self-glory, pride, disrespect, competition)
Submission to God (By submitting to his Word and the His Spirit)
*"Submit yourselves, then, to God. Resist the devil, and he will flee from you," James 4:7

*"Those who are led by the Spirit of God are sons of God," Romans 8:14

*"But if you are led by the Spirit, you are not under law…the fruit of the Spirit is love, joy, peace, patience, kindness, goodness, faithfulness, gentleness and self-control," Gal 5:18, 22-23

*"I am the vine; you are the branches. If a man remains in me and I in him, he will bear much fruit; without me you can do nothing," John 15:5 = "Not by might nor by power, but by my Spirit," Zec 4:6

*"And do not be drunk with wine, in which is dissipation; but be filled with the Spirit, speaking to one another in psalms and hymns and spiritual songs, singing and making melody in your heart to the Lord, giving thanks always for all things to God the Father in the name of our Lord Jesus Christ, submitting to one another in the fear of God," Ephesians 5:18-21

"Endure hardship as discipline; God is treating you as sons. For what son is not disciplined by his father? If you are not disciplined (and everyone undergoes discipline), then you are illegitimate children and not true sons. Moreover, we have all had human fathers who disciplined us and we respected them for it. How much more should we submit to the Father of our spirits and live!" Hebrews 12:7-9

Submission to One Another and to those in Authority (Especially to Spiritual Leaders)
"Submit to one another out of reverence for Christ," Ephesians 5:21

"It is necessary to submit to the authorities, not only because of possible punishment but also because of conscience," Romans 13:5

"Obey your leaders and submit to their authority. They keep watch over you as men who must give an account. Obey them so that their work will be a joy, not a burden, for that would be of no advantage to you," Hebrews 13:17

"Submit yourselves for the Lord's sake to every authority instituted among men," 1 Peter 2:13

11.   Holy communion-body and blood of Jesus– (among our weapons of spiritual warfare against all forms of evil, blood covering refuge, abiding in Christ and cleansing oneself)-
a) Holy communion
"For my flesh is real food and my blood is real drink. Whoever eats my flesh and drinks my blood remains in me, and I in him," John 6:55-56

"The Lord Jesus, on the night he was betrayed, took bread, and when he had given thanks, he broke it and said, "This is my body, which is for you; do this in remembrance of me." In the same way, after supper he took the cup, saying, "This cup is the new covenant in my blood; do this, whenever you drink it, in remembrance of me." For whenever you eat this bread and drink this cup, you proclaim the Lord's death until he comes," 1 Corinthians 11:23-26

"In him we have redemption through his blood, the forgiveness of sins, in accordance with the riches of God's grace that he lavished on us with all wisdom and understanding," Ephesians 1:7-8

"They overcame him by the blood of the Lamb and by the word of their testimony; they did not love their lives so much as to shrink from death," Rev 12:11

"In him we have redemption through his blood, the forgiveness of sins, in accordance with the riches of God's grace that he lavished on us with all wisdom and understanding," Ephesians 1:7-8

"Everyone born of God overcomes the world. This is the victory that has overcome the world, even our faith,"1 John 5:4

"The blood of goats and bulls and the ashes of a heifer sprinkled on those who are ceremonially unclean sanctify them so that they are outwardly clean. How much more, then, will the blood of Christ, who through the eternal Spirit offered himself unblemished to God, cleanse our consciences from acts that lead to death, so that we may serve the living God!" Hebrews 9:13-14

12.   Anointing with oil– (among our weapons of spiritual warfare against sickness, evil spirits, weakness and other burdens). The oil has no divine magical power. It is our faith and obedience to use it when and were necessary that enables God to do the miraculous work.

"When (not, if or in case) you fast, *put oil on your head* and wash your face, so that it will not be obvious to men that you are fasting, but only to your Father, who is unseen; and your Father, who sees what is done in secret, will reward you," Matthew 6:17-18

"They drove out many demons and *anointed many sick people with oil and healed them*," Mark 6:13

"Is any one of you sick? He should call the elders of the church to pray over him and anoint him with oil in the name of the Lord," James 5:14

"The Spirit of the Lord is on me, because he has *anointed* me to preach good news to the poor. He has sent me to proclaim freedom for the prisoners and recovery of sight for the blind, to release the oppressed," Luke 4:18, Isaiah 61:1

"How God *anointed* Jesus of Nazareth with the Holy Spirit and power, and how he went around doing good and healing all who were under the power of the devil, because God was with him," Acts 10:38

"And it shall come to pass in that day, that his burden shall be taken away from off thy shoulder, and his yoke from off thy neck, and the yoke shall be destroyed because of *the anointing*," Isaiah 10:27 (KJV)

"He (Moses) poured some of the anointing oil on Aaron's head and anointed him to consecrate him," Leviticus 8:12

"Take the anointing oil and anoint him by pouring it on his head. Bring his sons and dress them in tunics and put headbands on them. Then tie sashes on Aaron and his sons. The priesthood is theirs by a lasting ordinance. In this way you shall ordain Aaron and his sons," Exodus 29:7-9

"And take some of the blood on the altar (now done by taking Holy communion) and some of the anointing oil and sprinkle it on Aaron and his garments and on his sons and their garments. Then he and his sons and their garments will be consecrated," Exodus 29:21

"Anoint Aaron and his sons and consecrate them so they may serve me as priests. 31 Say to the Israelites, `This is to be my sacred anointing oil for the generations to come. Do not pour it on men's bodies and do not make any oil with the same formula. It is sacred, and you are to consider it sacred. Whoever makes perfume like it and whoever puts it on anyone other than a priest must be cut off from his people.'" Exodus 30:30-33

"You anoint my head with oil; my cup overflows. Surely goodness and love will follow me all the days of my life, and I will dwell in the house of the Lord forever," Psalm 23:5-6

"He allowed no one to oppress them; for their sake he rebuked kings: ***Do not touch my anointed ones***; do my prophets no harm," Psalm 105:14-15

13.   Praise and thanksgiving– (among our weapons of spiritual warfare against ingratitude, murmuring, complaining, a comparison attitude, doubt, doubt, fear, the "spirit of despair" (Isaiah 61:4)). This includes listening to praise and worship music, prayers of thanksgiving for answered prayers, prayers of praise and worship, and maintaining a thanksgiving lifestyle.

*"May the praise of God be in their mouths and a double-edged sword in their hands, to inflict vengeance on the nations and punishment on the peoples, to bind their kings with fetters, their nobles with shackles of iron, to carry out the sentence written against them. This is the glory of all his saints," Ps 149:6-9

*"Since my youth or God you have taught me and this day I will declare your marvelous deeds" Ps 71:17 (As spiritual children we can reflect on the time since we got saved and how God has kept us since our spiritual youth. Our physical age has little and no relevance to our spiritual lives)

*"O come let us sing to the Lord; let us make a joyful noise to the rock of our salvation: ***Let us come into his presence with thanksgiving***," Ps 95:1-2

"Rejoice in the Lord always; again I will say rejoice. Let all men know your forbearance (patience). The Lord is at hand. Have no anxiety about anything, but in everything by prayer and supplication with thanksgiving let your request be made known to God. And the peace of God, which passes all understanding, will keep your hearts and your minds in Christ Jesus." Philippians 4: 4-7

"I urge that supplications, prayers, intercessions, and thanksgiving be made for all men" 1 Tim 2:1

"Do not be grieved for, the joy of the Lord is your strength," Nehemiah 8:10

14.   Positive confession and guarding the tongue –(among our weapons of spiritual warfare against pessimism, self-proclaimed calamities (spiritual, social, physical, material, etc.) and weapon for creating desired matters)

(Luke 6: 45), mountains (obstacles in life which may be physical, circumstances, emotional, spiritual, social, financial -Matthew 17:20, 21:21), calamity

(Proverbs 21: 23, 13: 3), loosing problems (Matthew 16:19) death (spiritual, physical, social, material, financial-Proverbs 18:20-21), withholding God's blessings, ruining destiny (James 3: 3-6), Proverbs 13:2, Proverbs 18:7

15.   Generous giving to the work in the body of Christ – (among our weapons of spiritual warfare against greed, selfishness, insufficiency, poverty)
  *"Honor the Lord with your wealth, with the firstfruits of all your crops; then your barns will be filled to overflowing, and your vats will brim over with new wine," Proverbs 3:9-10
  *"Bring the whole tithe into the storehouse…and see if I will not throw open the floodgates of heaven and pour out so much blessing that you will not have room enough for it. I will prevent pests from devouring your crops…says the Lord Almighty," Malachi 3:10-11 (NB. Tithing not required in New T but the biblical principles of giving to God's kingdom interests still apply today. See section on financial healing in chapter on Deliverance and Healing)
  *"Command them to do good, to be rich in good deeds, and to be generous and willing to share. In this way they will lay up (in heaven) treasure for themselves as a firm foundation for the coming age, so that they may take hold of the life that is truly life," (1 Timothy 6:18-19
  *"The blessing of the Lord brings wealth, and he adds no trouble to it," (Proverbs 10:22).

16. The name of Jesus and our position in Christ –the helmet of salvation– (among our weapons of spiritual warfare against every curse and work of the enemy)
  Our position in Christ

<u>The name of Jesus</u>
  "Therefore God exalted him to the highest place and *gave him the name that is above every name, that at the name of Jesus every knee should bow, in heaven and on earth and under the earth*, and every tongue confess that Jesus Christ is Lord, to the glory of God the Father," Philipians 2:9-11
  *"The seventy-two returned with joy and said, "Lord, even the demons submit to us in *your name*," Luke 10:17
  *"Worthy is the Lamb, who was slain, to receive power and wealth and wisdom and strength and honor and glory and praise!" Revelation 5:12
  <u>Our position in Christ</u>
  "Therefore, if anyone is in Christ, he is a new creation; the old has gone, the new has come! All this is from God, who reconciled us to himself through Christ and gave us the ministry of reconciliation," 2 Corinthians 5:17-18
  "Therefore, there is now no condemnation for those who are in Christ Jesus, because through Christ Jesus the law of the Spirit of life set me free from the law of sin and death," Romans 8:1-2
  *"Christ redeemed us from the curse of the law by becoming a curse for us, for it is written: "Cursed is everyone who is hung on a tree." He redeemed us in order that the blessing given to Abraham might come to the Gentiles through Christ Jesus, so that by faith we might receive the promise of the Spirit," Galatians 3:13-14
  *"God made him who had no sin to be sin for us, so that in him we might become the righteousness of God," 2 Corinthians 5:21

"You are all sons of God through faith in Christ Jesus... There is neither Jew nor Greek, slave nor free, male nor female, for you are all one in Christ Jesus. If you belong to Christ, then you are Abraham's seed, and heirs according to the promise," Galatians 3:26,28-29

*"This mystery is that through the gospel the Gentiles are heirs together with Israel, members together of one body, and sharers together in the promise in Christ Jesus," Ephesians 3:6

"Praise be to the God and Father of our Lord Jesus Christ, who has blessed us in the heavenly realms with every spiritual blessing in Christ...In him we have redemption through his blood, the forgiveness of sins, in accordance with the riches of God's grace that he lavished on us with all wisdom and understanding.," Ephesians 1:3,7-8

17.   Faith-the spiritual shield– (among our weapons of spiritual warfare against doubt, fear, the "spirit of despair" (Isaiah 61:4), giving up, walking by sight, displeasing God)-

"Even youths grow tired and weary, and young men stumble and fall; but those who hope in the Lord will renew their strength. They will soar on wings like eagles; they will run and not grow weary, they will walk and not be faint," Isaiah 40-30-31

18.   Hardwork –(among our weapons of spiritual warfare against laziness, stagnation, neglecting utilizing or sharpening of given talents,   weapon against lack of promotion (from God))

"The man with the two talents also came. `Master,' he said, `you entrusted me with two talents; see, I have gained two more.' His master replied, `Well done, good and faithful servant! You have been faithful with a few things; I will put you in charge of many things. Come and share your master's happiness!'" Matthew 25:22-23

19.   Persistence –(among our weapons of spiritual warfare against impatience, despair, lack of commitment, lack of obligation)

"God "will give to each person according to what he has done." To those who by *persistence* in doing good seek glory, honor and immortality, he will give eternal life. But for those who are self-seeking and who reject the truth and follow evil, there will be wrath and anger," Romans 2:6-8

"Let us not become weary in doing good, for at the proper time we will reap a harvest if we do not give up,"   Galatians 6:9

Luke 11:5-8,

20.   Planning –(among our weapons of spiritual warfare against purposelessness, lack of direction, fruitless plans God plants in our hearts, real failure, wasted resources (time, talents, strength, finances, etc.), trial and error lifestyle):"Commit your plans to God and they will succeed," (Proverbs 16:6).

"Commit to the Lord whatever you do, and your plans will succeed," Prov 16:3

"Many are the plans in the mind of a man, but it is the purpose of the Lord that will be established." Proverbs 19:21

Appendix 2: Deliverance, Healing & Restoration Prayer

Appendix 2: Deliver us from the evil one," Matthew 6:12-13.

*"Forgive us our debts, as we also have forgiven our debtors. And lead us not into temptation, but **deliver us from the evil one**," Matthew 6:12-13 (NIV, ASV, NKJV, BBE).*

Please note that the following prayer is only a guide to seeking deliverance and healing from the erroneous spiritual warfare and deliverance teachings that advocate for direct confrontation against Satan. It's not intended to replace your own devotional prayers. It was compiled to make it easier for believers who may not understand how they may seek deliverance, healing and restoration.

You'll notice that it's heavy on scripture, and deliberately so. This brings more understanding on the extensive backing we have from scripture on deliverance and restoration. It increases our level of faith and understanding on the parts God expects us to fulfill before he can intervene.

For example, he wants us to forgive others before we can receive his mercies. He wants us to walk in obedience before we can see the disobedience of others to God's will overcome.

A prayer of appeal like this one is what we would categorize as our true spiritual warfare prayer and deliverance prayer. It is prayer directed at God, seeking his intervention in our battles in life. It is an indirect weapon of spiritual warfare and deliverance that seeks God to directly deal with forces that only he has the power and authority to confront.

When God intervenes Satan has no option but to follow God's decree. That's why our focus on God is the only solution and the only true spiritual warfare.

Like Daniel, we fervently confront God to intervene and deal with principalities wrestling against us. Once God acts the affliction in the area of petition is removed. As God's will is fulfilled we indirectly overcome the evil forces that were the source of the problems. No direct confrontation involved on our part. The Lord is the one that delivers "us from the evil one," Matthew 6:12-13. We cannot deliver ourselves without his intervention.

The prayer can also be applied to other areas requiring deliverance, healing and restoration –personally or corporately. It's however framed to be personal more than corporate. No need of feeling guilty about personal prayers –unless that's all you pray about.

Please bear with any repetitions or lack of flow in some areas. It's a prayer, like any prayer, written or unwritten, where English grammar is expected to take a secondary role. Though he wants us to ask the Lord knows what we mean and need even before asking (Matt 6:8). The Lord bless you.

It is okay to repeat this prayer as many times as you wish. It can also be helpful just by reading through it over and over again, week after week, just to grasp the scriptures relating to deliverance, healing and restoration.

Repentance to God and Forgiving of Others

Our Father and God, I come before you in the name of Jesus Christ. Lord, I now realize that I was not following your word in regard to spiritual warfare and deliverance teachings that advocate for direct confrontation against Satan. I realize I was merely slandering spiritual beings by attempting to confront them directly.

Your word says, "Bold and arrogant, these men are not afraid to slander celestial beings; yet even angels, although they are stronger and more powerful, do not bring slanderous accusations against such beings in the presence of the Lord. But these men blaspheme in matters they do not understand," (2 Peter 2:10-12).

I confess all my sins, including the ones involving the slander of celestial (heavenly) beings through practicing what I assumed were biblical spiritual warfare and deliverance teachings. Please forgive me for behaving so arrogantly and slandering celestial beings.

May the work of your son Jesus cover fro all my sins. Thank you that the work of Christ, who as your word says, "has freed us from our sins by his blood, and has made us to be a kingdom and priests to serve his God and Father," (Revelation 1:5-6).

Forgive my debts as I have completely forgiven the debts of all those who wronged me in thoughts, words or actions. These include some family members, relatives, friends, workmates, other acquaintances, strangers, those who persecuted or currently persecute me and even people that seem not to deserve forgiveness like thieves, criminals and so on. I humbly and obediently say this in line with the word of my master, Jesus Christ: "Father, forgive them for they do not know what they are doing," (Luke 23:34).

Having forgiven them, I therefore declare like Stephen that, "Lord, do not hold this against them," (Acts 4:60). Let none of them pay for their sins but make yourself known to them so that they partake of your salvation. May you grant them salvation like you did to Paul who supervised the stoning of Steven.

Deliverance, Healing and Restoration

     Lord you alone can quantify the extent Satan has been frustrating my life as a result of practicing the erroneous spiritual warfare and deliverance teachings. The following are some of the recent losses and hindrances that have been and some still are being experienced:

_____

_____

_____

_____

_____

_____

_____

_____

_____

_____

_____

_____

_____

     Whatever doors that as a result of my sins gave access to the enemy to attack me spiritually, socially, physically, materially and in any other way, I ask that you shut them from now onwards. May you bring healing and restoration in all the areas that were damaged or destroyed by the enemy as I humbly come praying before you and turning from all my wicked ways.

     Thank you that you're bringing healing and restoration as your word says, "'When I shut up the heavens so that there is no rain, or command locusts to devour the land or send a plague among my people, if my people, who are called by my name, will humble themselves and pray and seek my face and turn from their wicked ways, then will I hear from heaven and will forgive their sin and will heal their land. Now my eyes will be open and my ears attentive to the prayers offered in this place,'" (2 Chronicles 7:13-15).

     Lord I believe from your word that certain destructive matters have no basis to be in and around my life any more. There door of legal entry is now closed after stopping the erroneous practices, seeking your mercy and applying the true biblical spiritual warfare and deliverance teachings. Whatever Satan attempts against my life is now an attempt to steal what does not rightly belong to him. Your word says, "The thief comes only to steal and kill and destroy; I came that they may have life, and have it abundantly," John 10:10.

     In the name of Jesus I'm asking you to restrain Satan from prolonging his season of oppression and destruction over my life. Being your child, through

Christ, his time of dominion and influence in my life has past forever. Lord, please let the finished work of your Son Jesus bring the intended liberty in every area of my life. Only you have the power to ensure that the weapons of the evil fallen angels in the spirit realm do not prosper against me and those I'm interceding for.

Lord I pray like Jehoshaphat, "O Lord, God of our fathers, are you not the God who is in heaven? You rule over all the kingdoms of the nations. Power and might are in your hand, and no one can withstand you. O our God, did you not drive out the inhabitants of this land before your people Israel and give it forever to the descendants of Abraham your friend?.... But now here are men from Ammon, Moab and Mount Seir....O our God, will you not judge them? For we have no power to face this vast army that is attacking us. We do not know what to do, but our eyes are upon you," 2 Chronicles 20:6-7,10,12.

May you take judgment in my favor and enable me to live a victorious life. Your word says "I was watching and the same horn was making war against the saints, and prevailing against them, until the Ancient of Days came, and a judgment was made in favor of the saints of the Most High, and the time came for the saints to posses the kingdom," Daniel 7:21-22.

May such a judgment in my favor apply to all the areas the enemy was and is making war against me. Father, please ensure that Satan is overcome for all his criminal activities against every area of my life that in one way or another, has been or is still victim of manipulations from Satan and his agents through suffering from certain oppressions, hindrances and bondages.

Your word says he is "the accuser of our brothers (all believers on earth), who accuses them before our God day and night," Revelation 12:10. Thank you that your son Jesus is representing every case over my life against Satan's accusations. Your word says, "We have one who speaks to the Father in our defense--Jesus Christ, the Righteous One," 1 John 2:1.

It also says, "Because Jesus lives forever, he has a permanent priesthood. Therefore he is able to save completely those who come to God through him, because he always lives to intercede for them. Such a high priest meets our need--one who is holy, blameless, pure, set apart from sinners, exalted above the heavens," (Hebrews 7:24-26).

Your servant Job was able to declare concerning his affliction, "Even now my witness is in heaven; my advocate is on high. My intercessor is my friend as my eyes pour out tears to God," Job 16: 19-20. Father, I too say my Lord Jesus is my witness, for he is the one that died for my sins so that I can be set free from the devil. As my Witness stands beside you please look into every case in my life that the enemy is accusing me for, has brought suffering for or wants me to suffer for.

Heavenly Father, your word says, "They overcame him by the blood of the Lamb and by the word of their testimony; they did not love their lives so much as to shrink from death," Revelation 12:11. May my appeal to you be binding in heaven and may you settle matters in my life in such a way that Satan and his agents are completely overcome in all the areas of my life. I'm presenting to you the following as my testimony and case against Satan and his agents over every area of my life that's experienced losses and hindrances:

(cross out the ones you have no word of testimony –you can only lie to yourself here)

1)   I've repented to you, God, for my involvement in slandering and speaking abusively against celestial beings through what I thought were spiritual warfare and deliverance teachings. You've forgiven me for this sin. The penalty or consequence for this sin, like every other sin, was paid for on the cross by your Son Jesus and therefore the enemy has no claim or basis to bring any accusations or attacks any more.

"If we confess our sins, he is faithful and just and will forgive us our sins and purify us from all unrighteousness," 1 John 1:9,

"To him who loves us and has freed us from our sins by his blood, and has made us to be a kingdom and priests to serve his God and Father," Revelation 1:6

"Christ redeemed us from the curse of the law by becoming a curse for us, for it is written: 'Cursed is everyone who is hung on a tree,'" Galatians 3:13-14,

2)_____

_____

_____

3)_____

_____

_____

4)   I used a lot of my time to grow in spiritual matters and being involved in matters that are essential to the body of Christ. I've been trusting you Lord to add the material necessities in your own time and measure so that pursuing them does not distract or interfere with seeking your kingdom interests first and your righteousness,

"Seek first his kingdom and his righteousness, and all these things (material and basic needs) will be given to you as well," (Matthew 6:33)

2)   Been faithful in my income to kingdom and ministry matters.

"Bring the whole tithe into the storehouse...and see if I will not throw open the floodgates of heaven and pour out so much blessing that you will not have room enough for it. I will prevent pests from devouring your crops...says the Lord Almighty," Malachi 3:10-11,

"If you spend yourselves in behalf of the hungry and satisfy the needs of the oppressed, then your light will rise in the darkness, and your night will become like the noonday. The Lord will guide you always; he will satisfy your needs in a sun-scorched land and will strengthen your frame;" Isaiah 58:10-11,

"He who is kind to the poor lends to the Lord, and he will reward him for what he has done," Proverbs 19:17

5)   Where I've fallen short the blood of Jesus has covered and cleansed me from all sins and their consequences since I've repented from all sins and continue to walk in repentance.

"To him who loves us and has freed us from our sins by his blood, and has made us to be a kingdom and priests to serve his God and Father," Revelation 1:6

"Christ redeemed us from the curse of the law by becoming a curse for us, for it is written: 'Cursed is everyone who is hung on a tree,'" Galatians 3:13-14,

"If we walk in the light.. the blood of Jesus, his Son purifies us from all sins," 1 John 1:7,

"If we confess our sins, he is faithful and just and will forgive us our sins and purify us from all unrighteousness," 1 John 1:9,

6)   I have completely forgiven the debts of all those who wronged me in thoughts, words or actions. These include some family members, relatives, friends, workmates, other acquaintances, strangers, those who persecuted or currently persecute me and even people that seem not to deserve forgiveness like thieves, criminals and so on.

"If you forgive men when they sin against you, your heavenly Father will also forgive you. But if you do not forgive men their sins, your Father will not forgive your sin," Matthew 6:14-15,

7)   I'm now in Christ and thus under no condemnation from Satan, the accuser of the brethren. He now has no valid case against me since the blood of Jesus and his work on the cross paid for all my sins and their consequences,

"Therefore, there is now no condemnation for those who are in Christ Jesus, because through Christ Jesus the law of the Spirit of life set me free from the law of sin and death," Romans 8:1-2,

John 1:9,

"To him who loves us and has freed us from our sins by his blood, and has made us to be a kingdom and priests to serve his God and Father," Revelation 1:6

8)   I've Jesus Christ as my advocate, representing every case in my life and will ensure every case works to my good and that justice prevails against the enemy,

"If anybody does sin, we have one who speaks to the Father in our defense-- Jesus Christ, the Righteous One," 1 John 2:1,

"Even now my witness is in heaven; my advocate is on high. My intercessor is my friend as my eyes pour out tears to God," Job 16: 19-20,

"Will not God bring about justice for his chosen ones, who cry out to him day and night? Will he keep putting them off? I tell you, he will see that they get justice, and quickly," Luke 18:7-8,

9)

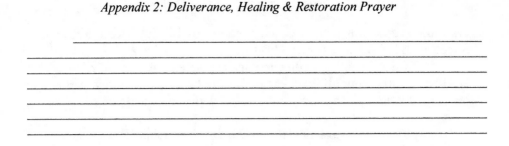

Our Father and God you said, "No one can deliver out of my hand. When I act, who can reverse it?" (Isaiah 43:13). Thank you that Satan can never reverse whatever you decree over my life including my salvation, fulfilling my callings and restoring all that he stole, killed or destroyed in my family, career and ministry, my time, finances, my body, spirit, soul and all that you entrusted me with.

In the name of Jesus please cause the evil spirits to be powerless over my life from now onwards. Your word says, "The Lord will grant that the enemies who rise up against you will be defeated before you. They will come at you from one direction but flee from you in seven," Deuteronomy 28:7.

May your angels pursue and overcome them as your word says: "May those who plot my ruin be turned back in dismay. May they be like chaff before the wind, with the angel of the Lord driving them away; may their path be dark and slippery with the angel of the Lord pursuing them." May your angels drive away every evil spirit that has been working against my life.

Please also reveal to me areas opening doors for the enemy to bring attacks. I ask according to your word: "Break the arm of the wicked that would not be found out," Psalm 10:15. By your grace through Christ Jesus remove and enable me to do my part in overcoming these areas.

Help me do away all inequity. Lord I ask like the Psalmist: "Open my eyes that I may see wonderful things in your law... Turn my heart toward your statutes and not toward selfish gain. Turn my eyes away from worthless things; preserve my life according to your word. Fulfill your promise to your servant, so that you may be feared. Take away the disgrace I dread, for your laws are good," Psalm 119:18, 36-39. Turn my heart towards your statutes and away from selfish gain and worthless things in your eyes.

You said, "If you do away with the yoke of oppression, with the pointing finger and malicious talk, and if you spend yourselves in behalf of the hungry and satisfy the needs of the oppressed, then your light will rise in the darkness, and your night will become like the noonday. The Lord will guide you always; he will satisfy your needs in a sun-scorched land and will strengthen your frame. You will be like a well-watered garden, like a spring whose waters never fail. Your people will rebuild the ancient ruins and will raise up the age-old foundations; you will be called Repairer of Broken Walls, Restorer of Streets with Dwellings," Isaiah 58:9-12.

Lord as I walk according to your word please repair and restore what has been destroyed in all the areas of my life be it in my family, career and ministry, my time, finances, my body, spirit, soul and all that you entrusted me with.

Your word says in Daniel 7:21-22, "I was watching and the same horn was making war against the saints, and prevailing against them, until the Ancient of Days came, and a judgment was made in favor of the saints of the Most High, and the time came for the saints to posses the kingdom." May such a judgment in my favor apply to all the areas the enemy was making war against me. Thank you for taking judgment in my favor and enabling me to posses the kingdom. Father please ensure that Satan is judged for every accusation he continues to bring before you, night and day.

Thank you Father for sending your Holy Spirit to come and live in me. You Word says, "Don't you know that you yourself are God's temple and that God's Spirit lives in you? If anyone destroys God's temple, God will destroy him; God's temple is sacred, and you are that temple," (1 Corinthians 3: 16-17). Thank you that you will destroy and overcome anyone including agents of Satan if they try to destroy your temple. May you cleanse me, your spiritual temple from all evil and deliver me from the evil one. May I be a house of prayer and worship that you can use to touch the lives of others in whatever way.

May the penalty and vengeance against Satan also include you anointing me with your Spirit in such a way that you'll use me to bring massive destruction against Satan's works and control in the lives of people. May I be one of your elect whom you'll use to deliver multitudes from Satan's works and control, be it in their bodies, souls, spirits, families and marriages, callings and vocations, finances, and all that the enemy has had control of. May it be an equipping for effective work in the area of my calling.

Your word encourages us to ask for whatever matters we desire and believe are consistent with your will. Our Lord Jesus said, "Whatever you ask in prayer, believe that you have received it, and it will be yours. And whenever you stand praying, forgive, if you have anything against any one; so that your father also who is in heaven may forgive your trespasses," (Mark 11:24-26). He also said, "If you remain in me and my words remain in you, ask whatever you wish, and it will be given you. This is to my Father's glory, that you bear much fruit, showing yourselves to be my disciples," (John 15:7-8). The following are among the major areas I'm asking for your provision.

(Please be as specific as possible on matters applying to you –spiritual, material, social or physical matters)

a) Spiritual Matters

1)   For character change that you transform me to not be self driven but to be fully led by your Holy Spirit and thereby fully produce his fruit and character of "love, joy, peace, patience, kindness, goodness, faithfulness, gentleness, and self-control," (Galatians 5:22-23),

"And this is the confidence which we have in him, that if we ask anything according to His Will he hears us," 1 John 5:14

2)   For the grace to grow and mature in using given spiritual gifts (e.g. wisdom, discernment, interpretation, healing, and so on, i.e. gifts and fruits of the Holy Spirit).

"We have different gifts, according to the grace given us. If a man's gift is prophesying, let him use it in proportion to his faith. If it is serving, let him serve; if it is teaching, let him teach; if it is encouraging, let him encourage; if it is contributing to the needs of others, let him give generously; if it is leadership, let him govern diligently; if it is showing mercy, let him do it cheerfully," Romans 12:6-8

"Now to each one the manifestation of the Spirit is given for the common good. To one there is given through the Spirit the message of wisdom, to another the message of knowledge by means of the same Spirit, to another faith by the same Spirit, to another gifts of healing by that one Spirit, to another miraculous powers, to another prophecy, to another distinguishing between spirits, to another speaking in different kinds of tongues, and to still another the interpretation of tongues," 1 Corinthians. 12:7-11

"We have not received the spirit of the world but the Spirit who is from God, that we may understand what God has freely given us," 1 Corinthians 2:12

"Follow the way of love and eagerly desire spiritual gifts, especially the gift of prophecy," 1 Corinthians. 14:1

"Settle it therefore in your minds, not to meditate before hand how to answer; for I will give you a mouth and wisdom, which none of your adversaries will be able to withstand or contradict," Luke 21:14-15.

"Work out your salvation with fear and trembling; for God is at work in you, both to will and to work for his good pleasure" (Philippians 2:12-13).

3)   Open doors of being used by you Lord in ministry oriented work on a full or part time basis, as purposed per time and matter throughout my life,

"Each one should use whatever gift he has received to serve others, faithfully administering God's grace in its various forms." 1 Peter 4:10

"How can they preach unless they are sent?" Romans 10:15

4)   Working with the right organization or team at every stage of my life,

"Being confident of this, that he who began a good work in you will carry it on to completion until the day of Christ Jesus," Phillipians 1:6

"Commit to the Lord whatever you do, and your plans will succeed," Proverbs 16:3

"I will instruct you and teach you in the way you should go; I will advise you and watch over you," Psalm 32:8.

5)   For the grace and anointing for witnessing and all commissioned obligations, including obligations to fast when necessary and interceding for certain people consistently if required. Also adequate preparation (spiritually, socially, materially and physically) for service, stewardship or leadership

"You will receive power when the Holy Spirit comes on you; and you will be my witnesses in Jerusalem, and in all Judea and Samaria, and to the ends of the earth," Acts 1:8

"The Spirit of the Lord is on me because He has anointed me to preach good news to the poor. He has sent me to proclaim freedom for the prisoners and recovery of sight for the blind, to release the oppressed, to proclaim the year of the Lord's favor," (Luke 4:18-19).

6)   For the grace to have enough time, commitment, energy, other resources, grace and anointing to fulfil all obligations –obligations to God, to the body of Christ (ministry), other ordained vocation, to spouse, to immediate family, to parents, and every matter entrusted with,

"Seek first his kingdom and his righteousness, and all these things (material and basic needs) will be given to you as well," (Matthew 6:33)

7)   For the grace, anointing and resources to grow in being a blessing to others – spiritually, socially, materially, etc,

"Seek first his kingdom and his righteousness, and all these things (material and basic needs) will be given to you as well," Matthew 6:33.

_____

_____
_____
_____
_____

b) Social Matters
(family, marriage, friendship, workplace and other interpersonal matters)

_____

_____
_____
_____
_____
_____

c) Physical health Matters

1)   Complete healing and deliverance from…….. (e.g. ulcers and all other illnesses and works of the enemy),

"May God himself, the God of peace, sanctify you through and through. May your whole spirit, soul and body be kept blameless at the coming of our Lord Jesus Christ. The one who calls you is faithful and he will do it," 1Thessalonians 5:23-24

"For everyone who asks receives, and he who seeks finds, and to him who knocks it will be opened." Matthew 7:8

"They drove out many demons and anointed many sick people with oil and healed them," Mark 6:13

"Is any one of you sick? He should call the elders of the church to pray over him and anoint him with oil in the name of the Lord," James 5:14

"Even youths grow tired and weary, and young men stumble and fall; but those who hope in the Lord will renew their strength. They will soar on wings like eagles; they will run and not grow weary, they will walk and not be faint," Isaiah 40-30-31

" Blessed is he who has regard for the weak; the Lord delivers him in times of trouble. The Lord will protect him and preserve his life; he will bless him in the land and not surrender him to the desire of his foes. The Lord will sustain him on his sickbed and restore him from his bed of illness," Psalms 41:1-3

_____

_____

_____

_____

_____

_____

d) Material Matters

1)   Open doors of financing of all obligations (esp. home bills, family needs, tuition where and when needed and funds for helping out in the Body of Christ)

"Seek first his kingdom and his righteousness, and all these things (material and basic needs) will be given to you as well," Matthew 6:33.

"My God shall supply all my need according to his riches in Glory in Christ Jesus," Phillipians 4:19.

" Blessed is he who has regard for the weak; the Lord delivers him in times of trouble. The Lord will protect him and preserve his life; he will bless him in the land and not surrender him to the desire of his foes. The Lord will sustain him on his sickbed and restore him from his bed of illness," Psalms 41:1-3

"The Lord will open the heavens, the storehouse of his bounty, to send rain on your land in season and to bless all the work of your hands. You will lend to many nations but will borrow from none. The Lord will make you the head, not the tail. If you pay attention to the commands of the Lord your God that I give you this day and carefully follow them, you will always be at the top, never at the bottom," Deuteronomy 28:12-13

"Bring the whole tithe into the storehouse…and see if I will not throw open the floodgates of heaven and pour out so much blessing that you will not have room enough for it. I will prevent pests from devouring your crops…says the Lord Almighty," Malachi 3:10-11,

"He who is kind to the poor lends to the Lord, and he will reward him for what he has done," Proverbs 19:17

2)   Miraculous provision of finances and other needs in all areas of need…… (e.g. for studies, home or car purchase, spiritual projects/assignments, etc.)

"Seek first his kingdom and his righteousness, and all these things (material and basic needs) will be given to you as well," Matthew 6:33.

"My God shall supply all my need according to his riches in Glory in Christ Jesus," Phillipians 4:19.

"Those who sow in tears will reap with songs of joy. He who goes out weeping, carrying seed to sow, will return with songs of joy, carrying sheaves (bundles of crop harvest) with him," Psalm 126:5-6.

" Remember this: Whoever sows sparingly will also reap sparingly, and whoever sows generously will also reap generously… And God is able to make all grace abound to you, so that in all things at all times, having all that you need, you will abound in every good work," 2 Corinthians 9:6,8

"If you spend yourselves in behalf of the hungry and satisfy the needs of the oppressed, then your light will rise in the darkness, and your night will become like the noonday. The Lord will guide you always; he will *satisfy your needs* in a sun-scorched land and will strengthen your frame;" Isaiah 58:10-11,

_____

_____
_____
_____
_____
_____

_____

e) General Matters

1)   For the grace, anointing and resources in fulfilling according to your will all matters, big or small, known or unknown, in my life, my family's lives, and other people's lives I've been commissioned to serve,

"Now to him who is able to do immeasurably more than all we ask or imagine, according to his power that is at work within us, to him be glory in the church and in Christ Jesus throughout all generations, for ever and ever! Amen," Ephesians 3:20

_____

_____
_____

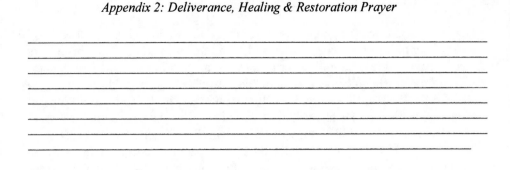

d) Thanksgiving

Thank you heavenly Father, in the name of Jesus Christ, that I am now set free from any influence of Satan and all his agents. Thank you that you will fulfill according to your perfect will the matters I've committed to you. By faith I believe it and obtain all your promises for my life and the lives of others. I'll therefore be thanking you that the matters are already fulfilled even though I may not currently see their fulfillment. I'll walk by faith and not by sight, depending on your faithfulness and your word, not on circumstances.

Please overcome anything that stands as a hindrance in the answers to my prayers, including areas of unbelief, compromise and disobedience in any area of my life. Enable me not to wonder in a wilderness because of unbelief, complaining, ingratitude, compromise or disobedience or anything that may bring stagnation in any area of my life and the lives of others. Thank you that it's your desire that I live according to your perfect will and live as your worthy servant, fulfilling all that you purposed to fulfill in and through me.

Thank you that no evil shall by any means befall me because you are now my refuge. Your Word assures me of your protection saying, "Because you have made the Lord your refuge, the most high your habitation, no evil shall befall you, nor shall scourge come near your tent. For He will give his angels charge over you in all your ways; they (the angles) will lift you up in their hands, so that you will not strike your foot against a stone. You will tread upon the lion and the cobra; you will trample the great lion and the serpent," Psalm 91:10 –13. Thank you for giving your angles charge over me in all my ways. Thank you that, through your Son Jesus Christ, Satan who is the great serpent mentioned above and his agents are now powerless over me. They can do me no harm.

Thank you that Satan cannot torment me because I'm now your blessed child. My family and everything around me is blessed from now and forever by you. Thank you for your word that says, "Blessed is the man who fears the Lord, who finds great delight in his commands. His children will be mighty in the land; the generation of the upright will be blessed. Wealth and riches are in his house, and his righteousness endures forever. Even in darkness light dawns for the upright, for the gracious and compassionate and righteous man. Good will come to him who is generous and lends freely, who conducts his affairs with justice. Surely he will never be shaken; a righteous man will be remembered forever. He will have no fear of bad news; his heart is steadfast, trusting in the Lord. His heart is secure, he will have no fear; in the end he will look in triumph on his foes. He has scattered abroad his gifts to the poor, his righteousness endures forever; his horn will be lifted high in honor," Psalm 112:1-9.

Our Heavenly Father and God, now that I am free from Satan's illegal influence I ask you in the name of Jesus that you sanctify me. Set me apart for your use as your servant and child. Please let your Holy Spirit be my ultimate guide, leading me to all truth. Seal me with your Spirit in Jesus' name so that I'll be able to clearly hear the voice of Jesus my Master, throughout the days of my life. I pray like Jabez, "Oh, that you would bless me and enlarge my territory! Let your hand be with me, and keep me from harm so that I will be free from pain," 1 Chronicles 4:10

Thank you Father for sending your Holy Spirit to come and live in me. You Word says in 1 Corinthians 3: 16-17, "Don't you know that you yourself are God's temple and that God's Spirit lives in you? If anyone destroys God's temple, God will destroy him; God's temple is sacred, and you are that temple." Thank you that you will destroy and overcome anyone including agents of Satan if they try to destroy your temple. May you overcome him and destroy his works against me and his attempts of defiling me, your temple, in whatever area of my life spiritually, socially, materially, physically and in all areas you entrusted me with.

Thank you for hearing my prayer Heavenly Father. May you accomplish exceedingly more than all I have asked and said in your hearing. May it be as Ephesians 3:20 says: "Now to him who is able to do immeasurably more than all we ask or imagine, according to his power that is at work within us, to him be glory in the church and in Christ Jesus throughout all generations, for ever and ever! Amen." In the name of Jesus Christ I pray and thank you, Amen.

Appendix 3: Other Authors on Spiritual Warfare and Deliverance

Appendix 3: Other Authors and Ministries Sounding the Alarm on Spiritual Warfare and Deliverance Principles

Our website has tones of resources on spiritual warfare and deliverance principles, including free audio sermons and online books. Our main website on spiritual warfare and deliverance matters is SpiritualWarfareDeliverance.com. You can access it through JesusW.com the main website for Jesus Work Ministry which is interlinked with SpiritualWarfareDeliverance.com.

Below are other websites and ministries, among many, that focus on distinguishing between true and false spiritual warfare and deliverance teachings. They may be worth visiting for more content and writing on spiritual warfare and deliverance ministry.

Their views are what we have embraced as spiritual warfare throughout history. It was only recently, in the early 1980's, that a few of our fellow evangelicals began to claim a new understanding to scripture.

On the other hand, a few of the listed websites and ministries are too critical of those that follow misinterpreted teachings to the point of labeling them as cults. As you've found in this book we do not agree with this approach of bashing fellow believers in the body of Christ. Please see our website SpiritualWarfareDeliverance.com for updates on selected websites and spiritual warfare related matters.

1.   Modern Myths about Satan and Spiritual Warfare, by David Servant
In this online book, Modern Myths about Satan and Spiritual Warfare, Servant covers on the major errors that surround the wrong spiritual warfare doctrine. The chapters are arranged along myths on misinterpreted scripture and wrong doctrine.
        http://www.shepherdserve.org/spiritual_warfare.htm

2.   Strange Spiritual Warfare, by David W. Cloud
        About binding and loosing Rev. Cloud says, "The devil can be resisted (James 4:7), but he cannot be bound today (1 Thess. 2:18 -We wanted to come to you--certainly I, Paul, did, again and again--but Satan stopped us)). Far from being bound, the devil is "walking about seeking whom he may devour" (1 Pet. 5:8). He will not be bound until he is cast into the Bottomless Pit when Jesus Christ returns to earth (Revelation 20). Ephesians 6 describes the whole armor of God against the devil, and absolutely nothing is said about binding the devil or identifying territorial spirits or any of the other practices in today's spiritual warfare movement..."
        http://wayoflife.org/fbns/strangespiritual.htm

3.   The Spiritual Warfare Movement, by Gary Gilley
Pastor Gilley covers on many areas of the assumed spiritual warfare. One of them is on what has been labeled as "Warfare Prayer." Gilley says "Since when are we to address Satan in prayer?... This concept is not drawn from the Scriptures. And when did we get the authority to command demons to do anything? Even Michael would only say to Satan, "The Lord rebuke you" (Jude 9)...."

> Part 1: http://www.svchapel.org/Resources/Articles/read_articles.asp?id=39
> Part 2: http://www.svchapel.org/Resources/Articles/read_articles.asp?id=40
> Part 3: http://www.svchapel.org/Resources/Articles/read_articles.asp?id=41

4. The Dishonoring of God in Popular Spiritual Warfare Teaching, by Bob DeWaay
Pastor DeWaay points out that, "The church was never commissioned to control the heavenlies. Consider this: Jesus told Peter that Satan had demanded from God "permission" to sift Peter like wheat (Luke 22:31). God, in His sovereign oversight of the universe, gave it to Satan, but it only led to Peter's conversion and subsequent ministry. Once we are in charge of the heavenlies will Satan have to ask us rather than God for such permission? Does the church have sufficient knowledge, wisdom, and power to rule a realm of being that is only partially described in the Bible and to rule this realm for everyone's good?..."

> http://www.twincityfellowship.com/cic/articles/issue48.htm

5.   Do We Have All Authority? By Mike Oppenheimer
Oppenheimer examines the spiritual authority believers have been given in the light of beliefs that propose unlimited authority for believers.

> http://www.letusreason.org/Latrain16.htm

6.   Spiritual Warfare: Biblical Binding and Loosing, by Mike Oppenheimer
Oppenheimer covers on topics like Binding and Loosing, Believer's Authority, Biblical Strategy in (spiritual) Warfare.   http://www.letusreason.org/pent13.htm

7.   Confusion on Spiritual Warfare, by Link Hudson
Hudson says, "There is no mention of doing the warfare by yelling at spirits up in the air...If this type of 'spiritual warfare' were so wonderful, why didn't Jesus do it, or teach us to do it? Why didn't the apostles practice it? Why don't the scriptures mention anything about it?..."
http://www.housechurch.org/cgi-bin/ubbcgi_hc/ultimatebb.cgi/ubb/get_topic/f/18/t/000010.html?

8. Spiritual Warfare Evangelism: How Did We Get Here? By Dr. Orrel Steinkamp
In the article Steinkamp summarizes the teaching and background of what has been called geographical or territorial spiritual warfare.

> http://www.deceptioninthechurch.com/orrel8.html

9.   Spiritual warfare - The true facts or fantasy?
A look at the new warfare techniques being taught in some of our evangelical circles.

> http://www.letusreason.org/Pent13.htm

10.   Deliverance and Spiritual Warfare, by Steve Fernandez, Pastor, Community Bible Church

This is booklet is published in the Reformation and Revival Journal. Pastor Fernandez covers on the spiritual warfare topic with such chapters as 1. The Distinctives of the Deliverance Model: a) The Believer's Authority, b) Christians and Demon Possession, c) Binding and Commanding Satan. 2. The Dangers of the Deliverance Model: a) A Diminished View of Conversion, b) A Minimizing of Sin and Personal Responsibility, c) A Misdirecting of the Believer's Focus, and d) A Denial of the Sufficiency of Scripture.
http://www.cbcvallejo.org/Deliverance_and_Spiritual_Warfare_NoFrame.htm

11.   Brief review of a book titled: Warfare Prayer: How To Seek God's Power and Protection in the Battle
To Build His Kingdom. Author: C. Peter Wagner. Reviewed by John Claeys Pastor
http://www.faithalone.org/journal/bookreviews/wagner.htm

12.   Spiritual Warfare, by Clifford Denton

Denton writes that, "I am concerned that there may be a movement growing which has a very unreal view of prayer and spiritual gifts but which is, nevertheless, trying to conquer Satan with human effort. Such approaches are dangerous and, I am thinking more and more, unscriptural. There seems to be a wide gulf between the intimacy of prayer from brokenness, humility and need, expressed in the articles of this journal and the headstrong ideas of some who would take the world by forceful spiritual power..." http://www.familyrestorationmagazine.org/tishrei/tishrei060.htm

13. The Real Soul War: The Battle for Victorious Life & Relationships, by Sid Galloway
With detailed scriptural references Galloway covers on what real spiritual warfare is. A major focus is on spiritual warfare over relationships. Dr Galloway directs a ministry for families known as Soulcare Family Ministries.
http://www.soulcare.org/Bible%20Studies/Soul_War.htm

14.   Just Give Me the Facts. Compiled by Renee Rodriguez
What is The New Apostolic Reformation? What is the Prophetic? What Is Strategic Level Spiritual Warfare? What About the Terms Used in Spiritual Warfare, What Do They Mean? What is Deliverance Ministry?
http://www.agetwoage.org/ApostolicJustFacts1.htm

15.   True and False Salvation, by W.B. Howard
This is part of a Bible course by Endtime Ministries. Howard begins by distinguishing between true and false salvation. Then he moves on to distinguishing between true and false spiritual warfare. http://www.despatch.cth.com.au/BCU/Unit8_main2.htm

16.   The Technology of Spiritual Warfare Evangelism, by Dr Orrel Steinkamp
"Mapping the spirit world and its internal organization is not the assignment of the church. The great commission is not, "Go into all the world and bring down principalities -- but rather "Go into all the world and preach the Gospel to every

creature." Mark 16:15. Our choice is very clear! We must follow the teachings of Jesus, and the practice of the Apostles as recorded in Scripture!..."
http://www.deceptioninthechurch.com/orrel9.html

17.   Territorial Warfare - Fact or Fiction? by Jeannette Haley, Gentle Shepherd Ministries
Haley covers on the teachings and background of what has been called geographical or territorial spiritual warfare.
http://www.gentleshepherd.com/articles/warfare/territorialwarfare.htm

18.   Territorial Spirits and Spiritual Warfare: A Biblical Perspective, by Eric Villanueva
About Ephesians 6, Villanueva writes, "The weapons he lists for battle are: honesty, righteousness, witnessing, assurance of salvation, belief in God, and proficiency in the Scriptures. But wait, isn't this simply obedient Christian living? Where's the mystical mumbo jumbo - the direct encounter with the supernatural?..."
http://www.equip.org/free/DS542.htm

19.   How Deliverance Ministries Lead People to Bondage, by Bob DeWaay
Pastor DeWaay writes from long experience in certain practices of deliverance ministry and spiritual warfare. http://www.twincityfellowship.com/cic/articles/issue78.htm

20.   Misguided Focus on the Demonic: Commentary on Spiritual Mapping and Strategic-Level Spiritual Warfare, by Rev. Kent Philpott
http://www.w3church.org/MisguidedDemonic.html

21.   My Beliefs About Spiritual Warfare, by John Paul Jackson
In this article, Pastor Jackson summarizes and defends what he wrote on spiritual warfare in his book, Needless Casualties of War. He says, "From the testimonies that our ministry receives, I am convinced that unnecessary heartache and harm is happening to many, simply because they are practicing spiritual warfare in a dangerous way..." Needless to say we do not agree with some extra-biblical teachings on the spirit realm that Pastor Jackson shares on his website. The spirit realm is indeed a controversial area. http://www.streamsministries.com/Warfare.html

22.   Charismatic Chaos - Part 6: The Third Wave by John F. MacArthur, Jr.
MacArthur, Jr. looks at the origins and development of what came to be know as the "Third Wave," movement and its related teachings.
http://www.biblebb.com/files/mac/chaos6.htm

23.   C. Peter Wagner - Quotes & Notes compiled by Sandy Simpson & Mike Oppenheimer
Lots of quotes that help trace the origins of the false teachings popularized by C. Peter Wagner and his followers. http://www.deceptioninthechurch.com/wagnerquotes.html

Book References

Bassett, Lucinda, 2003. *Attacking Anxiety & Depression: A Self-help, Self-awareness Program for Stress, Anxiety and Depression*, Oak Harbor, Ohio, Midwest Center for Stress and Anxiety, Inc.

Brown, Rebecca, MD and Yoder, Daniel, 1996. *Unbroken Curses: Hidden Source of Trouble in the Christian's Life*, Whitaker House (Used for research purposes -Book embraces false teachings on spiritual warfare)

Campbell, T. Colin, Campbell II, Thomas M. and Robbins, John, 2006. *The China Study: The Most Comprehensive Study of Nutrition Ever Conducted and the Startling Implications for Diet, Weight Loss and Long-term Health*, Benbella Books

Harshbarger, Jeff, 2004. *From Darkness to Light*, Bridge-Logos, Florida

Jackson, John P., 1999. *Needless Casualties of War*, Streams Publications, Sutton, New Hampshire

Keller, Phillip, 1984. *Power! The Challenge of Elijah*, Bridge Publishing, Chepstow, Gwent, UK

Servant, David, 1994. *Modern Myths about Satan and Spiritual Warfar*e, Pittsburgh, Ethnos Press

Stone, Perry, 2002. *Dealing with Hindering Spirit*s, Voice of Evangelism, Cleveland, Tennessee

Stone, Perry, "3:00 in the Morning: Tapping into the Spirit World," (audio) Voice of Evangelism, Cleveland, Tennessee

Wagner, C. Peter, 1988. *The Third Wave of the Holy Spirit: Encountering the Power of Signs and Wonders Today*, Ann Arbor: Servant Publications, (Used for research purposes -Book embraces false teachings on spiritual warfare)

Weiner-Davis, Michele, 1995. *Fire Your Shrink*, Simon & Schuster Audioworks.

BusinessWeek, May 29 2006, Medical Guesswork (article by John Carey)

Henry, Matthew, *Matthew Henry's Commentary on the Whole Bible*, 1997. Thomas Nelson Inc., Nashville, Tennessee

Henry, Matthew, *Matthew Henry's Commentary on the Whole Bible: Complete and Unabridged* (6 Volumes) Retrieved March 2004, from http://bible.crosswalk.com/Commentaries/MatthewHenryComplete/

Ancient Hebrew Sacrifices and Offerings
http://webstu.messiah.edu/~jh1220/nweb.html

Anxiety Disorders Association of America (ADAA)
http://www.adaa.org/GettingHelp/Glossary.asp

Day, Lorraine, http://www.GoodNewsAboutGod.com/studies/anthrax.htm

Page, Linda, Immune System, http://www.healthyhealing.com/immunesystem.html

Finney, Dee Building The Body's Immune System: Prevent Viruses From Taking
Over Your Body, http://www.greatdreams.com/building_the_body.htm

MacArthur Jr, John F., "Charismatic Chaos - Part 6: The Third Wave," 1991,
http://www.biblebb.com/files/mac/chaos6.htm

Wesley, John, *Explanatory Notes: the Old and New Testament*, BibleDatabase
(Versio 3.1 (Christian Software)). Download available at http://bibledatabase.org/

Elwell, Walter A. (Ed) (1996). *Baker's Evangelical Dictionary of Biblical Theology*.
Crosswalk.com. Retrieved March March & Ap 2004, from
<http://bible.crosswalk.com/Dictionaries/BakersEvangelicalDictionary/>.

Bible Library Ultra Edition (version 6.0 (Software)), 2001, Ellis Enterprises, Inc.,
Oklahoma City, Oklahoma

Easton, M.G. (M.A., D.D.) 1897. *Easton's Bible Dictionary* (Illustrated Bible
Dictionary), 3rd Ed, Thomas Nelson, Public Domain, Retrieved March and April
2004, from http://bible.crosswalk.com/Dictionaries/EastonsBibleDictionary

The International Standard Bible Encyclopedia (4 volumes) 1988. Bible Library
Ultra Edition (version 6.0 (Software)), 2001, Ellis Enterprises, Inc., Oklahoma City,
Oklahoma

The Holy Bible, *New International Version* (NIV). Copyright© 1989-1998 by
International Bible Society. Zondervan Reference Software (Version 2.6), Grand
Rapids, MI

The Holy Bible, *King James Version* (KJV), 1611. Electronic conversion by
NASCO. Copyright 1988. Electronic Work Product. Bible Library Ultra Edition
(version 6.0 (Software)), 2001, Ellis Enterprises, Inc., Oklahoma City, Oklahoma

The Holy Bible, *American Standard Version* (ASV) 1901. American Bible Society.
Electronic conversion by NASCO. Copyright 1988. Electronic Work Product. Bible
Library Ultra Edition (version 6.0 (Software)), 2001, Ellis Enterprises, Inc., Okla-
homa City, Oklahoma

DeWaay, Bob "How Deliverance Ministries Lead People to Bondage," http://www.twincityfellowship.com/cic/articles/issue78.htm

Mercola, Joseph, Monsanto Pushes Hormones on School Kids in Their Milk, http://www.mercola.com/2001/aug/25/milk.htm

The Harris Poll® #97, December 8, 2004, http://www.harrisinteractive.com/harris_poll/index.asp?PID=526

G. Richard Fisher, Walking in the Shadow of The Walk, http://www.pfo.org/francisfrangipane.htm

Richard LaFountain, Grove City Alliance Church, Pennsylvania, http://www.grovecityalliance.org

National Institute of Mental Health (NIMH), http://www.nimh.nih.gov/HealthInformation/anxietymenu.cfm and http://www.nimh.nih.gov/publicat/anxiety.cfm#anx9 (accessed May, 2006)

WebMD, Inc www.webmd.com/content/article/60/67144.htm (accessed May, '06)

Thomas A. Richards, The Social Phobia/Social Anxiety Association, http://www.socialphobia.org/whatis.html#whatis1 (accessed May, 2006)

The Foundation for Informed Medical Decision, http://www.fimdm.org

Henderson, Lynn and Zimbardo, Philip quoted by Peter Jaret, CNN with WebMD, archives.cnn.com/2000/HEALTH/04/06/social.phobia.wmd/ (accessed May, '06)

USA Today, Psychiatric Drugs Fare Favorably When Companies Pay for Studies (article by Marilyn Elias), May 25, 2006, p. A1

Index

About the Author

Dr. Eric Isaiah Gondwe is the founder of Jesus Work Ministry, a primarily online based Christian resource and outreach ministry (JesusW.com). He is a born again and ordained evangelical pastor.

Like many serving in areas they least expected Eric Gondwe found himself applying his gifts in a never imagined field - deliverance ministry. His staunch past involvement in spiritual warfare and deliverance teachings popular in some evangelical circles formed the stage to receiving his call into deliverance ministry.

Eric Gondwe's firsthand experience, extensive biblical research, and eventual deliverance after prolonged prayer and fasting periods have equipped him with the "tools" that fellow Christians find to be of immense value in the area of spiritual warfare and deliverance.

In this book on spiritual warfare and deliverance you'll learn the do's and don'ts, what works and what doesn't, what's biblical and what's not, what brings deliverance and what invites bondage. The principles shared will save you from avoidable spiritual attacks that some, including Eric Gondwe, have encountered and learnt the hard way.

He's also a professional writer, web developer, and a consultant in information technology (IT) and management (including nonprofit management).

From the secular academic world Eric Gondwe has an undergraduate degree in mass communication, print media concentration, from University of Zambia (Lusaka, Zambia). His graduate program was an MBA, IT and marketing concentration, from United States International University ((USIU) Nairobi, Kenya). His second graduate program was in management, IT concentration, at Harvard University (Cambridge (in Boston), USA). He has a number of certificates in theology and in various disciplines.

His primary (junior) and secondary (high) schools were Kamwala and Olympia Primary Schools in Lusaka, Maamba Private School in Southern Province, Zambia, and Peterhouse School in Zimbabwe.

CPSIA information can be obtained at www.ICGtesting.com
Printed in the USA
LVOW08s2046081113

360635LV00002B/634/P